Family in Six Tones

ALSO BY LAN CAO

The Lotus and the Storm

Monkey Bridge

Family in Six Tones

A REFUGEE MOTHER,
AN AMERICAN DAUGHTER

Lan Cao *and*

Harlan Margaret
Van Cao

VIKING

VIKING
An imprint of Penguin Random House LLC
penguinrandomhouse.com

LIBRARY OF CONGRESS CATALOGING-IN-PUBLICATION DATA
Names: Cao, Lan, 1961– author. | Cao, Harlan Margaret Van, author.
Title: Family in six tones : a refugee mother, an American daughter /
Lan Cao and Harlan Margaret Van Cao.
Description: New York : Viking, 2020.
Identifiers: LCCN 2020002313 (print) | LCCN 2020002314 (ebook) |
ISBN 9781984878168 (hardcover) | ISBN 9781984878175 (ebook)
Subjects: LCSH: Cao, Lan. | Novelists, American—20th century—Biography. |
Women refugees—United States—Biography. | Vietnamese American
women—Biography. | Cao, Harlan Margaret Van. |
Mothers and daughters—United States—Biography.
Classification: LCC PS3553.A5823 Z46 2020 (print) |
LCC PS3553.A5823 (ebook) | DDC 813/.54—dc23
LC record available at https://lccn.loc.gov/2020002313
LC ebook record available at https://lccn.loc.gov/2020002314

Printed in the United States of America
1   3   5   7   9   10   8   6   4   2

Book design by Daniel Lagin

To William Van Alstyne and Harlan Margaret Van Cao
And the American Dream, whatever that is

Lan Cao

For my father and mother. And for girls with eccentric brains,
weird personalities, and too much to say.

Harlan Margaret Van Cao

Do I dare
Disturb the universe?
In a minute there is time
For decisions and revisions which a minute will reverse.

For I have known them all already, known them all:
Have known the evenings, mornings, afternoons,
I have measured out my life with coffee spoons;
I know the voices dying with a dying fall
Beneath the music from a farther room.
So how should I presume?

—from "The Love Song of J. Alfred Prufrock," by T. S. Eliot

Family in Six Tones

INTRODUCTION

In my life, there is Saigon, my childhood city, and there is Harlan, my daughter. One is loss and the other is love, although sometimes loss and love are intertwined. Both are volcanic, invasive experiences, their own particular battle zones, full of love and warmth. All-powerful, all-encompassing, searing, awakening. Once experienced, they take over your life, altering the very cells in your body, both in the moment and in retrospect.

I am writing as a refugee who lost a country and as a mother whose love is vaster than even the vast parameters of loss. In Vietnamese, the word for country is a combination of earth and water, elemental and archetypal. Traditionally, the Vietnamese are tethered to their ancestral home, born of land and sea, the way newborns are tied umbilically to their mothers, sharing one swollen, tightly packed body, ferociously, bound almost despotically by flesh and blood.

For all of us refugees who enter America with our contingent lives, there is the all-powerful, all-venerable American Dream. Do we follow it? Are we trespassing when we enter it? Or do we float into the dreams we invent ourselves? Having witnessed so many refugee families struggling to make it, I wonder whether the American Dream is really for dreamers. Are you dreaming if you're working twelve hours or more a day?

It might seem strange that being a refugee and being a mother feel so similar to me, but both involve a tortuous and lifelong drive in search of home and security—in one case for oneself; in the other, even more furiously, for one's child. The journey of a refugee, away from war and loss toward peace and a new life, and the journey of a mother raising a child to be secure and happy are both steep paths filled with detours and stumbling blocks. For me, both hold mystery. It is like crossing a river on a monkey bridge. The bridge, indigenous to the Mekong Delta, is handmade, with slender bamboo logs and handrails. It is frail and slippery, and crossing it requires agility and courage; it is both physical and mental. I have not made my crossing alone but have had fellow travelers on this bridge—we could call them darker selves that emerge from the hidden, almost mystical shadows.

Carl Jung saw shadow selves as selves that are cradled in the darkness and lie outside the light of consciousness. But what I think of as my shadow selves are denser, perhaps more fragmented from the self than Jung's original use of the term. They might seem like strangers at first, unknown, unknowable, and as a result frightening, a presence manifesting unruly states that had to be fought with or unshackled from. Over time, with a deeper reservoir of understanding, I have come to see them as guardian angels, as they are now more integrated with me than not.

After more than forty years in the United States, I still feel tentative here at times. And after seventeen years of being a parent, I continue to venture through motherhood as if it's a new culture. No matter how many parenting books I have read or how much advice I have received, I still feel like an immigrant in the universe of motherhood. As I tentatively make my way through this landscape, I find that I vacillate more than I am certain, shifting my terms of engagement more than digging in. Like an immigrant newcomer, I am ambivalent. I question myself, especially when my precocious kid sarcastically unleashes comments like "Great parenting, Mom" after I make a decision she doesn't like. She sounds so sure in her skepticism, and her certainty stands in stark contrast to my inner uncertainty.

Even something as basic as language—mother tongue, which for me is Vietnamese—posed a dilemma. I wasn't sure whether I should speak it to Harlan when she was a newborn. Even something as beloved as a country or a language could be a burden. And I wondered whether it was better for her not to be hyphenated or fragmented in any way. My husband, Bill, didn't speak Vietnamese. There would be no conversation. She would hear only my monologue. So I didn't stick to a Vietnamese-only regimen with her. I wanted to give her what I did not have and have not been able to achieve: wholeness. I wasn't sure I wanted her to be disjointed and bifurcated like me. By the time I changed my mind and saw hyphenation as an unconventional form of wholeness, as having a set of twos instead of multiple divided halves, her little brain had become an English-language brain. Now she would have to learn Vietnamese and any other language as a second language. That delayed decision remains a moment of regret.

Harlan was born in the United States, far from Vietnam, but I have bequeathed Vietnam to her whether I wanted to or not, sometimes as a gift, sometimes as a burden, but always as a marker or an imprint. I lost Vietnam when I was thirteen years old, in 1975. Forty years after the fall of Saigon, in 2015, my daughter herself turned thirteen, which for me meant the past had turned to the present, bringing itself to me in a singularly haunting act once again.

This was deeply poignant to me, perhaps because I saw it as life coming full circle, like a serpent swallowing its tail. Or maybe it is because humans need to find order and symmetry in life, and the tick, tick of calendar and clock in increments of five and ten creates the illusion that we can organize and mark time in comprehensible segments. For this momentous fortieth anniversary of the fall of Saigon, we went to see Rory Kennedy's film *Last Days in Vietnam* in Westminster, California, home to one of the largest Vietnamese diaspora outside Vietnam.

The theater was packed with Vietnamese who, like me, nurtured a deep elegiac longing from afar for the country we had left. Having watched Vietnam the country and Vietnam the war dissected in slanderous misproportion by Americans all these years, all of us, made to feel uncertain of our knowledge and our memories, returned yet again for another American interpretation of Vietnam, full of hope that something would be told right this time.

Seeing the film was one way for me to share my family's history with Harlan. We'd talked so much, but she'd never seen Vietnam on TV or in a movie. We held hands and we cried. We saw one city after another fall as the United States stopped supplying guns, ammunition, and even replacement parts. Come what may, whatever the consequence, whatever the wreckage, the war had to end, as far as America was concerned. After the first few minutes of the movie, however, I closed my eyes, casting myself adrift in my compartmentalized head, insulating myself from the screen. I was at the movie theater, but not really. I could be there, but also not. I knew how to detach, float away, without letting on that it was happening. Forty years ago, I too had witnessed these apocalyptic events from a TV in the living room in Avon, Connecticut, where I had been sent to live with an American family before the country's collapse.

I couldn't help but wonder whether I would be able to send my daughter off, away from country and family, to live with another family without any certainty that I would ever see her again. What would have to happen in our lives for me to take that action?

Harlan Margaret is my one and only child. In a dreamlike way that turned out to be real, I felt she was alive inside me almost as soon as she was conceived. Before the pregnancy was even advanced enough to be confirmed by a test kit, my body already changed, reconfiguring to make room for this new nudging, jostling, carnivorous being. Swollen breasts. Tender belly. Voracious hunger. Insatiable desire to nap. And from the moment the pregnancy was confirmed, I found myself measuring time not by reference to it in my own life but rather into the projected future of hers.

Both Bill and I were law professors. And so our daughter was named after one of the great justices of the United States Supreme Court, the august and magnificent Justice John Marshall Harlan from Kentucky. In 1869, he rejected separate but equal, the prevailing principle in the United States used to justify racial segregation, when he alone dissented from the majority in the infamous *Plessy v. Ferguson* case. I also wanted to give my daughter a gender-neutral name, and incidentally, the name Harlan also has Lan in it. In that way, we are intertwined with and embedded in each other.

The name Margaret came from Aunt Margaret, who had taken me in and cared for me when my parents sent me off in 1975. I was to be adopted by her and her husband, Fritz, our precious family friend, if South Vietnam fell and my parents couldn't make it out. Margaret was also the name of my daughter's grandmother on her father's side: Margaret Ware, a precocious, independent, intelligent woman who grew up in Santa Rosa, California, and entered Stanford University at age sixteen, graduating in three years. A California state park has a dedicated redwood grove and commemorative plaque carved with her full name, Margaret Ware Van Alstyne. The family had bought hundreds of acres of redwood forests to save them from commercial lumbering and donated them to the Navarro River Redwoods State Park. Until Bill died in 2019, trips to and stories about the redwood forests were part of Harlan's family heritage.

I also gave her a Vietnamese name, Nam Phương, which means "in a southern direction"; that is, toward "Nam," Vietnam. It was also the name of Vietnam's last empress, a figure considered a symbol of national unity and pride in Vietnamese history.

I thought if I had to carry a child for nine months, the child should take my last name, but in the interest of equality, I generously suggested using both our names. My husband's last name is Van Alstyne; mine is Cao. And so we made a new last name for Harlan: Van Cao, which seemed egalitarian enough. But in reality, although he probably didn't realize it, I won because Van merely means "from" in Dutch, and what we have in the end is Harlan Margaret "from Cao."

She might be, biologically speaking, from me, but from the moment I was pregnant, it felt as if we were sinewed together, as if I were also from her—motherhood and babyhood mixed together. The Vietnamese also believe that the mother and child relationship begins when the child is in the mother's womb. The relationship can be nurtured and developed as the child grows, and when the child is born, it is already one year old. It was natural for me to talk to her, to place the CD player close to my belly when I played music, to read out loud to her. We were very sensitive to each other's movements. I could feel her head against my belly, and sometimes I could almost grab her elbow and heel with my fingers to move her to a position more comfortable for me. My coughs were usually followed by intense, almost violent hiccups on her part—more than 150 once. Sometimes I could summon her by tapping on my belly rhythmically, and I could feel her respond to my call—our private code—by moving more vigorously.

Because I was almost forty when I became pregnant, it was recommended that I have an amniocentesis. What happened during the procedure turned out to be a fairly accurate predictor of Harlan's personality. Naturally, I was nervous because the procedure is invasive and carries a risk of inducing miscarriage. Amniocentesis could not be done earlier than sixteen weeks, and by that time, I had already fallen in love and bonded with the baby, having felt her movement and the shape of her body pressed against mine. This way in the morning, that way in the evening. Calm and unperturbed when I read or listened to music or when I took a warm shower. Energetic and agile after I ate a large meal. Would I be able to go through with an abortion if the procedure showed a developmental abnormality?

With ultrasound guidance, the doctor inserted a needle through my abdominal wall and uterine wall to reach the amniotic sac. I concentrated on the ultrasound picture on the monitor, trying to make out the baby's shape against the grainy black-and-white background. Suddenly, the doctor stopped her probing, sterile gloves immobile against my belly. She rushed out of the room and came back excitedly with a colleague. I was frightened, thinking she had seen a problem. Instead, she told me that even though she had inserted the needle in an area far from the baby, Harlan was miraculously aware of its presence, even moving her hand as if attempting to grab the needle. "You have a really special and sensitive baby in there," the doctor said.

This turns out to be true—not that I am boasting, because all mothers think their babies are special, but Harlan is very sensitive, in terms of being quite discerning and aware. When she was only two, I was reading a book with her about a baby whale that had gotten lost. We were at a part where the baby has a joyous reunion with its parents, and she asked me, pointing to the illustration of the two parent whales, "Which one is the mommy and which is the daddy?" I looked carefully, and seeing just two gray whales of equal size, I said I didn't know. She gleefully pointed out that one in particular was the mommy. I asked her why she made this choice, and she pointed to the whale's eyelashes. "This one has longer eyelashes." I would never have noticed such a thing. Her ability to discern the most minute detail, however, means that she is able to detect my weaknesses and my lack of certainty in many matters, and as a result, she has been able to exploit them to her advantage. As you can guess, I have not been able to impart the Vietnamese cultural norms that rank the parent immutably higher than the child. She knows my ambivalence and can work to throw me off-kilter.

According to Vietnamese folklore, a child's personality is shaped by her mother's pregnancy and birthing experience. Even a tiny baby can receive her mother's memory, weaving and absorbing it into her blood, sinew, neurons, the very genes themselves. As an example, my brother Tuấn had struggled all his life until his death at the young age of forty. According to my mother, he suffered the effects of the war not only when he briefly joined South Vietnam's army at age nineteen, but even when he was inside my mother's womb. He had been cursed by his fetal memory of her pregnancy trauma—the bombings, explosions, and artillery shelling, which had made her anxious and jumpy. When pregnant with Tuấn, my mother was with my father in North Vietnam, as he had been stationed in Hưng Yên Province, before the 1954 partition of the country into a Communist North and a non-Communist South. She said she could feel the baby's agitation and distress. Her anxiety and fear were in turn assimilated by the baby, calcified in his very being.

When she was in her seventh month of pregnancy, the bus she was on was ambushed by insurgents. The bus driver and conductor, seeing that she was pregnant, told her to scramble under the seats as they tried to shield her. After a fusillade of bullets and grenades, my mother felt the limp and heavy bodies of the two men pressed against her, blood gushing out of deep wounds.

There were three survivors that day. My mother was one and the baby she carried was the second. The third survivor and my mother limped out of the debris of the charred bus and made their way around rows of nearby gutted cars. They found a stream and ran to it, hiding behind the muddy banks as blasts of gunfire continued around them. The water turned out to be leech infested. My mother found an engorged leech in her nose and many clinging to her belly, their bodies embedded in the soft flesh. The baby inside her kicked furiously, almost as if he could feel the predation of bloodsuckers coming for him.

When she pried the leeches off, their slimy blood-sucking heads were still stuck in her flesh. My mother was frightened that the leeches had infected her unborn baby. When she found her way back to the city, she went not just to a regular medical doctor for checkups but also to a traditional medicine man, who warned her about restless fetus syndrome, explained that the baby was not at peace, and prescribed herbal concoctions for her to boil and drink. She was convinced that although the remedy prevented a miscarriage, the baby's emotional equilibrium had been damaged by her own anxiety and by the surrounding violence. My father was skeptical and often said that my mother was simply coddling her black sheep son and making excuses for him.

Fortunately, my pregnancy was smooth and uneventful, but the birth was difficult and even distressing. It's been seventeen years since I gave birth, or, more precisely, since I tried to expel the baby from me. My grandmother had given birth eighteen times, even if not all her babies had survived. One of my mother's babies, birthed a year after me, died in the same hospital I was born in. My aunt, Mother Five, died giving birth to her daughter after three normal, healthy childbirths. This is what can happen to women when we bring life into the world, like the match that gave life to fire and then died. This is why even under the best of circumstances a mother is on the alert for her child's safety, and why the child is often oblivious to and sometimes even irritated by the mother's fears—the child does not remember how life and death were intertwined at the very moment of her birth. Her own birth recedes to the margins of her life, but it continues to stick to the birth mother's very being.

The first contractions I felt were in the evening of August 2, 2002, and they were so strong they made me collapse on the floor with the most intense pain I'd ever felt. I went to the hospital around two a.m., and after an hour I was sent back home. I hadn't dilated enough and the contractions were not close enough together for me to be admitted. I was told to time the contractions to see if they lasted between forty-five and sixty seconds and were no more than five minutes apart. When I got home, I threw myself on the bed because the pain was so acute. I struggled to remain alert enough to accurately time the contractions, which were becoming regular, though always seven to ten minutes apart and lasting only about thirty terrible seconds, not the requisite forty-five to sixty seconds. This continued until the morning of August 4, when the intensity, acceleration, and length of the contractions changed, and off we went to the hospital. I was relieved to be admitted at last.

But trouble followed every part of my birthing experience. Even when I received the welcomed epidural, complications abounded. The doctor had trouble inserting the needle into the numbed area surrounding my spinal cord in the lower back. He also struggled threading the catheter through the needle. I could see blood on the compresses that he applied to the area even as he apologized profusely for the difficulty. For the next ten hours, I was told to push and push. The baby's spiky tuft of hair could even be felt, but she refused to come out—or to put it another way, I couldn't get her out. We clashed even then.

At four thirty p.m., there was a huge commotion, and I was told the baby's heartbeat showed distress and that the doctor had ordered an emergency C-section. From then on, everything happened at a rapid clip. I was wheeled down the hall into a room, a blanket draped over me, although it was summer and we were in the South. My obstetrician huddled with others on the team. I was introduced to the attending pediatrician. I felt pressure against my lower abdomen below the bikini line. Then I heard the most beautiful sound on earth—the cry of a baby, the spark of life—which made the whole ordeal and every pang of pain that had preceded that cry worth it. I was elated and so eager to see her. My husband, who was a constitutional lawyer but knew enough tort law to know how often surgical mishaps occur in real life, kept reminding the doctor to remove all medical paraphernalia from my body before closing me up. The comment, softly delivered, could be interpreted as humorous and provoked much laughter among the medical personnel.

And then suddenly all laughter ended. I could sense a complete shift in the energy of the room. The baby was whisked out. The room became quiet, and I was immediately stilled by the silence. I began freezing and felt my entire body vibrating and my teeth chattering nonstop. This was a normal side effect of the anesthesia used during the C-section, my doctor said, but it alarmed me. I was swaddled in another blanket and wheeled back into my hospital room. When the pediatrician and obstetrician came in to see me, they told me that Harlan had pneumothorax. It happens when there is a tear or rupture in the alveoli, the tiny air sacs of the lungs, allowing air to escape into the chest. The doctors went through the many possible causes, one of which was vigorous crying and screaming, which can cause the alveoli to rupture. Yes, the pediatrician told me, some babies can cry and scream hard enough to cause this condition at birth. I was reassured Harlan would be fine—the doctor had removed the collected air by inserting a chest tube through her chest wall and into the air space. However, to be absolutely safe, he had ordered that she be transferred to a children's hospital one hour away in Norfolk, Virginia, to be monitored in the neonatal intensive care unit. I did not get to hold my baby until more than twenty-four hours after her birth.

When she was transported from the intensive care unit and returned to me at the hospital, I felt an all-consuming, howling kind of love that was brand-new to me. It's the kind of love that makes mothers throw themselves into danger to protect their children the way we instinctively use our hands and arms to shield our more essential and vital parts—head and heart. The nurses carefully placed her in my arms and positioned her just right, so that she could suckle. My body had fed her when she was in the womb, and now it was ready for the next stage, breastfeeding, which became a source of both food and comfort for her. I didn't wean her completely until she was three. Each time I tried, she cried so hard, and although many books advised that mothers should teach babies to self-soothe, I believed that if I could comfort and console her with something as easy as offering her what she craved—her mother's breast, and consequently sanctuary, security, and a sense that she mattered—I would. Why not? There would be plenty of opportunities later in life when nothing I could do would solve her problems. This was an easy one for me.

Months later, when I supplemented her nursing with solids, I remember feeling that this was a profound marker in both our lives. I realized she was growing older and becoming a separate being every day. She was now able to eat mashed carrots and peas. She no longer relied on my body alone for sustenance. It was a moment I celebrated and mourned. One moment she was wholly and completely inside her mother's body, entangled and intertwined, and the next she was outside as a separate being, and becoming more separate by the day.

Every question I had was followed by another question. Do I share the world's beauty with her and leave it at that, the unmarred, simple beauty of a sunrise, a sunset, a shiny young leaf, its autumn counterpart, the blazing orange shades of gold and copper and ocher and vermilion that spread across what was once green? Or do I warn her about the world's danger, the violence and evil on earth?

When Harlan was born, I was entering a stage of life that I considered to be a stable one, anchored by a house, a mortgage, and a good job that I loved. I had not wanted to have a child until I felt economically secure in America. My life was my own, and I could, if catastrophe struck again, survive. Alone.

Which paradoxically made me ready to be a mother. But motherhood, of course, meant the opposite. Since her birth, since my baby's first plaintive cry that demanded a mother's immediate attention, I have embarked on a journey with Harlan that by its nature is not autonomous and alone but immersed and together, with all that is unpredictable, a cursive loop filled with highs and lows of every emotion conceivable, each felt intensely and profoundly. Two beings entwined.

I used to think the mother delivers the baby. But the truth is the opposite: It is the baby, the child, who creates her mother, reinforcing the mother's primal role as protector and nurturer and then rejecting that role as too suffocating and off-putting. And then somewhere, sometime, the two are reunited under different terms.

Harlan and I are often not compatible. We clash and boomerang through each other's lives. When she was about two and I transgressed against motherhood, leaving her for a stretch of many hours for a full-day job interview, she wailed nonstop, and no singing, rocking, or pumped breast milk could alleviate her distress. When I returned and held her and devoted myself completely to her service, she stopped crying immediately. But if I focused too much on her, she could feel the anxiety and would cry.

And of course, it's the child's prerogative to defend itself against the encroachment of parental rules.

I don't remember feeling this way about my parents. And if I did, I did not indulge in the feeling, much less feel entitled to it. Is this because I was a Vietnamese child, raised according to strict traditional rules? Or because we were a refugee family and I was afraid of disturbing their fragile psyches?

Although I don't believe that a birth sign determines destiny or personality, it is noteworthy that I was born the year of the buffalo and Harlan the year of the horse. The buffalo is slow, steady, persevering, plodding— exhibiting all the attributes necessary for an animal that is used for plowing the fields. The buffalo is traditionally prized in Vietnam given the country's agrarian economy and the primacy of rice in the Vietnamese diet. It is also known to be stubborn and narrow-minded. It's certainly not known for its flashiness, flamboyance, or brilliant wit. By contrast, the horse is artistic, magnetic, and engaging. It likes to prance and show off. It is also known to be rebellious and carefree, with a dash of childishness. No wonder the Vietnamese zodiac says horse and buffalo tend not to be compatible. In almost every area of life, I have multiple contingencies in case my plans fall through. In almost every area of life, Harlan has one plan because she is certain that singular plan will succeed. Whenever I have tried to engage in gentle correction, I am met with resistance, sighing, eye-rolling, huffing and puffing. Sometimes it escalates into outright arguing. Like a horse bucking to throw someone off her back—exhilarating and exhausting.

By nature, Harlan is more like her father—relaxed, basically happy, essentially carefree, believing plan A will work and that having a plan B is excessive. Given my history, Bill was a good counterbalance for her, and it was a sad day for us and particularly for her when Bill died, during Harlan's junior year in high school. The exuberant American part of her life, the part that she could easily relate to and identify with, was gone. After all, she is an American kid, even if she has a Vietnamese mother tied to the darker sufferings of Vietnam. Although many of my formative years and my grown-up years were spent in the United States—indeed I have lived many more years in this country than my compact thirteen years in Vietnam—I do not really feel completely American. Or at least I still struggle with what "American" means.

I am considered the 1.5 generation—born in Vietnam but coming of age in the United States, cussed and interlocked between two or more selves. Like others, I've carried my own and perhaps even my parents' bad memories, trauma, and grief, which have echoed in their lives and mine. We have tried to deflect but have also absorbed the past. And sometimes our bodies and psyches become reluctant chroniclers of disturbance, spawning fractals of division, compartmentalized personalities, wounded souls—shadow selves, one could say, with distinct names like Cecile. Things that have happened to many of us in this generation have left their mark on each of us, although the same event can affect our individual brain pathways and our neurotransmitters differently. But pain is pain, whether it is remembered and felt as a dull ache or as a pang, and even if it's not visible to others, its vessels and capillaries are there in the body's hollow space.

Sometimes the past can take over and swallow the present. Other times the past can be suppressed, magically cast aside until it inevitably finds a way back. Over the years, therapy has unlocked for me and for the darker shadow selves within me a path, neither linear nor one-dimensional but circular and multidimensional, so that I can move away from refraction and fragmentation and finally toward reconciliation and healing. Because there is something tender and special about sitting in a room with another person who holds you in your pain and with whom you have forged a sacred trust, a person who is surely educated and trained, but whose unique relationship with you transcends degrees and techniques.

Growing up partly in the United States, I have also experienced the exuberance and gloom of migration and assimilation. As a teenager, I was immersed in American life through school and television, which I was allowed to watch only because my parents believed it was a way for me to work on my English. On television, especially on sitcoms, I witnessed standard-issue teenage rebellion, American-style. I saw that children regularly questioned their parents and talked back in quick, snappy retorts that usually garnered the most laughs from the studio audience. A kid came home from school, walked straight to her bedroom without saying hi to her parents, and then slammed the door. Parents tiptoed around their children's moods. Children remained seated or continued slouching on the living room couch when their parents' grown-up friends visited, casually acknowledging the visitors' presence with a breezy hi. Kids talked to their parents with their feet on the coffee table, bottoms of shoes conspicuously exposed. No one did a single one of those things in my home (or in homes like mine). My parents watched these shows too, but they never had to tell me they did not approve of such behavior. It was simply assumed that the way I had been raised would inoculate me against such insolent insistence on individual rights. And although I was thirteen, the age when susceptibility to peer influence was supposedly strongest, I never challenged my parents. At home I was all Vietnamese. In the world, with others, I was divided, hyphenated, fluctuating sometimes toward the Vietnamese and other times more toward the American side.

That is not Harlan's experience.

She has the confidence and assertiveness of an American kid, which a part of me fully supports and encourages. I want her to have her own voice, even if I have to struggle with many frustrating moments of defiant belligerence. Living in the United States reinforces certain ideals about parents and children and children's personal growth processes that are foreign to the Vietnamese. Because I was ambivalent about the hybridity of Vietnamese American, I sent mixed messages to Harlan even in small daily struggles. She was neither born nor raised in or near a large Vietnamese community. When she was born, I lived a three-hour drive from my father, who was living in Falls Church, Virginia, a center of the Vietnamese diaspora. I was basically the only Vietnamese Harlan was close to. There was not enough Vietnameseness in her environment to serve as a countervailing force to the more dominant Americanness that I myself also felt ambivalently drawn to.

As a child I took piano lessons, and when I wanted to quit because I hated finger exercises and scales, my parents spent less than one minute telling me that I was not allowed. No. "You will appreciate the piano when you are grown-up and need music. Being able to play the piano alone is different from listening to music on the radio alone." I was obligated to continue. And as it turns out, I am glad I was forced to do so. Being Vietnamese, I did not insist on arguing with my parents and deciding for myself what I should or should not do. But Harlan believes she has the right not to like something and to act on her feelings. When she wanted to quit the violin, our struggle was not a simple one. I wanted her to want to press on, but I did not want to make her feel obligated. I wanted her to know she had the right to quit but nonetheless choose not to. I could have made her stick with the violin, but it would have meant exerting my will over hers while she bucked the entire time. Every practice was marred by raised voices and even outright shouting. I capitulated. She quit. I felt bad. She felt good, at least for the time being.

I had more cultural support after my friend Mai came to live with us in Williamsburg, Virginia, from Vancouver, Canada. Mai is my age and her family and mine had been intertwined in Vietnam. We were childhood friends in school in Saigon. We had been separated when South Vietnam collapsed. I fled, while her family was stuck behind. We only connected decades later, thanks to the internet. Mai came for a visit and stayed, eventually becoming enmeshed in our small family. We adopted her and she us, and we became the Four Musketeers, an unconventional family that we created together. She brought Vietnam memories of her own with her, which sometimes felt like they were mine as well. Having Mai reenter my life when we were in our midforties was like a return to Vietnam for both of us. Harlan was about six when Mai joined us, and she began referring to my friend as Mother Two.

Mai is also of the 1.5 generation, and she, like me, is not completely Vietnamese. Neither she nor I was uniform or consistent in our thinking about which Vietnamese values should be nurtured and passed on to Harlan. Respect for parents and the elderly was bedrock, but beyond that, it was sometimes a dash of this, other times a dash of that, with the three grown-ups making things up as we stumbled along. From the beginning, Harlan was sassy, feisty, and, to me, sometimes pugnacious, which to her was standing up for herself. What a Vietnamese family considers correcting their children and teaching them, she would use as proof that I was never satisfied with her.

Once, Harlan showed me a watercolor painting she had made in a weekend art course. I offered a mild suggestion about composition and color as we walked hand in hand from the class to the parking lot. In a tone that was both tart and sweet, she retorted, "You're not the boss of my painting." What struck me was the tiny ankle boots she was wearing. She was still struggling with tying laces, so the boots were fastened with

Velcro. She could not have been more than five. And yet the voice was sassy and presumptuous. *Impertinent* was one of the first words she learned because we used it often to refer to her. I should have had a better inkling of our relationship then.

Perhaps our turbulence also comes from our circumstances—from my Vietnamese roots, which cannot find peace on American soil. I myself have an uneasy, often incoherent relationship with Vietnam. Vietnam means culture and history, but also war and loss. Add all that to motherhood and you have complications, or, to put a more positive spin on it, complexities. Mongrelized, hybrid, chaotic, unstable. "Not a normal family," Harlan says with the careless confidence of an American. Vietnam remains powerful, exerting both its centrifugal and centripetal forces on me. Because my discerning and perceptive child knows I haven't found equilibrium, she is poised to take advantage, ready to resist and strike, using perfectly honed American logic.

Lan

My American life started with loss.

A few months before Vietnam fell to the Communists in April 1975, my father and an American family friend I called Papa Fritz took me in our black Opel sedan to Tân Sơn Nhứt airport in Saigon. I knew the route so well that the drive there, past streets shaded by tamarind trees and low-slung buildings, felt normal, routine. My father was in uniform: camouflage fatigues, red beret, polished standard-issue military boots. The city had been under rocket attack night and day. The streets, restless and swollen with people going about their business, were singed in smoke.

The last time the war was this close to us was during the Tet Offensive in 1968, and the memories of Tet's devastation and its mix of the mundane and the deadly still frightened me. Tet firecrackers sounded exactly like gunfire, allowing the Vietcong to hide their attacks behind Tet festivities. Our house was in Cholon, which I thought of as Saigon's twin city—Saigon's other, shadow self. Our house was also close to the Phú Thọ race-track, which had been seized by the Vietcong. Suddenly, the flat, open grounds where we used to watch horse races was the site of one of the fiercest battles of the Tet Offensive. This seemingly innocuous area had become a strategic compound because it could also function as a helicopter landing zone and an artillery base. Americans and South Vietnamese forces fired thousands of rounds into the area, followed by house-to-house combat in the racetrack's vicinity as the Vietcong tried to retake it. The noise was deafening. My cousins and I cowered in the bathroom in the back of the house while the grown-ups decided whether we could make it to Saigon, which was also under attack but less so.

This time, the fighting was not as close to our neighborhood as it had been in 1968. Still, we could feel the city shake when surrounding areas were shelled. After a particularly violent series of explosions that sounded close to our house, my father explained that the Vietcong had detonated a bomb-storage area and destroyed an ammunition depot in Bien Hoa, about twenty miles from Saigon.

Even war can be normalized, especially a long war, like the one in Vietnam, which lasted more than twenty years. Sometimes it was very close to us and sometimes it was farther away. Throughout my childhood, the war pervaded my everyday consciousness, often with pointillistic precision. As a commander of South Vietnam's elite airborne troops, my father was regularly away on combat duty for several days or weeks. He would come home and life would seem normal again, until the next combat operation.

My first clear memory is of my body being swollen and itchy and feverish from chicken pox and my father picking me up and wrapping his arms around me. He pinned my hands, which were swaddled in cloth pouches to keep me from scratching. There was the smell of the earth and leaves and soil rising from his uniform. There was the small majesty of his by now familiar boots, which were big and still caked in mud. There was the low-key lullaby that he sang to calm me, about a woman who held her child while waiting for her husband to return from the war. The husband had been ordered into battle by the Emperor. She waited and waited for him to return, for so long that she became a stone.

I knew the scars on his body did not come from schoolyard games. They came from a battle near the Cambodian border in which his troops were ambushed. I knew he had cyanide pills sewn into the hems of his uniforms, just in case he was ever captured or tortured. He would be able to bite the hems and swallow the poison even if his hands were cuffed. War made its mark on his body and his mind, and the ghosts of war stayed with us like whispered prayers inside our hearts, in the backs of our minds, in the marrow of our family consciousness.

Even when it was far away, the quiet engine of war could still be felt. Many of my father's airborne troops were stationed right behind our house. My father told me the camp was off-limits to me, but I often entered it secretly. All that separated it from our back garden, with its lush frangipani and lantana plants and bougainvillea, was a metal door, which I could open from my side because the troops often forgot to lock it from their side. And I would secretly spend time with the soldiers, and was even allowed to touch their guns. Sometimes the clicking noises of the guns as cartridges were inserted and removed frightened me. Sometimes I saw one of the soldiers act boisterously, almost crazily, and he had to be held down by others as if they were fighting each other in an out-of-control brawl, but I was told later that they were doing this so they could console him.

Beyond our house it was also easy to be reminded of war. Outside our neighborhood at the Jeanne d'Arc Catholic church that stood at Six Corners, where six streets converged, there was always a young man with no legs—just one stump below the knee and the other above the knee—who sat on a patch of grass with his military medals laid out on a blanket, strumming a guitar and singing Creedence Clearwater Revival. "Have you ever seen the rain," he sang in a grizzly rasp of a voice. I had perfect pitch, and I would go home to my piano and listen to the music hidden inside its body, appreciating always its intonation, its muscle memory, trying to eke out the right notes. Sometimes when the urge to find the tune was uncontrollable, I even ventured into the church itself, past the vestibule and baptismal. There, you could smell the different aromatic oils used for baptism, confirmation, ordination. I would run past the nave, with its rows of dark polished pews, straight to the sanctuary, where I would find the piano nestled by the altar and tabernacle. The priest, with a strange expression— scowling, smiling, sneering, waving me in—was nearby. A small fan oscillated quietly, and his black robe fluttered as he coaxed me in. At a certain time of the day, every object in the church had a twin, rows of perfectly cast shadows, and despite the dark eeriness of the space, I allowed myself to go in because of the piano.

From there, in the somber quiet, I could hear the beggar man right outside singing. Like he was trying to recover God.

When the beggar man was not singing, he used his arms to propel himself across the sidewalk with alacrity, asking for loose change and telling people where he had fought. A part of me loved the frantic acoustic guitar licks, part sorrow, part pure ecstasy. Another part of me was terrified by what was unsettlingly not there—the missing body parts—and what was unsettlingly there—the tender stitched skin, wrinkled yet stretched over bony, fleshy nubs. I was transfixed by the songs that came out of his mouth—or, rather, out of some mysterious cavity deep in his chest—like the Rolling Stones' "19th Nervous Breakdown": "Here it comes, here it comes, here it comes, here it comes, here comes your nineteenth nervous breakdown." It wasn't fraught or foreboding like a threat, but more like the jangle of a promise. Whatever it is, here it comes.

One of my mother's beloved brothers was blown up by a mine while he worked overtime in a minesweeping unit. We called him Father Three, or Ba Ba, like a stutter. He was second in order of birth, but the firstborn was always referred to as the second to fool demons who had a tendency to grab a family's first child. The mine had been cleverly wrapped in plastic or maybe was made of plastic; such mines are less expensive, more durable, and harder to detect. My grandmother went to collect her son's splattered body—days later, she could still find bits of flesh under her nails and matted in her hair when she unraveled her chignon. His daughters vanished from our lives, as his widow was lost in her own madness and grief and wrath and stopped coming to visit.

My grandfather, a well-known landowner in Sóc Trăng in the Mekong Delta, had been captured by the Vietcong and killed; landlords were deemed rapacious evildoers. They held him for quite some time, and my father had tried to parachute into the rumored vicinity to free him, but Grandfather could not be located. He might have been moved just before my father landed. Or he'd already been killed. I also remember my brother coming home one evening covered in blood because he had dined in a restaurant on Tự Do Street and a Vietcong on a motorbike had lobbed a grenade onto the patio. He was scolded for not knowing better. Right away, my parents instilled yet another lesson into us: Never sit at the front of stores or restaurants.

Still, there was an ebb and flow to living. Although my childhood markers all had something to do with the war, we managed to find normalcy in the interstices of daily life.

WE DIDN'T JUST FIND NORMALCY, ACTUALLY. We even found magic.

I daydreamed about magical things and had a magical view of the world, immersed as I was in the realm of dreams, visions, premonitions. In 1974, my older brother Tuấn was nineteen and enlisted in the Army of the Republic of Vietnam, and my mother, worried about his safety, rushed to see a fortune-teller. She left the house filled with anxiety but returned home feeling buoyant and reassured by a faint torch of hope. "The war will be over soon. Your son won't be in it for long and he will be safe," the fortune-teller declared.

That was an extraordinary, almost magical statement, that peace was loosely feasible. The war, sprawling, wrenching, with its many twists and reversals, had been going on for twenty years with no end in sight. The supernatural notwithstanding, what the woman declared seemed wholly realistic. My mother believed her. "He will be safe" was a verse she kept in her heart. Tuấn was the soft, soulful type who loved to strum the guitar and sing love songs. His voice was deep and warm. He carried his guitar with him and made me wish my piano were portable. How wonderful that he could have his instrument with him anytime.

Tuấn used to sing with a band called Shotgun, and I loved his renditions of famous American songs like "My Way" and "For Once in My Life," French songs like "L'Amour C'est Pour Rien," and other Vietnamese songs of the melancholy kind my mother loved, such as those by Khánh Ly and Thanh Tuyền. Tuấn was not a soldier or a warrior, in other words. I knew he wanted to be a singer, which to my parents was just as bad as being an actor, or even worse.

When my mother told me what the fortune-teller had said, I was not skeptical either. I was happy to believe what my mother believed. It was magical but not impossible. Indeed, her prediction was correct, and my mother was granted the grim satisfaction of a magical wish come true. The war did end, although it ended with our loss. And my brother did survive, physically unscathed.

Even my father listened attentively when my mother told him what the fortune-teller had forecast. He did not snicker, even though he must have known the facts. I was twelve, and my friends and I read the daily newspapers with a measured mix of dread and detachment. My parents did not flinch from real-world discussions at the dinner table. The fact was that South Vietnam had been forced to sign the Paris Peace Accords of 1973, a peace treaty it didn't want to sign because it allowed more than 145,000 North Vietnamese troops to remain in South Vietnam, ready to pounce and ambush when the Americans turned away. Our newspapers called it the "leopard spot" treaty. It didn't feel like a real peace agreement, but it allowed the Americans to declare that there was now peace with honor—and that after a decent interval, long enough to absolve the United States, the North and even China could just come and claim us.

And after the treaty was signed, fighting continued as usual and intensified in the Central Highlands. Still, my father seemed to take my mother's story seriously, as if he could allow himself a bit of magical thinking too. I happily took my cue from him.

My father devoted himself to yoga and Buddhist meditation. He told me that after years of practice, he had miraculously developed a secondary lifeline on his palm that ran parallel to the primary one. It was long, deep, and rosy. I ran my finger over it and felt its indented groove. I was happy because it signified that he had a strong spirit filled with vitality. Sometimes he invited me into his yoga room and we meditated together. The shadow side of life seemed so far away. I felt light and almost carefree. Even Buddhism seemed magical.

The *One Thousand and One Nights* stories my father gave me and that I read before bed, often surreptitiously under the blanket with a flashlight because it was past my bedtime, kept me alive in the fairy-tale world of the fantastic and the fabled. I was enchanted by Scheherazade, who had a mythmaker's understanding of the power of stories, which she told night after night to save her life. Her stories were fabulous, filled with mythological and phantasmagorical elements, and blended seamlessly with the wushu movies and novels that were beloved in Asia and Vietnam. We, both children and adults, were addicted to the acrobatic style of fighting and swordsmanship. We flocked to see their film versions the same way people today love the Harry Potter movies.

As in the movie *Crouching Tiger, Hidden Dragon*, male and female martial arts fighters in these films sail and somersault across rooftops and land on tree branches in spectacular defiance of the laws of physics. Poison-tipped arrows fly with parabolic ease and hit the intended target straight on. Warriors unsheathe their swords and the crisp metallic blades glimmer. The hero or heroine, usually an orphan or a suffering child, must find a beloved teacher, a strict disciplinarian, a revered sage, just and fair, willing to impart fighting secrets so that the disproportionately more powerful enemy can be vanquished. The chosen disciple must exhibit a natural proclivity for a certain code of righteous conduct, one that celebrates humility and patience, respect and order, rectitude and loyalty. We children absorbed these values.

The most famous of all and the one I was most addicted to was a series of martial arts–themed books by the Chinese writer Jin Yong called Legends of the Condor Heroes, featuring two heroes, Guo Jing and Huang Rong. Guo Jing, or Quách Tinh in Vietnamese, was forced to flee with his mother to the desert after his father was killed by foreign armies; he grew up there with Genghis Khan's Mongols. Huang Rong, or Hoàng Dzung in Vietnamese, is a beautiful, stratospherically intelligent, magnetic, and mischievous young kung fu fighter whose father was himself a legendary martial artist and who for mysterious reasons falls in love with the bumbling, not naturally gifted, not particularly dashing Quách Tinh.

I threw myself on the bed with piles of books and followed their exploits. How I wanted to live in the Mongolian steppes.

A wide cast of characters ranging from heroes to rogues roams across the pages. Who could resist the delirious charm and eccentricities of Quách Tinh's martial arts teachers, the Seven Freaks of Jiangnan? My cousins and I took turns adopting their fabulous personas: the blind elder, best at staff fighting, dart throwing, and nighttime fighting; followed in descending order by six others who were connoisseurs of pickpocketing, fan fighting, horse riding and whip fighting, palm and pole fighting, spear and lance fighting and the youngest, the sole female among the seven, sword fighting.

Who wouldn't be dazzled by such elaborate and intricate fighting routines, with fabulous names like Eighteen Dragons Subduing Palms and Nine Yin White Bone Claw, in which combatants can pierce skulls with fingers and magically paralyze opponents by merely touching their pressure points? Fighting scenes abound, with momentary pauses for philosophical contemplations on love, loyalty, honor, and betrayal. Each chapter begins with a couplet of poems and ends with a heartrending cliff-hanger. That was how I first learned to love poetry.

Although magic was everywhere, I treated it as everyday normal. That was its beauty. My nine cousins, children of Father Six, and I immersed ourselves in that world. We believed it was indeed possible, at least once upon a time, to take momentary leave of the earth, even to fly. Shaolin monks could do it. Wing Chun nuns who invented the martial arts style that Bruce Lee practiced could do it.

I was a martial arts student myself. South Korea had sent hundreds of thousands of soldiers to South Vietnam. My father knew many South Korean officers, who introduced him to a Tae Kwon Do master willing to teach me. Because I played soccer, I had considerable leg strength. I was a natural at Tae Kwon Do, which emphasizes kicking more than other martial arts such as karate, which centers around hand blocks and punches. Soon enough, I learned and mastered the art of the kick—hook kick, ax kick, flying side kick. I imagined myself gliding over rooftops and landing on bamboo branches.

My father loved traditional martial arts. When he could find me an aikido teacher, I started learning this soft style in addition to the harder style of Tae Kwon Do. They are not opposites but more like yin versus yang. The movement is circular and smooth and involves more turning, pivoting, and joint locks than kicks or punches. In both martial arts, there are individual moves to learn, which are combined into exercises and then patterns to perfect form, position, and technique. Eventually you learn how to keep the form, break the form, and leave the form. It's just like learning the piano, learning the form by doing scales and finger exercises, and then leaving it to make beautiful music.

I had reached the rank of red belt, merely one belt away from black, when I left Vietnam. And I was on the verge of being able to play Chopin's *Fantaisie-Impromptu* after many hours of practice. But when I left, I also left my piano behind.

Years later, I would eagerly watch my child practicing her own martial arts moves in Virginia as if I were watching my childhood wushu heroes running up walls or gliding on rooftops with extraordinary flair. This was especially so when Harlan had to perform katas, or kicks, blocks, and punches assembled and stylized into patterns she needed to memorize to achieve the next belt. I reluctantly came to realize, however, that the innate, latent sense of spirituality and morality that is a vital and compelling part of martial arts, that gives martial arts its pointed intensity, is hard to impart when martial arts is taken out of its cultural home. Yes, there is always the thrill of the form. But without everything else—the ingrained ethics, the drumbeat of right and wrong, duty and obligation—the story is incomplete.

When we moved to California, Harlan was on the verge of a black belt too. The Tae Kwon Do schools in California refused to recognize her belt and rank from Virginia, and she would have had to start all over as a white belt. She too ended up with no more than a red belt. She didn't want to continue, and I didn't have the oomph it took to make her.

One minute I would think: It would be a good thing to teach Harlan to follow through and persist until the end. And then I would retreat: Or maybe it wouldn't be a good thing, since martial arts is my Vietnamese dream and not hers. In America, I should let her find and make her own dream, not ventriloquize or impersonate mine.

AS MUCH AS I LOVED THE MYSTERY OF MAGIC, what was most magical about my childhood in Vietnam was not the mysterious or the fantastical but everyday life, strange as that might sound, because our daily lives were crosscut by the echoes of war. What was it like to be one part of a rollicking swell of schoolchildren running from the classroom into the courtyard to immerse ourselves in the pouring monsoon, drinking rain and screaming in unison with delight? What was it like to be part of the hectic rhythm of beautiful Saigon, to hold hands and audaciously cross the streets together, an exercise that gave real-life meaning to the saying "going with the flow"? Neither cars nor motorcycles bothered to stop for pedestrians, and the art of the crossing depended on doing, venturing not back and forth but decisively forward and not thinking too much.

Acquiring Topaz, my German shepherd pup, qualified as a magical feat. My mother, alternately giving and withholding, would not allow me to have a dog. She said dogs and buffaloes—she and I were both buffaloes—were incompatible and that having a dog would bring us bad luck. Topaz was a secret gift from my father, who presented me with the pup for my twelfth birthday, a most significant birthday because it was the completion of my first cycle through the lunar year zodiac. Topaz couldn't live with us, so my father built a big doghouse for him in an army lot down the street from our house. My father put the dog, a sweet secret, in the middle of my daily life. I could visit Topaz before school and before bed. When I first saw him, he was a mere scrap of a creature. Fluffy baby fur, round, with four huge paws. He liked to be read to, and he liked to give barking encouragement when I dribbled and kicked a soccer ball.

Collecting stamps from the world's countries—Hungary, Poland, Burma, Mongolia—was also magical. Prying the soft, pulpy tamarind flesh out of their pods after they fell, bulging and ripe, from the huge trees that lined my street was magical. Befriending a wounded cricket and nurturing it back to life in its new home, a matchbox that I'd punched holes all over so the cricket could breathe, was magical. Balancing myself under a banyan tree as I tried to walk on its massive spread of giant roots protruding aboveground was magical. I imagined it was the same banyan tree as the one the Buddha had sat under and achieved nirvana. Running up and down Saigon's first escalator with my two cousins close to my age in the city's first air-conditioned indoor mall, Crystal Palace, was magical. And even though they often scared me, visits with my mother to the local military hospital, where severely wounded soldiers were cared for, were also magical—especially when someone the doctors thought would die somehow survived.

AT SOME POINT, MAGIC FAILED. The magic of fairy tales and supernatural martial arts. The magic of wishful thinking and imagining. And the magic of the everyday, which, for a country at war, felt especially magical. Magic of every kind failed to change history or politics. This time, this month, this year—1975—my parents behaved differently. The war had taken a turn different from all those prior. Tet 1968 had been abnormal, but 1975 verged on the catastrophic.

Before sending me off to the airport, my mother, fittingly gentle, reminded me that Papa Fritz was only taking me on a short trip to Nước Mỹ, the Vietnamese word for America, which means "pretty country." Going to a pretty country with a close family friend sounded like an adventure, an innocent escape.

It would be cold, I thought excitedly. I wondered if I would see snow, white and pure, something I had only ever seen in films like *Doctor Zhivago* and *Love Story*—the train ride through the gorgeous snow-covered Ural Mountains and the whiteness of Harvard Square, respectively. Sitting in class, armed with the sharp end of a compass for math lessons, we carved "Love means never having to say you're sorry" on our desks after hearing Ali MacGraw say it in the movie.

I had only a small suitcase and a backpack. It was to be a short trip, after all, my mother assured me—a temporary respite from the daily gunfire and explosions. But without a return date, a part of me felt unsteady. I tucked several of my favorite stamp albums into my backpack, along with an envelope of hastily chosen photographs and my autograph book, which was filled with photos of classmates and their personal notes, drawings, and poems. I had not had a chance to say good-bye, and I did not know when I would see them again. I felt strange leaving the country without telling my friends. It felt as if I was doing something illicit.

For what was to be essentially a vacation, my mother approached my trip fussily, fretfully. My father had given me a small Buddha that had been infused with a special protection spell by a Cambodian paratrooper in his airborne brigade. Despite my protests, my mother and Papa Fritz pushed several of her jade bracelets up one of my wrists and 24-karat gold bracelets up the other. They also insisted that I wear several strings of my mother's pearl necklaces. I was thirteen and a tomboy who loved soccer and hated anything decorative on my body. I was not sure why I needed to take jewelry with me, but if I must, I would rather stuff it in my luggage instead. My mother had on her serious face. "It's better you wear them," she insisted, and Papa Fritz nodded in agreement.

Papa Fritz was the commander of the 199th Light Infantry Brigade and had been wounded in 1967 when enemy fire hit his helicopter. My mother had volunteered, every morning from five to nine, at the Cộng Hòa military hospital in Saigon and I sometimes accompanied her, especially after the 1968 Tet Offensive, not every day or every week, but frequently enough for my father to object and for my mother to ignore his objections. Years later, these were the images that stayed with me, like flames that torched and turned dreams bloodshot into the night. Like the searing memory of a young soldier with sunken eyes, legs partially bandaged and held up by a metal apparatus. The next day his legs were gone.

In the hospital, I saw not war but the horrifying moments after: the dreamers who volunteered and the conscripts, some meek, some crazy, some grateful to be alive, and some angry not to have died; the ever-present smell of burned skin, hot and raw, blistered and weeping with fluid when the burn was fresh, and thick and crusty when the burn was older; the clatter of metal against metal, scissors, scalpels, skin hooks, tissue nippers;

the fevers and pallor and sputum and wracking coughs; the simmering pots of congee on the floors cooked by wives and mothers of the wounded; the hiss and sizzle of an intermittently functioning refrigerator used to store blood; the spray of water from a hose aimed at dead skin to remove decay and infection. There were never enough beds or wheelchairs. Along the narrow verandas, young men lay on the floor, some on stretchers, waiting to be put back together.

Papa Fritz had been in a different, less familiar hospital, the U.S. Army's 3rd Field Hospital, reserved for American servicemen. We were there only to visit him. I could hear planes taking off and landing because the hospital was very close to the main gate of Tân Sơn Nhứt airport. Papa Fritz had his own bed, and his leg was kept raised in a device that looked like a metal sling. There was a lot of commotion in the room because he was the commander of a brigade that had lost twenty-four men killed in action only a few miles north of Saigon, during an assault with South Vietnamese rangers. The step-up in guerrilla attacks so close to the capital was meant to disrupt the presidential elections planned for September 1967.

I remembered our visits to this hospital, followed by Papa Fritz's frequent dinners at our house after he was released, until he was sent back to the United States a few months later. The time he spent with us was short, but the connection I made with him was instant and deep. We spoke French with each other and sometimes mixed the French with my rudimentary English. When we flipped through the comics, we had Snoopy and Dennis the Menace to cheer us up and make us chuckle.

In 1975, he returned to Vietnam to take me out. He was like someone who drove the wrong way on a one-way road to save a puppy. He was flying into Vietnam when everyone was desperate to fly out.

My mother did not accompany me to the airport. She waved good-bye almost coyly as the car drove away. We made our way like the hundreds of people around us on foot, in cars and rickshaws, on motorbikes and bicycles and three-wheeled machines, each fighting for every centimeter of street and sidewalk. I was leaving the country, so I observed the central boulevard, the shoppers and merchants, almost as if it were for the last time.

When I headed with Papa Fritz to the tarmac toward the giant plane, heat rising from asphalt seams, I turned back and saw my father with a sad look on his face. His military uniform was crisp and starched, filled with tension. I still remember the black gleam of his polished military boots, the same ones Santa would put gifts in on Christmas Eve. One of my favorite presents, hidden in the toe area of the boot, was a velvet box containing the first-day-of-issue stamp of the last empress, Nam Phương.

In my mind, I was but a tourist in 1975, passing through customs in Manila, then Guam, then Hartford, Connecticut. Papa Fritz held my hand and told me everything was fine as he filled out our forms. One of the immigration officers in Guam eyed the bracelets stacked on my wrists. Papa Fritz stiffened but relaxed when the officer said, "My daughter loves to pile it on too." I wanted to say I hated them, but Papa Fritz took control and told the officer that we had bought them from a skilled artisan in Saigon. "They look almost real," the officer complimented in a steadfast and professional voice. I sported a big dumb smile on my face despite the anxiety I felt inside.

AMERICA, AMERICA, AS IN ALL THOSE FAMOUS SONGS, like "America the Beautiful" and "God Bless America," which I remembered from the American television channels and radio stations in Saigon. I didn't know much about America. A few weeks after I arrived in Avon, Connecticut, it snowed. It was just a dusting because it was late March, but I was thrilled. I was with Papa Fritz and his wife, whom I called Aunt Margaret. The air was fresh and felt newly minted. The back deck had an accumulation of no more than an inch. Outside the sliding glass door, the world was almost all white. A bushy-tailed squirrel, which I had only seen drawn in fairy tales like "Snow White," was perched on the railing, staring at me fearlessly. I leaned into the wind, which chilled my face.

Aunt Margaret had bought me sweaters and jackets. I was bundled up and went outside, and for the first time in my life, I saw the delicate flakes of a new snowfall floating down in slow motion. Wonderstruck, I touched the snow with my fingertip. It tasted pure in my mouth.

There was even a flight of Canada geese. Black head, bill, and neck, with a startling white patch down the cheek like a chinstrap, the birds lining up in V formation and honking raucously as they made their way across the Connecticut sky. For years, as a child, I was intrigued by the movement of life: the flight of birds in the sky, their black wings flickering like delicate lace, the migration of monarch butterflies in Mexico and Canada geese in North America, the run of salmon from vast oceans to the upper reaches of rivers and the spawning ground of their birth, and of course the indelible image of the 1972 exodus of South Vietnamese refugees from Quảng Trị Province on what we have since called the Avenue of Horrors—refugees on Highway 1, trapped on an eleven-kilometer stretch between two rivers and two collapsed bridges. Our TV charted the chromatic blacks and blues of silhouettes in retreat from direct artillery fire aimed straight at them.

Later, Aunt Margaret drove her mother, Grams, to the doctor. We sat in the waiting room together. Aunt Margaret was scribbling on a yellow notepad. Together, Grams and I watched *The Mike Douglas Show* and then *Dinah!* on television to pass the time. When the nurse came for Grams, Aunt Margaret followed them and left me alone for a few minutes. The notepad was conspicuously left on the chair, and because her handwriting was large, I could see my name in black ink. It read: "She has no idea Vietnam is going to fall."

My entire body froze, my heart rate accelerated, and I was overcome with a feeling of impending doom. I knew that battles were sometimes won and sometimes lost, but I never believed a loss would be irreversible.

That night, I could not sleep. There was a pain in my heart, and I felt it one wing beat at a time. Aunt Margaret got into the bed and held me.

From that day on, the television became my connection to Vietnam, its screen glowing in the gloom of the evening. There were no more letters from my parents after the first two arrived in quick succession. We were all transfixed by the sight of a country ignited and falling, its government supplicant and helpless. On the evening news, you could watch the fall of Ban Mê Thuột, Quảng Trị, Hue, Da Nang, Qui Nhơn, Nha Trang. Like a scene from a disaster flick, a plane carrying orphaned babies crashed during takeoff and jackknifed into a green rice field. Newscasters droned on with their bloated and formulaic pronouncements; commercials nattered in between. With speed and compression, catastrophe was heading south, closer and closer to Saigon. President Gerald Ford's speech in 1975, delivered at Tulane University on April 23, was featured on the evening news. From American officialdom itself, I heard that the war "is finished as far as America is concerned." The long-brewing end had finally arrived. I remember that moment, like anyone who has ever loved and lost. It was the moment when I transmogrified from visitor to refugee.

A week later, as time grew shorter, the American Armed Forces Radio Service broadcast its prearranged signal, "The temperature in Saigon is 105 degrees and rising," paradoxically followed by Bing Crosby's "White Christmas," as a covert Morse code call to alert Americans to Saigon's impending end and the beginning of the United States' surreptitious evacuation plan for them.

Of course, it was not Christmas in April, and there was no snow in Saigon—only a city that was harried and fretful and squirming with rumors.

This was why my parents said Saigon fell in the winter. It happened almost in one fell swoop. Just like that. Like prey seized by a hunting bird making its rapid descent.

As for my beloved dog Topaz, the tragedy of abandoning him is one that can hardly be written. I left my dog-blessed life behind. I missed even my humblest possessions that I had hoarded: mid-autumn festival lanterns, paper kites, lion masks. And I realized very quickly that there had never been one self within me that was permanent. Only a life sentence of multiple selves that must nimbly adapt to new ways, new borders, new countries, new homesteads. As we moved forward, I flailed about, this way and that, here and there, not always neat and straightforward, despite appearances to the contrary.

To soothe and reassure me, Papa Fritz showed me adoption papers my parents had signed, turning me over to him in case the feared but wholly foreseeable occurred. I was one of the lucky ones who made it out, but it was hard to think of luck when Saigon fell.

Despite the passage of time, I don't think I have truly budged from that moment in 1975. When NPR's *Morning Edition* aired a StoryCorps clip in 2018 of an interview I did called "Former Refugee Reflects on the Vietnam War's Tet Offensive 50 Years Later," I was startled by the description "former refugee." After more than forty years in this country, I still feel as much a refugee now as I did then, still holding on to a heartbreak that started long ago but reverberates to this day. "Life is what happens when you're busy making other plans," John Lennon sang in "Beautiful Boy." I, on the other hand, see life in terms of loss to be overcome, danger to be dodged.

Many Vietnamese friends continue to reel from the events of April 1975. We don't talk about it, but acute things are revealed in casual, innocuous moments. When a close childhood friend was sick and wanted me to check his email for him, he shared his password with me. The numbers at the end of the password were 1975—catastrophic and permanent. Those digits show up again and again in our usernames and passwords, much more than our own birth years or some other personal signifiers. It seems to loom perpetually in our collective hearts as something forever defining. We are here, but also still there, improbable survivors mauled always by 1975.

Harlan

I once saw a goose I thought was pretty and confidently approached it at the park and said to it, "Hello, goose. My name is Harlan Margaret Van Cao, okay?"

And that was that. The goose and I were best friends. I was three.

If I only had that same confidence as I got older, I'm convinced I never would have become so isolated.

This isolation that I feel isn't depression, and it isn't unhealthy. I actually love being Harlan. I'm always wrapped in this special blanket.

Back when I was fifteen, there was a girl at my high school whom people talked about as if they knew everything about her, when they really knew nothing. And she couldn't bring herself to walk down crowded hallways. Between periods she would stay in the bathroom until everybody was in their next class, and she would always be late. The growing string of tardies was worth being able to walk across campus without the judgmental stares on her. Even as she walked through the silent halls, the hostile voices in her head whispered and slowly got louder, finally stopping when she came to her classroom. It was impossible to separate delusion from reality, and so she chose to stay by herself.

And every day the teacher would shake her head in disappointment and say, "Maybe if you cared more about your education you could show up on time, Harlan."

That's how I saw myself—separated and apart. Harlan was someone who had nothing to do with me. I began to think of myself in a third-person point of view. It made it easier to shed responsibility for pain. My blanket was that extra perspective. It was a shield, and it was soft like rabbit ears.

I used to be able to go an entire day feeling nothing inside. Numbness seemed to be a thick skin I would never shed. Then, the next day, I would feel everything at once for eighteen hours, to the point where I'd have to hold my temples to quiet my insides, which unraveled and knocked at my brain from the inside of my skull. Between the two of us, other Harlan and myself, I think I should have had more control over myself, but I really didn't. My decisions became impulsive and so difficult to explain that I blamed it on the other part of me, which I had totally detached from myself.

My mother and I are a lot of different ages at once. She can be fifty-five, but also fifty-four, fifty-three, one, two, three, four, etc. And the different-age selves have their own voices that speak to me. She once sent me a text message: "Did you sit on my side of the bed?"

"Yes. For a second this morning," I replied. "Why do you ask?"

"Why'd you sit there?"

"Mom, I don't know. I was putting on socks?"

"It wasn't Goldilocks?"

"What are you talking about?"

"We were hoping Goldilocks had come to see us."

I didn't even bother to answer her. I knew she was doing anything but joking.

When I got home, she explained to me that Goldilocks often came through our house and would eat from our bowls; my mother had apparently been waiting for her to come to pay us a visit. She was a master at detachment.

My mother and I are both detached from ourselves and yet also very attached to each other. We are silent bleeders. We bleed separately, but we share the blood.

My father died a week before his birthday. I was sixteen years old, and he was eighty-four. He had been ill, so there was a webcam in the downstairs room in our house in Huntington Beach, California, so my mom could check in on him when we were gone, even if we were just five minutes away. After his death, she never unplugged the camera in that now-empty room. Now all it sees are my late-night visits to the floor space where his bed used to be, where I lay myself down and cry.

I actually went to school the day I found him dead, because his bed had been leased from a medical company and I knew that they would insensitively roll it away the minute his body was gone, and I couldn't stay and watch them go: first the body of my dad and then the bed he'd slept on.

On his birthday, when the clock struck twelve, I descended the stairs and held myself in my Harlan blanket on that space on the floor. And I hiccupped and I wept.

I felt him then. He held me and it felt just like him. The heaviness of those watches he'd always wear sat upon me. He told me it was okay. "I'll never forget you," I told him.

The Rolling Stones, one of his favorite rock bands, was all I played for months.

"You can't always get what you want . . . but . . . you just might find you get what you need."

What did I want? To have him back.

But what was it I needed? Maybe it was to find myself without him.

My mother continued to plug in his phone when it was dead, and I found myself texting his number, a conversation all in blue.

The family dynamic beyond my immediate family was a little ridiculous, because my father had three other children from his first of three marriages. His son, who lived in Massachusetts, had two boys, my father's only grandchildren. The boys were my nephews, but I was younger than them by a couple of years, and they tormented me. When I was very little, they came into my room and dug through my bed, which was protected by a white mesh canopy and many pillows. They took my beloved stuffed animals and ruthlessly cut off their heads, carrying the stuffing around the house and yelling tribal chants to make themselves seem bigger than they were.

My father, who had been bullied as a little boy by his older brother, took this very personally, and after sewing the heads back on for me, he said that he resented the fact that he'd have to include them in his will.

WHEN I WAS IN SECOND GRADE, my teacher called me up to her desk and asked me why the spacing on my spelling cards was so strange. I looked down at the paper and saw nothing wrong.

The dog ran a way from the truck.

The word *the* meant nothing, but the word *dog* was grainy and wet, like soil after a thunderstorm. And even though I had begun to lose my sense of smell around age six, I could tell it also smelled like rain. The dog ran, and *ran* was a milky word. But only the type of milk that's in those cute cardboard cartons, not the plastic bottles. I kept *dog* and *ran* together because they were compatible. Both of them were flowy like water.

Away made me upset. The word was a squirrel with big eyes on the bottom branch of a tree, all sad that it couldn't climb higher. But *a way* was like the sky with no clouds, so I wrote *away* in a happier format.

From was meaningless also. It was a string in the wind, and *the* was still air. I figured putting them together would bring the string down; the stillness in *the* would calm the wind in *from*.

And *truck* was kind of lonely, but he also was sociable. So I put him relatively close to *fromthe*.

When I was in third grade I began to see sounds and feel letters and taste smells . . . and I started seeing a purple cat. The lilac kitten trailed behind me when I walked to the bus stop under the wet trees of my street. And I became jealous of it because it never grew up. I chose never to name it or assign it a gender. That would make it real and me nuts.

Just like I chose not to mention to anybody, not even to my other self, that the word *bison* reminded me of corduroy pants and ladybugs. Every word actually reminded me of something else. *James* was a cherry covered in coconut whipped cream, and *Michael* was sunshine on the side of a building—one of those mysterious buildings that are so heavily tinted and hard to see into that for all you know, the Mafia could be operating inside. Going through daily conversation was alienating and awkward. I had to mentally translate everything within milliseconds before speaking.

Harlan was navy green sand. As if someone had taken each tiny grain on the beach and painted it dark green like the color of a redwood needle. I would have liked for my name to be like a Monet painting; the lily pads on the beautiful blue pond is still the most peaceful image I've ever seen. But that wasn't how it was. I couldn't choose which words and names reminded me of what. And the only reason why I didn't ask to go to a child psychologist was because I was sure at the time that I was normal; everybody's name must remind them of painted sand.

But it doesn't. Everybody doesn't have synesthesia, which is what I diagnosed myself with. Kandinsky often painted odd colorful shapes that seemed musical and spooky on the canvas because he had it and didn't know what else to do.

I was born with eyes that were bigger than my actual body, which is saying a lot because I was born nine pounds, twelve ounces. Nothing but rolls of fat and spiky black hair covered me; it took two years for me to stop looking Asian and to start looking half or more than half. And my type of childhood was different from what the other kids at school had, and not just because of the painted grains of sand.

I found myself, at age five, already becoming enraged by people who called my dad my grandfather and my mother my nanny. Now looking back on it, I can see why they would assume the seventy-three-year-old man next to me was my grandfather, but I'm still going to stay angry about it because I can and because I sometimes sit and think about how unfair it was to my family: to my mother, who knew that she would eventually need to be not only the mother but also the father; to my father, who knew he could never give me what most other kids had, which was defined by little things that became big as he got older. And I felt sad for him because I knew that the agony of a parent knowing they are not enough for their child must have been brutal. He drove me to preschool each day in his Mazda, the only sports car on the market with back seats that actually could fit a car seat big enough for my chubby self. So there I sat, in my expensive custom outfit and matching hat, in the passenger's seat of my dad's midlife crisis, with the taste of spilled coffee and leaking pens between the seats.

Then after school I was hauled by my mother to a house that resembled the cottage Snow White's dwarves lived in. My violin teacher, who lived there, was approaching her last days of living, which she spent with her four cats. As I got older I saw the reasons behind my mother pushing me so relentlessly into music: She could never play the violin, so she wanted me to. When I told her I hated it, she took it personally; she told me it was a privilege to be so in touch with music, and so I played until my fingers were sore. And then when I turned fifteen, I quit once and for all.

As I grew older, I had long curly brown hair that looked blond in the sun, and abnormally chubby cheeks and arms. My family called me Susu, for "sumo wrestler," and my eyes looked like enormous puddles, especially when I cried, which was often because honestly I was overly sensitive to anything that didn't go my way. I cried the first time I saw roadkill. I cried when I dropped ice cream on the floor. I cried when I realized I was literally the last person in my preschool class to learn to walk; up until then, all I could do was stand in the middle of the room, clinging to a nearby chair.

I never learned how to crawl either. And when I say "never learned," I mean that I couldn't learn and I insisted instead on scooting around the house on my butt while wearing a small basket on my head as a hat.

At the grocery store people gave me adoring glances, asking my mother how old I was, telling her how adorable her daughter was. She immediately pulled me aside and went through the many safety drills I had learned around the same time I learned the alphabet.

"Harlan Margaret. What do you do if a stranger tells you they have lots of candy in their van?"

"I don't follow them."

"You kick and scream and you run. Now, what about if they have a puppy?"

"They're lying, right?"

"Well, yes, but even if they were telling the truth, a puppy is not worth being locked in a windowless van by a child molester. Do you understand, Harlan Margaret? *Child molester.* Does that sound like something you want?"

It was always that phrase, "child molester." I had to watch out for those, along with all the other disasters my mother prepared me for each day.

"No?"

I was told that if I got lost, I was to find a woman with children, another mother, who would most likely help me. When I was six and we went abroad, my mom made a tag typed with the necessary information: my name, her email, her phone number, the fact that I am a U.S. citizen and could be returned to the U.S. embassy if needed. The tag was attached to my clothes with a safety pin.

My childhood was all about self-defense. I was aware of every possible way that someone could die in their own home; I knew that when a pot was on the stove, the handle should never be facing out because an infant could easily knock it over and get "burned to death." I would go to my friends' homes and turn all the handles in and give them a lecture about all the ways they could die while taking a bath in their own houses if a blow dryer was nearby. Every weekend, I played the piano and painted with watercolors and went down to the pond and fed bread crumbs to the swans with my father. My mother quickly warned him about hidden electrical wires near the water. And flesh-eating bacteria in lakes. While my mother showed me all corners of the world and cultured me enough to prepare me for college, her fists were always up in front of her face, sparring, blocking punches, dodging bullets that she anticipated, even if they never came.

And now that I'm seventeen, she doesn't go everywhere with me. I ride in cars with kids my age and I sit in the passenger's seat unbothered by things that would drive my mother over the edge.

I was put into Tae Kwon Do lessons when I was four years old. I could kick higher than my head when I was eight, and the orange belt dragged along the floor as I squirmed in front of the punching bag, working toward the black belt my mother never reached. My mother had a red belt with three stripes, which was the rank right before black belt. But she left Vietnam before she could get a black. I know that was a big regret of hers.

To be honest, I liked going only because I was good at it. I wanted to get ahead of the other kids and prove I was good enough for myself.

I went up and down the room in rows and columns, kicking and punching the air in a haze of dark purple.

I went three or four times a week. I think, looking back, that my mother was more excited about it than I was. It was as if she was re-creating her own childhood; her investment in my success in music and martial arts was more than just the typical tiger mom obsession. I didn't truly care that much when I broke a stack of boards in half with my kick, but I saw my mother sitting there in her chair with perfect posture, watching me intently with pride while the other parents barely looked up from their cell phones. And so I did it for her.

The issue with this wasn't that Tae Kwon Do tired me out or caused stress, but that I felt that it should have been a way for me to relieve my anger. Instead, all eyes were on me constantly. My mom had actually wanted me to do aikido, because her father had made her do it, but because we lived in a town the size of the White House, it never worked out. It didn't stop there; I have always felt all eyes on me, even a decade later.

I went home each night and lay in bed with her. It was the same bed she had put me in when I was a baby; I was placed away from my father so he couldn't roll over in his sleep and suffocate me to death. She lay there, in the middle, probably with one eye open to make sure I survived the night. I knew it was the Vietnamese way. When my pediatrician, the one who saved me at birth when I couldn't breathe, asked my mother about my bed, she told him I slept with her. She adored this doctor and always told me he saved my life. But when we got home, she told my father she was exasperated with him. "Not everyone in the world has separate bedrooms and separate beds. Not everyone wants this kind of independence. He should focus on medical advice, not get involved with cultural issues."

My pathological concern with myself and my own body is actually worrisome. The number of times I've stared at myself naked in the mirror is ridiculous, and I've always said I don't want my body wrecked by the labor of childbirth. Maybe this is because of my emotional insecurities, which I compensate for by my *lack* of physical insecurities. I always swore that if I got pregnant, then I would just do a C-section right away.

On top of that, when I first became obsessed with Woody Allen movies, I discovered there was a name for what I was feeling: hypochondria. This self-diagnosis finally made me feel somewhat normal. My symptoms included the fact that I didn't have to read WebMD in order to convince myself I had cervical cancer; all it took was one missed period. I could cough and assume it was time to start inviting people to say good-bye to me on my deathbed.

On my thirteenth birthday, I got out of the shower and noticed that one of my breasts sat lower than the other and seemed to be slightly smaller. It took me half a minute to crawl onto my bed in emotional agony, whispering to myself, "I have breast cancer and the doctor's gonna cut them off."

Clearly I didn't realize that underdeveloped breasts, or just breasts in general, tend to vary in size. I knew nothing and convinced myself of everything.

And yet, that concern for myself didn't show itself where it was needed; I couldn't remember to look both ways while crossing the street. My mother still held my hand until I was eleven or twelve.

I could fit my entire body on her torso at one point in time. I once noticed the scar on her body below the bikini line, a long gash at the bottom of her stomach. That was where they had cut me out. I noticed how they had strategically placed the cut in a hidden place, away from others' eyes. It was like a secret only the two of us knew, along with everything else we cried together about.

"I'm sorry," I told her.

"For what?"

"For the cut. It's forever."

"I want it to be forever. I hope it never goes away," she told me.

The following nights were spent sharing tears and stories. She cried and trembled underneath me when she spoke of how much she missed her father and how she wished mine wouldn't be so difficult when it came to raising me.

My parents had complete opposite personalities, and therefore two different ways of raising their only daughter. My mother couldn't drive ten feet without strapping the seat belt onto me. She wanted it to be a rule that absolutely could not be broken, even if we were driving from one end of a parking lot to the other. My father wouldn't think twice about racing around in his Mazda with me in the car seat demanding that he go faster than the other cars on the highway. He only wanted me to love him and to tell my friends how cool my dad was, which I did. My mother only wanted me to be careful and safe. She didn't care what I told my friends, as long as she went to sleep at the end of the day knowing she had been a good parent. This is not to say that my dad wasn't, but then again, he hadn't spent half his childhood in a bomb shelter holding his head to protect it from bullets.

When my mother and father stood next to each other, neither one of them looked their age; they both looked much younger. She has very good skin, like all Asian women. It's common knowledge that white women who age poorly practically wish they could peel the skin off an Asian and paste it onto their own faces to look younger. And then my dad, the love of my childhood, was very tall, and although I was born when he was sixty-eight, he looked forty-five and had the muscular frame of a bodybuilder.

When I was in the third grade, a boy who was known for being quite crass and overly knowledgeable about sex came up to me and asked me where my dad had bought my mother online. I frowned at him and walked away.

In my house, everything is saved. Almost forty-five years after 1975, my mother still lives the way her own family lived when they first arrived. They washed and reused plastic utensils, ziplock bags, and aluminum foil. And so now, each paper towel, unless it is on the verge of death, is reusable for some purpose. It's borderline hoarding. I wipe my wet hand with a paper towel. I don't put it in the wastebasket. I put it somewhere for my mom to use again when she has to clean a spot on the floor. Basically, our kitchen cabinet has a corner of used paper towels to be revived and reused. If I spill sriracha on the floor, I go to the pile and pick out the best-looking towel and clean it up. Even then, the towel can still go back to the pile.

Soap never runs out. When one of us notices that we are running low, all we have to do is fill the container with water and shake the bottle and we can get the last little bit out of the bottom.

There is no such thing as single-use paper, and our kitchen doesn't have one of those fancy family calendars for writing down schedules, like "Wednesday: take Sarah to soccer practice." Everything is written on the back of old paper, usually some law review article stained with coffee.

My father didn't follow this rule. He had a carefree personality and was like water. He would flow from one thing to another, to whatever pleased him or whatever someone introduced him to that intrigued him. He liked to break rules. He said that it's good to break at least one rule a day. That way, people don't just follow and obey the government like sheep. The accidents he had gotten into on the freeway didn't stop him from riding across the country many times on his motorcycle. When he first taught at Duke Law School, there was no parking spot for motorcycles. And usually the parking spaces for cars were all taken. He parked his in the space for bicycles and would get a ticket. He asked the university to create a space for motorcycles but after months, nothing was done. So he took it upon himself to pull a "motorcycle parking" sign from somewhere else and went to the law school parking lot in the middle of the night with a shovel. He planted the sign in front of a space and made it a motorcycle space. Everyone thought it had been done officially or that it had been there all along. It's still there to this day.

I grew up with two professors. My parents were my teachers, and everything was an opportunity for me to learn a new life lesson about society or human nature or even the law. My mother, especially, was all about education, repeating to me what her parents had told her: "You can lose a house, even a country, but no one can take away your education."

I was the last girl to learn how to ride a bike. I had memorized the artist of every painting from the 1500s to the 1900s. Titian, Matisse, Edward Hopper, Jasper Johns, and Degas all lived in my infant memory, while Elmo and Big Bird lived in the memory of everyone else my age.

My mother told me that when she arrived in college, a professor asked the class to write an essay based on a painting by El Greco. She had never heard of him, but every other student in the class had, and her self-confidence went way down. Of course, she knew the famous works of the Chinese painter Han Gan of the Tang dynasty, but that information was pretty much worthless. So I was given a classical education at home, and on the way to school, my parents put on CDs of every minuet and concerto ever written for the violin or piano. By the time I was nine, I really couldn't stand it.

Car rides were also opportunities to play Spanish-language DVDs on the little TV screen in the minivan. If I had a dollar for every time that little cartoon mouse jumped around on the screen repeating, "Cómo estás? Muy bien? Bien," I wouldn't have to work. It was even worse than the classical music, and up until I entered my teen years and began my obsession with romance, I despised the language. I began to think of it as something worth pursuing only when I was older and realized it's a love language; each word sounds like two people dancing together.

I WATCHED MY FIRST WOODY ALLEN MOVIE, *Annie Hall*, at age seven, and by the time I was twelve, I had memorized every single piece of dialogue from *Annie Hall*, *Hannah and Her Sisters*, *Husbands and Wives*, *Manhattan*, and *Midnight in Paris*. I could hum the entirety of Vivaldi's symphonies and Bach's waltzes and recite half of T. S. Eliot's "J. Alfred Prufrock." My childhood experiences were stifled by lessons from adults, and even things like Disney movies were an opportunity to get educated about feminism. *The Little Mermaid* was my favorite. The ending consisted of the main character, the mermaid, turning into a human so she could be with Prince Eric, who lived in a castle on land.

So there we were, my mother and I, sitting in the family room surrounded by stuffed animals, mostly German shepherds, and a blackboard that I had been practicing addition on. As I watched Ariel wave good-bye to the mermen in the sea while her ship sailed away with Eric by her human side, my mother scoffed.

"You see that? Huh? Ariel gets legs and goes onto the ship with Eric in order to live on land. Why doesn't she demand that *he* change into a mermaid so he can be with her? See that? Women constantly altering themselves for the men."

Even at the age of five, I was already rolling my huge eyes. "It's called a mer*man*, not mermaid. Eric is a prince."

"You're missing the point, Harlan Margaret."

My mother is an expert on the dangers of assimilation, especially assimilation into standards invented by men or white people.

I went to school and shared my new insights with my classmates, who weren't so thrilled that I was trying to ruin their childhood experience and their fantasy of being carried away by a prince with, yes, *legs*, not fins.

The greatest lesson of Disney movies was from *Beauty and the Beast*, in which Belle fell in love with the Beast. Sure, this may constitute bestiality, but that was not the point my mother made to me.

Her point was that Belle accepted the Beast for basically being the ugliest creature alive, but would it happen the other way around? In other words, would a good-looking boy fall in love with a hideous woman?

According to her, no.

And so, as I watched Belle dance in that poofy yellow gown with the love of her life, I also listened to my mother. And I learned that because of society's unfair expectations, no boy would be with me if I weren't beautiful. Therefore, I have to be beautiful.

But it was more complicated than that. I find that it is very hard to win either way. When you aren't beautiful, you aren't wanted. When you are beautiful, you are wanted and then thrown away.

Growing up, I realized that I'd rather remain unknown to people than be special. Because being special meant that one day I'd be unspecial. And this sort of thinking, coming from a ten-year-old, was frowned upon, which made me dig my heels in even more. I became pessimistic and lonely as I approached puberty. It wasn't until age sixteen, when I had moved on from the tormenting awkwardness, that I realized I was too special to be treated like I wasn't.

TO CELEBRATE MY FIRST BIRTHDAY, one hundred Vietnamese people ate a whole roast pig. It's a Vietnamese tradition. The pig, a baby, had been special-ordered by my mother's cousin, who held the party at her house in Falls Church, in Northern Virginia, where my mother grew up. There's this weird game Vietnamese people like to play where they set objects in front of the infant: a pen, a mirror, etc. The objects all supposedly represent the infant's future focus and personality. If the baby picks up the pen, the whole family looks at the mother as if she has the best baby fortune. I picked up the mirror. It represents vanity. One can imagine how that went.

Williamsburg, where my parents and I lived at the time, was about a three-hour drive from the rest of my mother's family. I have never understood why, after she finished college and law school, she didn't return to her family and the Vietnamese community in Falls Church. She would say her separation began when she left for college. I think of my family as this big tree that was transplanted in Virginia with a lot of branches all spread over Falls Church, and then to one side there is a branch that swerved out by itself, all lonesome and alone. My mother is that lonely branch and I am a stem that came out of it. We belong to the tree but not really.

My mother ate a lot of spicy food when she was pregnant. I was told that it was because she had hoped her baby would be as Vietnamese as possible, which meant that I would have to like spicy food. Imagine her disappointment when her daughter didn't join everyone else in smothering their food in Tabasco or sriracha or some other Vietnamese hot pepper sauce that is so hot it is filled with seeds.

There was a lot of other food besides the pig, and my mother told me most of it was hot. My Falls Church family loves sriracha, the one with the bright green cap and the rooster on the bottle. Apparently there are many srirachas, but we only buy that one. It is made by a Vietnamese refugee who was born the year of the rooster, lived in Saigon, and escaped on a boat called *Huy Fong* after the Communists won the war. So he named his American company after his refugee boat and once again grew chili peppers, as he did when he was in Vietnam.

Eventually, as I grew older, I noticed the comments people in the family would make if I seemed bothered by spicy food, so I simply stopped being bothered. I didn't allow myself to drink water with the hot sauce that I made a big show of putting on my food. I do love spicy food now, or at least I think I do, because I put hot sauce on things that shouldn't even be near spiciness. Chances are, I wouldn't have even bothered to force myself into that if it hadn't been for my family and the expectation to be as Vietnamese as possible.

So what does that mean, exactly, to be "Vietnamese"?

It means that in the back seat of our Honda van, the little DVD player would be on a constant replay of Vietnamese children's musicals, during those times when my mother didn't feel the urge to turn on the Spanish movies. Each disc carried half a dozen tunes, all of which taught children how to count and how to exercise, and, most important, how to respect their elders. I sang all of them religiously to my mother as she blow-dried my hair each night.

In front of the glass walls of our house was the gigantic flag of South Vietnam, yellow with three red stripes, side by side with the American one. I also sang the Vietnamese national anthem—South Vietnam's anthem, of course. My mother showed everybody that her half child was in fact cultured and taught to be respectful and always listen to orders, even when those orders made me want to turn the entire dinner table over.

About a year ago I rewatched old family videos.

September 2005:

There I am, in my little bucket hat with the matching outfit that my mom bought duplicates of, except that each outfit had a different pattern. Her favorite was tan velvet lined with brown ribbon covered in tiny pink roses. In the video, I'm sitting in front of the ninety-inch flat-screen television in Falls Church that played literally nothing except golf. And Ba Hai, my mother's cousin (Second Father or Father Two to me), who loved golf, had set up a tiny patch of fake grass to practice his swing on. I was terrified of him. They say that babies' intuition is incredible, but in my case, neurosis was already taking over.

So I guess it makes sense that I was scared of my Ba Hai. I honestly can't describe the feeling I got when I heard his shoeless feet padding down the hallway toward the front room. I say shoeless because every Vietnamese I know religiously takes off their outdoor shoes, leaves them at the door, and walks around with bare feet in the house. Does my terror make sense? As it turns out, my second father was a special forces soldier in South Vietnam's army and had actually spent years in rice fields at night killing the Vietcong. He carried with him an intense vibration that I must have sensed, because I have footage of my three-year-old self scooting away frantically prior to his arrival, which was a whole five minutes after. I was like a cat who could sense an earthquake before it arrives.

Falls Church was where we went to make me more Vietnamese.

Whenever we drove to Falls Church, we stayed at Ba Hai's house, which was only a few blocks from the rest of the relatives. As I got older, my mother filled me in on the details of her relatives' lives, such as the deadly missions Ba Hai had been sent on. On a night that was moonless and pitch-dark, Ba Hai and his team were dropped into this village where government officials were actually secret Vietcong terrorists. They were ordered to capture everyone in a government house. To make sure they would not kill each other by mistake, they literally ran around naked. Anyone who had clothes on was the enemy. To make sure there was no noise, they did not use guns. They had only knives and tomahawks.

Basically, I was toddling away from a man who had run naked in the killing fields of Vietnam covered in the blood of his enemies.

Growing up with so many war stories, no wonder I was never that intrigued or frightened by fairy tales about witches or monsters. Hansel and Gretel and a witch in a gingerbread house cooking the children in a cauldron? That sounded tame compared to Ba Hai being in a hut all naked and covered in blood that was not his. Or Ba Hai being chased by his own father, a Vietcong agent himself, knife in hand, when he found out his own son had joined the special forces for the South.

My family members have no trouble talking among themselves about the war. They'd talk about it in one sentence and in the next they could start a heated debate about politics. They talked about these things freely at dinner, while drinking tea, while watching television.

But they never talked about their feelings. They might talk about my mother's brother who joined the army, became strange, and died at age forty, but I never heard anyone talk about how they felt about him or his death, or what he might have been feeling. I noticed that. My mother has always told me that I am a very sensitive child and that I am super observant. I don't remember this, but it's a story she's told me many times, so I feel like I have the right to say it is part of my memory:

"Mommy?"

"Yes?"

"The person next to our table is a transvestite." I wouldn't use this term now, but according to my mother, I was about four or five at the time.

She was startled. She didn't realize I even knew what a transvestite was. I was five, for heaven's sake. *Shrek* was a movie of irony, as my mother had taught me a year before, and I loved it. Prince Charming was bad; the ogre was good; the princess was ugly and in the end didn't wish to be pretty. What gave this transvestite away, I had noticed, was the slightly larger thing on his neck, which she told me was called an Adam's apple, and the beauty mark that had obviously been painted on the top corner of his upper lip.

When we visited family in Falls Church, we would also go to the nursing home where my grandpa lived. It was a five-minute drive from Ba Hai's house, and he had a lot of visitors, but still, my mother always felt bad that he was in a nursing home. She wanted him to come live with us in Williamsburg, but she didn't insist because she knew that Williamsburg was so far away from the rest of the family and the Vietnamese community. And he always said he did not want to move. So we paid him regular visits. My grandpa suffered from terrible pain in his entire body and could not walk. He was always lying in bed when I came to visit him. Because my dad also visited, Grandpa spoke to him in English, which meant I could also understand what was going on without my mother's translation.

I picked up bits and pieces. After he was shot during a battle near the Cambodian border, he was given a blood transfusion, but he was given the wrong blood type because the doctor was clearly an idiot, and from then on the pain became too much for him. But if we asked him how he was doing, he would always answer, "Fine," with a smile. He was a Buddhist and everything was always "fine." He didn't want my mother to push me either. He thought I was fine just the way I was.

My mother told me that when they first arrived in this country, her father told her, "Put a curtain down and don't think about anything from Vietnam."

A part of me thinks it is so amazing that all these people in my family, like my mother, fled to a new country and started over. And a part of me also thinks that really gives me no chance to mess up, because if they didn't mess up after what they had gone through, then I have no right to mess up, the way normal children are allowed to.

One of my mother's favorite sayings is from Alcoholics Anonymous: "Act your way into right thinking." Her brother was an alcoholic. She said it meant you had to ignore your thoughts, thoughts that weren't good for you, such as those that screamed in your head that you wanted a drink, and act as if you didn't have those thoughts. And then if you did that long enough, you would start to think correctly and your actions would flow, maybe even effortlessly, from correct thinking.

This is probably why people in my family don't share their feelings. Whether they know it consciously or not, it's how they have survived. My family members live as if they have already practiced this skill when it comes to Vietnam. As my grandpa said, put the curtain down. If their feelings get in the way of right thinking, they don't talk about their feelings. Maybe it's cultural, maybe it's the war, maybe it's my family. But what that means for me is that when I come to talk to my mother about something that happened at school that made me upset, her first instinct is to think about it "correctly" and then take action—fix it. But Vietnam is much farther away for me, and I don't have to run away from it or from my feelings. Sometimes all I want to do is feel—to the point where I'll put on "Love on the Brain" by Rihanna just so I can cry over a boy not texting me back.

I don't want it to seem as though I am rejecting the ways of my family or Vietnamese culture, because there are many things about it that I am deeply proud of. However, there is another thing that has always bothered me, and it is about how my rigid family hierarchy system is. Because the moment we set foot in Falls Church, it is all about birth order and rank.

My great-grandmother gave birth to eighteen children, but only eight survived. My grandma was the third one born. But to fool the devil or the demons, the firstborn, who is considered the most precious, is always referred to as number two. So my grandmother would be called Sister Four, or, depending who is talking, Mother Four. Her sister, Sister Five, had four children (one of whom is the dreaded Ba Hai) but died giving birth to the last child. One brother, called Brother Six, had nine daughters. Yes, *nine*.

Each daughter would be ranked from eldest to youngest. The eldest is my mother's oldest cousin. I also call her Mother Two. The youngest would be called my tenth mother. I grew up with the habit of just referring to them as Two, Three, Four, Five, Six, Seven, Eight, and so on. In fact, I call my mom Mother in daily life because she is just Mother, mine. If she makes me upset, I always have the other nine, right?

This obsessive ranking bothered me because I felt as though my family was just a smaller version of the caste system in India. My mother's mother, called Sister Four, was older and thus higher ranking than, for example, her brother, called Brother Six. So that means that my grandma's line of descent would always be "higher ranking" than her younger siblings' lines. This is why I am higher ranking than most fully grown adults on the cousin side of the family.

I feel there is more to a person than simply a number or a ranking. Nevertheless, if a stranger walked into my second mother's house, which is a lot like a hotel for the entire family, because anyone can just drop in uninvited anytime, they'd never be able to tell that there is actually a very intricate and tightly knit system involved. A few months after my mother left Vietnam, my entire family on her side fled and were put in a refugee camp in Fort Chaffee, Arkansas, for three months. They were there until my grandma's best friend, Fritz, sponsored them and helped them get resettled in Virginia. They picked Virginia because it was close to Washington, D.C., and, as the capital of the United States, it was, for them, the safest city in the world.

The original generation that came over consisted of my mother and her brother, my grandparents, my grandma's siblings, which included Brother Six and his nine girls, Brother Eight and his wife and one daughter, Ba Hai (who is the son of Mother Five and her Vietcong husband) and his wife and two children, my mother's grandmother, and two housekeepers who had been with the family for generations. I know it is really confusing because I was confused myself. All of them lived in one rented house, and their bedroom was an open basement where they placed mattresses, one next to the other, like tiles, until most of the floor was covered. That was how they all slept, curled next to each other, until a neighbor complained to social services that there were too many people living in one house and they were ordered to scatter. Someone official came, measured the square footage of the house, counted how many people were living there, and Explained America to Them.

Maybe that is why, before I started objecting last year when I turned sixteen, my mother never knocked before entering my room. In the house, inside the family, we do not practice independence. Independence is just a posture we adopt when it comes to the outside world. And yet when I ask her to help me find a spatula in the kitchen, she threatens me with my life, saying that if she finds it then it shows I'm lackadaisical. Honestly, that word means nothing to me anymore because of the number of times she's called me that.

From the outside, we just seem like a family of four generations with all the third-generation women married to white men who probably had no idea what they were getting into. Hence, I am not the only half-breed in the family. But until I was about five, I was the only one my age who couldn't do "simple" Vietnamese things.

I remember being told that I had to learn how to use chopsticks earlier because I was higher ranking, and Ariana, who was lower ranking, had already learned how to eat even rice with chopsticks. "She can pick up each *grain* of rice," I was told. And after I learned, I was told that my fingers had to be higher on the sticks. If I showed reluctance, Mom would point out one of the other cousins whose father was also white and who could easily use chopsticks.

After that, I used chopsticks for everything. In fact, even now, when I force myself to eat spicy Cheetos in order to immunize my mouth against Tabasco, I pick up each piece with chopsticks.

My favorite Vietnamese dishes are pho and spring rolls. For my family, spring rolls have to be made with rice paper, which is more delicate than the thicker Chinese egg roll paper. I knew the difference, but my Vietnamese family was not impressed. Pho and spring rolls are what Americans order in a Vietnamese restaurant. They wanted me to like food that is "more Vietnamese," like bún bò Huế, a soup from Central Vietnam with white noodles like pho, except the broth is not soothing like pho broth but aggressive and spicy and flavored with stalks of lemongrass. Or roasted pig, served with its body splayed out on a big platter with its head still attached. You could even see the little tongue sticking out of the pig's throat sometimes, which makes me gag.

So when we ate pho, my mother didn't want me to "just" have pho the way mere Americans order it. She always ordered the "special pho" on the menu, which meant it had everything: rare beef slices, well-done beef flank, fatty flank, meatballs, and something else that I called "spiky noodles." It was sliced thinly and it had spikes. I noticed that relatives we ate with seemed impressed when I ate spiky noodles. Only later did I realize that this was really the inner lining of a cow's stomach, and I screamed at my mother for letting me eat that "product of animal abuse," which really makes no sense if you're already eating the rest of the cow corpse anyway.

Despite our trips to Falls Church for serious Vietnamese immersion, I'm what I call merely "nail salon fluent" in the language. I understand enough Vietnamese to know what the nail technicians say about the clients. They refer to pregnant women as "the fat one" and call every blond woman "white person."

I can understand 60 percent of what I hear from my mother, but I cannot speak. Of course I have the accent and the six tones down, as I've been reciting those Vietnamese songs since I was a baby, but I cannot say that I am fluent in any way. I feel good about myself that I can actually produce those six tones. Unless you have absorbed it as a child, it is very difficult to make the tone shift. One wrong tone and higher-ranking "big sister" becomes lowly "head lice." *Chị* (big sister) versus *chí* (louse or lice).

When we moved to California, I went to Vietnamese school on the weekends, during what I like to call my "ostrich years," between eleven and twelve, when I walked like an awkward animal. To me, the ostrich is the most self-conscious animal there is. Just look at them. They know they're ugly.

At this Saturday school, I learned to read and write with all the accents—up, down, wavy, S, and so forth. Obviously those aren't the actual names of the accents, but that's how I remember them. Over the eighteen months that I attended, my Vietnamese grew by 20 percent, and then going into eighth grade I quit. That's what made sense to me.

My mother's own relationship with her past is mixed up because she isn't sure how much she wants to pass on to me. Maybe she isn't sure how much she wants to keep it herself. Maybe she just makes it up as she goes along. At the very beginning, she didn't want me to be "hyphenated," so she did not speak much Vietnamese to me when I was a baby. Maybe she thought I could be whole, undivided, and pure American. Until my 2009 trip to Saigon, my Vietnamese was limited to phrases such as "Mom, please get me ice water" and "I love my dog."

But then she suddenly regretted not teaching me more. Learning Vietnamese was not something that I put much effort into. I picked up what I heard, I paid attention to what was said about me in Vietnamese, and sometimes I would repeat back phrases. But I never became fluent. And she cares more than I do.

I RESENT MY MOTHER FOR THE WAY SHE SHOWS LOVE. I've always felt that her unwillingness to let go of the war has prevented her from showing love in the way that I need.

And she believes that I despise the Vietnamese playlist she plays every day in the car because, for about four months when I was twelve, I went through a phase of self-hatred in which I plugged my ears with earphones to block out the dramatic and poetic voices of the artist Khánh Ly. She won't let that go. She doesn't pay attention to all the times I hum the chorus of each and every song perfectly or all the times I turn the music up in order to prove her wrong. She thinks I don't care enough about her culture to remember Tet, but when I come with her to the Vietnamese New Year

festival, she is too busy honking at drivers who cut her off to notice that I
know where all her favorite pho restaurants are. We had to drive two hundred miles to Falls Church to get to these restaurants.

I resent her for thinking I don't know her. I know. She might be doing
her right thinking, right acting business, but her feelings are always there
too. I know that when we lived in Williamsburg, my mother was completely isolated from her community. So she immediately latched on to
this Vietnamese family, probably the only one in the city—two sisters,
each with white husbands, one of whom knew Spanish and would teach
his children conjugations at home. Each sister had a daughter, both of
whom were half, but other than that, I had nothing in common with them
except that all of us had some Vietnamese blood given to us by our mothers. Nor did my mother have anything in common with the two Vietnamese sisters, who spoke English with a really heavy accent and came from
an area in Vietnam that was not near where my mother grew up. That's
one way of saying they were "lower ranking" than my mother's ranking in
Vietnamese society.

My mom told me she wanted me to learn Spanish from the father of
one of the girls, which is why we spent so much time there. I knew, though,
that the real reason was she was just really sad. She was sad that she had
survived the war with her family and still was an outsider because of distance. So every week, we went to that family's house supposedly for my education. The emphasis my family places on education is a burden on both my
mother and me. On the zodiac wheel, my mother is a buffalo. She carries
a burden whether it is necessary or not. A lot of times, it is not necessary.
Education is not a burden to her; however, education, especially education
the Vietnamese way, became that for me as I began to be bothered by small
things. Yes, I was proud that I was the only first grader who could do long
division for six-digit numbers (along with subtraction and addition, both
of which were done using the "Vietnamese way"), but I felt slightly isolated
from the other kids who were still living in their infant days.

The Vietnamese way of subtraction and addition was taught to my mother when she was four or five. To this very day, I honestly have no idea how to add or subtract "normally." The Vietnamese way focuses entirely on teaching students that everything should go back to where they found it, that everything borrowed should be returned. Somehow even in math, values are sneaked in. Basically, digits are shifted between numbers to help students during a problem, but those digits need to be returned later on and the student needs to keep track of that.

In third grade I was called up to the board to subtract one hundred and four from two hundred and sixty eight. I knew I was expected to have gone into third grade knowing the "American" way, but I went ahead and did it my mother's way. Even the teacher had issues following what my little tally marks meant while I was working. I spent the remainder of class on my feet in front of everyone trying to explain, reciting what my mother had told me.

I got the right answer. But nobody understood.

It wasn't even that they didn't understand the method, but I knew that nobody else saw things the way I did. Nobody heard the word *shed* and got carsick. The word *victor* didn't remind anybody of rotten meat, just like *care* wouldn't make them think of shiny hard plastic.

I AM NOW IN HIGH SCHOOL. I realize that my mother's greatest fear is that I'm going to fail—mostly at school. She does everything she can to make sure that I have a good education. The way I see it, she gave birth to a child and raised that child, and now she just wants her investment to pay off. In fact, she is so frightened by my potential failure that the moment my grades dip below an A-, she begins booking tutors four days a week. She doesn't tutor me herself anymore because we fight and because I am now doing calculus and she doesn't know that subject.

She tells me stories of job interviews; she says that nobody wants to hire someone who has never failed. And yet I know that she will never have the self-control to allow me to collapse. My fear is that I will never be able to learn the art of picking myself up, because I have never once had to do that; she will not let me.

On the other hand, she has finally accepted that I will never take piano or violin seriously. My mother started playing the piano when she was five. She had an upright piano at home. She took her stamp collection when she left Vietnam, but she also wished she could take her piano. This was another reason why she got me to play the violin: It is portable. Because of this, lucky for me, she took it with us whenever we went on family vacations, so I could practice. I started playing the violin the moment I had enough strength in my neck to keep it in place between my chin and shoulder. My first violin was size $\frac{1}{16}$ and was only nine inches long. As I got older, my mother got me the $\frac{1}{8}$, then $\frac{1}{4}$, $\frac{1}{2}$, $\frac{3}{4}$, $\frac{7}{8}$, and then full size. I still have all of them in my drawers, even though my mother suggested we sell them, probably out of spite to make me feel bad. It didn't.

Although she has let the violin go—we had too many fights about it— she will forever be annoyed by the fact that I don't have the same driving force inside me that she has: anxiety. Instead of being thankful that she has not passed down her refugee anxieties to her child, she is anxious that I am not anxious.

My dramatic lack of anxiety keeps me from planning out the week, studying for tests, taking homework seriously. The existence of her anxiety is what divides us. I know that she wishes I was capable of feeling the emotion of stress, but I don't. She walks by my bedroom every day after school and sees me lying on my bed with my eyes on the computer, totally unfazed by the fact that I have seven hours of homework to do that night. She is aware of every little thing assigned to me, because her phone buzzes every time something of mine is graded. Most of the time, she knows that I got that horrifying B+ on my calculus test even before I do.

She is bothered by the way I shrug my shoulders when she asks how much work I have to turn in the next day. My lack of stress prevents me from feeling even the slightest desire to start my project the day it is assigned. To her this is absurd, because her commitment to school when she was my age was overwhelming; therefore my lack of commitment is underwhelming and unacceptable.

She is proud of my 4.6 GPA, I know, and of the difficult classes I have chosen to take: Honors Precalculus, AP Calculus, AP Statistics, and other honors and AP courses. I have not opted for easy classes in order to score good grades. And yet I also am worried that she isn't proud of *how* I have that GPA. I know I don't deserve it, considering that most kids work much harder than I do.

I slept in the same bed with my mother every night up until I was thirteen. In her culture, each family member, regardless of age or gender, shares a bed with another. She was incredibly hurt when I began sleeping in my own room, which had been furnished with a queen-size bed and paintings and posters on the walls. She didn't truly understand why I did this, and to this day, she sleeps only on the right side of the bed, as if she is leaving room for me to come back and take my place on the left.

My world has been and will always be a snow globe, and from inside it I'll see my mother as a faint sliver of moon outside, dangling like a sea horse from the sky.

Lan

When I rejoined my family after they made it out of Vietnam, I found myself in the drab purgatory of Falls Church, Virginia. Alone, without Papa Fritz or Aunt Margaret to show me the way, I was clueless as to how to handle most situations, even the most mundane ones. I knew nothing about Falls Church except that it made a minor appearance in the song "Dancing in the Street," at least the version sung by the Mamas and the Papas, who jested about its relative anonymity and insignificance when shouting out a list of cities that by contrast required no explanation: Philadelphia, L.A., Baltimore, until they got to Falls Church. Falls Church, the lead singer shouted. Where's that, the backup asked. Where's that?

It was where star apples, sapodillas, star fruit, rambutans, and mangosteens could not grow. It was where we of the younger generation learned to wrench ourselves from our antiquated history by moving on to a tacit destination. Even if far from family and parents.

In their logical refugee calculation, my parents had searched for the names of American towns that were close to the nation's capital. This suburban space and its orderly rows of houses and manicured lawns were now home to me, with an illusion of permanence, even if Saigon was anything but manicured and orderly. Home could be anywhere. Any world. Any moon.

Plus, Falls Church was almost tethered to Washington, D.C., and therefore safe, safe, safe enough for the entire extended family, a veritable clan of more than twenty relatives. My mother's mother was the oldest and the titular head, by rank and age, followed by my mother, fourth in birth order but the eldest among the surviving siblings, and my father. There were Grandma's close and faithful "servants," who had worked for our family's multigenerational brood for decades (we were to respect them the way we were to respect Grandma); Grandma's two remaining sons, fifth and seventh by birth order, called Father Six (and his wife and nine daughters, some with their own husbands and children in tow) and Father Eight (and his wife and daughter); my cousin (and his wife and two children), who was the son of my Vietcong uncle whom I called Father Five and who of course did not flee because his side had won; and my brother Tuấn, who had joined the army a year before the war's end.

Tuấn was the most fluent in English, so he was charged with leading our extended clan on a pilgrimage out of the tented compound of Fort Chaffee, Arkansas, to the ark of Falls Church, Virginia. Papa Fritz officially submitted his papers and sponsored every single one of them out of the camp, promising to be responsible for us in our melodic glide into new lives. Missing from our lives were Father Three's three daughters, who were yanked from our family by their mother after he died a gruesome minesweeper's death.

My parents were lost souls and couldn't offer any concrete help on how to navigate American life. The whole family had never been squished together like this before. We had space, surface composure, and white-gloved distance in Vietnam, allowing each of us—or at least the older generation, each with their own profound wounds, some mutually inflicted—to escape the other. Here, now, there was no room to flee.

My father was an only child born in Laos to parents who were small shopkeepers in Vientiane. They would be considered the merchant class, the last of the four Confucian classifications (Sĩ, nông, công, and thương—scholar, farmer, artisan, and merchant). He left Laos when violence was meted out against the minority ethnic Vietnamese. When he met and married my mother in Vietnam, she had just divorced her first husband, whose parents were landowners on par with her own parents. Even though both sets of landowners had lost almost all their land and had their houses burned down by Khmer bandits in the Mekong Delta, they continued to be treated in accordance with their prior status—grand landowners.

My father, on the other hand, was a luckless staff sergeant, an itinerant from a poor and unknown family in a foreign country. My parents fell in love irrationally, heretically, like a fish falling for a bicycle, defying all conventional expectations. My mother's parents and family disapproved of the marriage and disowned her, reclaiming her and swaddling her in the family's center only when my father rose through the ranks of South Vietnam's military. Family is not always haven. Even family—or especially family—disappoints.

And, paradoxically, it was because of my father's connections and status that the whole extended clan was able to flee in 1975.

Father Eight had his own fragile relationship with his mother. He had apparently been banished or, rather, erased from his family at birth, at my grandmother's direction, because he had been born in the "wrong" year and hour and would have brought bad luck to the entire family. He was raised by his parents' distant relatives, or maybe it was the family's gardener, and never even knew about his birth family until years later. Father Eight tried three times to kill himself; on his last attempt at self-obliteration, he almost succeeded. His body was put in a morgue. My mother and her seventh brother went to look at the body to identify it, and when the mortician opened up the morgue fridge where his body was being stored, everyone was startled to see Father Eight alive and moving.

For the sake of family cohesion and due to everyone's obedience to old-fashioned Confucian manners and morals, Father Eight set aside his long-forbidden memories and acted his part as one of the family's many dutiful sons. But he refrained from intimacy and closeness and maintained a willfully artificial albeit respectful relationship with his mother. It helped that they did not live close together.

But in 1975, past and future were held together not by the present but by grief. And, of course, by Confucian protocol, so we could all sidestep hurt and live together like one big happy family. The key to survival, my father told me, was to know what one ought to remember and then forget it immediately. Don't look back. Don't pick at what's passed. Let go. I can't tell if this advice provided illusory or real relief. But I took it in. There is only the present. Which is why *always* is an illusory word.

My mother told me the opposite: You cannot have the future without the past. Remember.

I told myself we were just shedding skin like animals. It was a normal process of life. Reptiles were expert at molting. I could be like them. In 1975, everyone was in the chaotic togetherness of the same small house, shape-shifting and privately nursing our own between moments of sadness and loss. Living our resolutely new lives in a provisional kind of liberation, with reticence, and heading toward a hard-edged future. Pretending old family fractures had healed and unlikely emotions had vanished, long, long ago, replaced with diplomatic good cheer. And, of course, trying to forget the war—the one that Americans called the Vietnam War and the victorious Vietnamese of the North called the American War. It's just the war to us here in Falls Church.

It was hard to get our house in order when we had to live together in such a small space. But my mother did not allow disorder. Everything was in its place. Even the drawers must be tightly shut, not left ajar. Indoor slippers and sandals were lined along the baseboard. No one needed to flip on the light switch at night; we knew where things were. It was about keeping a sense of order and basic courtesy.

My first experience with an American school was at Swanson Middle School in Arlington, Virginia. For just one month, May 1975. But that one month was both too short and too long. It was too short for me to learn much of anything about American ways. And it was too long because being the new kid from a bad war, I was ostracized. I was a dumb cow on display, sitting, standing, wondering; confused animal eyes provoking curiosity and laughter.

My arms weren't strong. I couldn't climb the rope. I couldn't throw a softball. I didn't understand first base or home run or the teacher's constant reference to the World Series. In the bright, clear light of spring, the other students watched, fascinated by my stutters and false starts. I was always the last girl standing as the team captains went round and round trying to figure how to not get stuck with me. Later, we had to partake in the strangest ritual. "Hit the shower," the PE teacher shouted. I didn't know what it meant. Disrobe, strip down, and soap up. Naked and in plain view. But I didn't want to carry these little tragedies with me, or let them fluster me. I classified them as minor so I could detach and compartmentalize them, put them in a miniature box and dismiss them. "It's just a stupid game, baseball. Not like soccer or the World Cup. Why do they call it the World Series when hardly any other country cares about it?" But these daily humiliations actually deepened the searing sense of loss and failure for me, loss and failure I saw duplicated or mirrored in the loss and failure of South Vietnam itself and of my parents and of all of us bumbling refugees. The American Dream—it could be flawed, maybe even a myth, but I wanted it and it was never going to be mine. This is a country for winners, and we were losers.

When I was little, I colored inside the borders. Now, in a similar way, I kept vigil, maintained boundaries—it was very important to—and no feelings were ever spilled across the lines. No one was to see or sense such mawkish sentimentality.

I even struggled with milk cartons in the school cafeteria. The first time I saw one, I picked it up, held it in my hand, looked at the spout, tried to open it—first the wrong end, then the right one—and even then I could not manage it. A girl stared at me and snickered. It wasn't clear if she was snickering at my exotic embroidered satin shirt, sufficiently prized that my mother had put it in my suitcase when I left, or at my obvious defeat before a mere inanimate object. I looked around, searching for someone to emulate. Two steps: The wings had to be separated and pushed back to deepen the crease, followed by a forward push and pull to make a spout. I looked at the arrows printed on the carton. "Open here." It seemed simple, but the cardboard wings were sticky and hard to separate. I pushed against the wings but the act did not produce a spout, only a spectacular spill that splashed against the bright red flower on my shirt.

Every day I gathered myself to prepare for everything that was new. Our crowded family settled in for the deceptively peaceful opening of a new Virginia life, except we children were the ones in charge when we ventured outside into the American world. There, motherhood failed. My mother's tentative, accented English miniaturized her.

My mother was a strong woman, and I was surrounded by other strong mothers from our extended family. Our family had always orbited around itself. Although the vast majority of Vietnam is Buddhist and the rest practice Catholicism, Taoism, and Confucianism, almost all Vietnamese follow some form of ancestral worship at home, premised on the ritual expression of filial piety. In our Virginia family room, there was a dedicated space for mythmaking and memorializing the parent-child connection—an elaborate altar of carved mahogany lacquered in glossy red, where pictures of dead relatives were displayed. We know that our own lives are linked to those of our parents, grandparents, and even great-grandparents, and their stories are bequests that are passed down from one generation to the next. Family karma is almost like DNA.

The most famous pagodas in Vietnam are sanctuaries dedicated to mothers. The older generation is respected by the younger. Parents, both mothers and fathers, sacrifice for their children, and happiness can be attained through this sacrifice.

For the most part, even in America, I accepted my parents' approach to parenting with completely reflexive respect, and I did not question their expectations, which are culturally sanctioned and reinforced—the good old-fashioned Asian model transposed onto America.

Listen to parents.
Be polite when talking to parents.
Listen to teachers.
Be polite when talking to teachers.
Education comes first.
Hard work is the key to success.
Play always comes after schoolwork.

One of the most famous Vietnamese poems is about the relationship between parent and child and the quiet debts owed; all Vietnamese children knew the poem by heart by the time we started kindergarten. The translation to English blunts its poetic flow and makes it sound clunky and didactic. And there are some words that have no synonym or parallel in English, which makes even the best translation incorrect.

Công cha như núi Thái Sơn
Nghĩa mẹ như nước trong nguồn chảy ra
Một lòng thờ mẹ kính cha
Cho tròn chữ hiếu mới là đạo con

Roughly translated:

Father's deeds are as great as Mount Thai Son
Mother's virtue is like spring water gushing from its source
From one's whole heart is Mother to be revered and Father respected
So that the child's way may be rounded and completed

In everyday life, this means the child owes an enormous debt to the parents, no matter what. And this is key: no matter what—just by virtue of their being parents. They gave birth, the first big debt-generating act. And they raised the child, the second big debt-generating act. They didn't have to do a perfect or even a good job. The way to pay them back is to repay the debt by whatever means, which always includes, at the very least, taking care of them in their old age. This is nonnegotiable.

When I went back to Vietnam to teach contracts, one of the Vietnamese law professors told me what he thought of American damage calculation. My lecture was on the principle of good-faith performance and on contract enforcement. The professor had a slight smirk on his face. He explained, "The best way to enforce a contract is to make sure you enter into a contract only with someone you know will perform it in good faith. Because otherwise, it's very costly to sue for breach in a court of law." I nodded. True, there are transaction costs in everything, including enforcement costs. "Do you know how you can tell if someone will honor a contract?" he asked. He didn't wait for me to answer. "By seeing whether they perform their first duty. Did they—are they—taking care of their elderly parents? That is the first and most important contract in life." You pay your debt to your parents. Not doing so is a moral stain.

One of the most beloved Vietnamese songs is about a mother's love—as vast as the Pacific Ocean, as gentle as the sound of a stream, her voice as soft as the rustling wind through a field of rice, her lullaby in the shadow of a full moon's light, and so on. Yes, in English, it's a bit over-the-top and mawkish, but in Vietnamese, it's quite beautiful. Vietnamese children grow up in an environment where every cultural institution supports and elevates the parent-child relationship, idealizing it as a paragon of love and harmony.

That model of mothering and parenting—not personal to us or our family but institutionally and culturally reinforced—persisted without question inside our home. True, your own footprints make the road. But there is an exception. The Asian road to education is not individually carved but rather culturally standardized. There is a template, and it is ironclad. And no Vietnamese parents can be stripped of authority when it comes to their children's education. My parents expected me to get good grades—or more precisely, all they wanted in their life now that we had left everything behind was for me to get good grades. Good grades meant As, not Bs. This was never stated, but it was clear because the choices they made through their actions centered around my homework requirements, which always came first. In our culture, the deepest things were the things not said—just like telling me they loved me. Our cultural inclination was to subdue chatter and embrace action instead.

My family moved through their first six months in this country with muscled intuition and precision. There were things to do—getting driver's licenses was first on the list. At the beginning, my father was the only one who could pass the test, so he was our designated driver. Two uncles, Father Six and Father Eight, tried multiple times and failed. Father Eight was diminutive and frail and shorter than all of us, including me. When he sat straight up, his head was barely above the steering wheel. Therefore, my father did all of the driving.

With Papa Fritz's help, my mother opened a Vietnamese grocery store in a somewhat depressed area of town. It's what ethnic refugees have done throughout the ages; our own food is the one thing we still know in a new land. But no errands related to the store could take precedence over anything related to my school, such as my need to go to the library to perfect my homework assignments. And not just the neighborhood library. My father insisted that we go to the central library, whether or not it was necessary, where the collection of books and microfiche was vast and thus superior. They both agreed that my mother would take a taxi or wait for a friend to drive her to work if I needed a trip to the library. And on the weekends, they preferred that I spend all of Saturday and Sunday ensconced among books instead of helping my mother with chores at the store.

They did not understand T. S. Eliot and "The Love Song of J. Alfred Prufrock," but they preferred that I read books, any book, rather than take on extra tasks. The first line in the poem made me cry. Just the words "Let us" . . . let us, let us anything. "Let us go then, you and I." "You and I" sounded so oddly out of reach for me. The only "you and I" that I could think of was my father and me. And he no longer knew what I was becoming.

My parents did not know what I did in the library exactly (reading about the war and noticing what was not there—the Vietnamese in Vietnam; history had been spliced, cut, rearranged, and we were becoming a casualty of someone else's sideways chronicle of war). It was enough that I spent time there. For them it was like taking your kid to a park on the weekend, except it's a park for the mind. Wandering and aimlessly looking at books on bookshelves, being moderately curious until I found the poetry section.

That education came first was so obvious, it did not need to be said.

I accepted the Confucian-rooted Vietnamese devotion to education. This was a traditional value, but in the United States, my parents saw it with fresh eyes, additionally indispensable, like something written into the cosmic code. And I followed it without question. Becoming American or at least something that was not refugee was going to be a protracted process. I developed a meticulously structured routine, a discipline, a method to create order to my day. There were segments, in minutes and hours, for homework and for extra work that went beyond what the teachers assigned—way beyond, just in case a trick question would be eked out of secret parts of a book. There was immersion in vocabulary books—one of my favorites was *1001 Words You Need to Know*, reminding me of *One Thousand and One Nights* and the magic of Aladdin and other stories told by Scheherazade to save her life. These new 1,001 English words would save my life like the 1,001 stories saved Scheherazade because they would give me access to the world of novels and poetry and short stories.

My English was assembled from a kit. I had my precisely allotted moments for Strunk and White's *The Elements of Style*, the antidote to grammatical and overall cluelessness like mine. Rules can console. I relied on the commands and decrees and prescriptions issued by the book's authors to give me some sense of the firm fundamentals of the English language—elementary principles of usage and composition. I stuck with this routine and never deviated from it. This discipline was going to be my way out.

Years later, when my own child entered high school, I tried to push Strunk and White on her first by telling her to read it with me. To coax her into wanting to spend more time with me, I forced myself to stop pointing out each time she said "like" or "um" when she talked. When that did not work, because she was never available ("I'm busy with homework, Mom"), I slyly put my treasured copy on her night table. It stayed in the same fixed position for months. I saw only dried yellowish water marks on it. She was using it as a coaster.

My father used to say anyone can be smarter than you; that's not something you can control—but you can always control being the one who works the hardest. In this way, he was just like other Vietnamese parents, who never tell their children they are intelligent. Intelligence isn't in anyone's control, but hard work is. All throughout high school, I was quite aware of my limits. I also followed rules. Always work before play. Never procrastinate. Give myself time to do any task in case something unexpected happens. Do extra-credit work as insurance against a bad test.

Perhaps I took it all too much to heart, because even my mother was concerned about me. She used to order me to stop looking for the missing pen cap or Tupperware lid, the misplaced pencil, the lost book, and just grab another perfectly adequate substitute instead. "You're wasting your time looking for something for hours now," she said all too rationally. But she didn't understand what was at stake: my own sense of urgency; my desire for precision and resolution; my rigid discipline and steely resolve, which I developed only as a reaction to the shock of America. In Vietnam, I'd had a world alive with magic and spontaneity, not study routines. My parents had wanted me to go to one of Saigon's elite French language schools, but I couldn't pass the entrance test. I found out when the list of those who failed was publicly posted at the school for all to see. I was what I would now call lackadaisical, or even lazy. But in Virginia, my daily ritual was defined by staying on track, by keeping everything tightly scaffolded, so I would not be derailed, as someone like me was quite prone to be. I was not wasting time just because I was spending it—lots and lots of it, repetitively, compulsively—to maintain the established infrastructure of order and predictability.

It was not going to be a straight line. I would have to swerve and dodge. But I would get out of purgatory. I would leave behind loss and betrayal and memories of amputated legs in military hospitals.

Maybe I could leave this paranoid husk of a self and allow a different self to emerge, a child self, more fun, more like the imaginative child I had been in Vietnam, believing in 1,001 kinds of magic, the Seven Freaks of Jiangnan sword artists who defy gravity and fly in the air and live by a righteous code of conduct. As a mother, now and then, I try to show Harlan a flash of that playfulness and spontaneity that these characters from my childhood once elicited in me. I think it would be just the "right" amount of fun, even frivolity, when balanced against my more entrenched sense of discipline.

My parents thought I was being a good, dutiful Vietnamese kid, devoted to school in the traditional way. Their immigrant dream centered around a conventional, good old-fashioned kind of security.

But I also decided to embrace education on my own—not to continue with tradition but to break from it, subvert it, and use it for liberation. For me, education was not the epitome of Confucian piety but rather my escape from it. It was my way out—out of American derision and disdain, and a sanctioned way out of the Vietnamese bunkered enclave, with its embarrassing ways. I had seen how Americans struggled to understand my parents and uncles and aunts, speaking down to them, adopting the body language, voice, and tone used when addressing children. Despite their slow, cautious diction, my parents could not get rid of their accent. In fact, it only made the accent more noticeable. Despite their plainness of speech, salespeople couldn't understand them. English—tuneless, toneless—was their third language.

Once, in the summer of 1975, Mrs. Moore, the nice neighbor from across the street, made it a point to welcome us with homemade cookies. My mother was squatting as she kneaded flour, pressing her entire body weight on the mix. We were all wrong. I was wearing jeans too high in the waist. My mother was doing the unnervingly uncouth Asian squat—a deep, flamboyant squat, feet flat, weight fully on heels. I could do it too, quite easily, in fact, and hold the position for a long time. It was comfortable for me. But all I could think of when the neighbor witnessed my mother's squat was the identical squat by Vietnamese villagers as they huddled in the background while big, tall GIs marched through their villages. People who squatted like that used holes in the ground for toilets and were called gooks.

Mrs. Moore marveled at my mother's flexibility, but I was mortified. My mother, of course, was oblivious. That we were one of them, staring at our own faces, ours and not ours, reflected on the television screen. When I later told her that no one in America squats, she scoffed. "That's why they're unhealthy here. They can't squat." My father nodded in agreement. He practiced yoga. He considered the Asian squat, like the cross-legged lotus position or even kneeling, an archetypal posture, a grounding force.

They made no effort at even entry-level assimilation. I could only marvel at how they were not self-conscious at all, even though I could tick off all the many reasons they should have been. I was jealous of their apparent indifference to American judgment.

Their worries were more inward than outward. Our family was permeated with the language of loss, specifically the emotional weight of loss rooted in betrayal, which left its brackish residue on us all. When other Vietnamese visited, it was to build upon a friendship reinforced by bereavement and by the huge gash of dysfunction and clannishness. The murmured stuff of discussion during the course of a jovial dinner was, more often than not, centered around blame and fault and sadness.

Here was the little living room with everyone in it—my big family and my parents' collection of friends, the cringing dispossessed, each using memory to revive Saigon perpetually and drown in its wreck. Pain was familiar and easy. As each person entered, I was told to do the obligatory bow; I crisscrossed my arms on my chest. Afterward, I retreated to an unlit corner of the living room. Thinking I could not be seen or noticed, I watched from there, making up my own bliss. Sometimes, in unexpected moments, I took out my slim notebook and wrote down the lyrics of Vietnamese songs I never thought I much cared for. But now I was worried that it was already too late, that I had forgotten them or would forget them soon—songs sung by artists like Khánh Ly and Thanh Tuyền, songs my mother listened to, songs I had shrugged off but absorbed without knowing they had entered my consciousness. I needed to save them in some form more tangible than memory. And I realized with gratitude that the soul of Vietnamese songs, its deeply searing and arresting beauty, had revealed itself to me all along. Here in America, these were the songs that returned the Vietnamese language to itself, to our souls. The progression of refrains became my private obsession, circling and circling without end or resolution.

There was always music when history became too much. I could almost hear my old abandoned piano, itself frozen in time and place, playing these notes in a distant song somewhere in Vietnam.

More noises. There was the clattering of rice bowls, rackety washing of utensils, metallic sounds of forks, knives, and spoons. My father was not very talkative, preferring solitude and meditation, keeping his hardened battlefield memories inside him. But sometimes he remained downstairs instead of retreating to his bedroom. Father Six was a paratrooper colonel who got a job as a cleaner at a bowling alley. Father Eight, emotionally fragile, was an artist, a painter, but got a job at a local Virginia company that made maps. Both liked to discuss politics with like-minded friends. The visitors had once been journalists, priests, monks, military people.

I was more interested in the Winter Olympics in Innsbruck, Austria. I had never seen an ice rink, much less figure skating. Dorothy Hamill was her characteristically nervous self, so said the announcer Dick Button. She would try to land the double axel. There was much chatter about being all-American. And the American Dream.

There are so many ways to understand dreams. Dreams are what we see in our sleep. They are also what haunt us and keep us from sleeping. But the American Dream seemed more like a promise repeating itself in our brain. E pluribus unum. From the cacophony of the many, the multitude, the ornery, and the varied, one shiny country, like a city on a hill, would emerge.

Is the bò kho good? Is there enough star anise, lemongrass, ground annatto? No one objected to the flagrant interjection of politics into the intimacy of mealtime. The main point of these gatherings was the talk— the slow, brooding hours centered around a rapidly receding past, a deeply remembered war that heaved itself into every conversation—not the food—even if my mother and Mother Six spent hours preparing it.

Sometimes some of my nine girl cousins from Father Six would join me. We would laugh about the time we hid on the roof and used water pistols to squirt people below. Or how we aimed pebbles at conical hats worn by passersby and giggled when the unsuspecting victims were startled and jumped.

"It was a political, not military, consideration," Father Six declared. In my house, time-jumping moments were common. It could be the 1972 Easter Offensive or the 1968 Tet Offensive or the 1971 Operation Lam Son 719 they were talking about. Or it could just be a general statement about everything to do with the war itself. Our mental calendars were marked not by birthdays or holidays to celebrate but by historical constraints to remember and mourn.

History unfurled almost every weekend at our house. A reckoning of the geopolitical wheel, a brick wall of facts and figures and theories, rejecting American convention. Henry Cabot Lodge, Richard Nixon, Henry Kissinger, Robert McNamara, falling one by one in the crosshairs. Each name a broken-off end of a fragmented history, antagonistic, provocative. Each name pronounced was followed by silence, as if each came with its own echo we needed to hear.

"Every strategy had to be approved by the Americans," someone would say, followed by talk about how the Vietnamese were supposed to be obedient serfs, saying nothing even when we understood most of everything.

"They had a strategy? What do you call American strategy?"

"Making and avoiding potholes?"

"It's doing the same thing over and over and expecting a different result." I sometimes thought they were talking about a person or a failed relationship, not about the war or the United States.

"Why?" someone would ask.

"Why Vietnam? Look at South Korea. Indonesia. Malaysia. All still there. All three survived Communist guerrillas."

It was easy to be driven to madness. Every meeting, every meal was the same damn meeting and the same damn meal with the same damn question: Why? "I didn't see it coming. Did you?"

"What went wrong, then?"

When someone turned the conversation around and suggested it would do the Vietnamese good to look at ourselves, I could hear a rising chorus of yes. Yes, yes.

"We are an unfortunate race, the lowest of all the Asian races."

"Or at least of the chopstick-using countries."

"Always puffing our chest. Only good when there are invaders to unite against." Father Six turned and made a dismissive sound.

There was another snort of ridicule. "We are an unfortunate, gossipy, backbiting race. Like crabs in a barrel. The moment one is about to crawl out, the others pull it down."

"We will never be like the Japanese."

No. They kept shaking their heads, belittling their own people.

And then someone would say something—in question form, though it was not meant as a question—to test their collective memory. "Do you remember that year when I planted the peach tree? It was the same year that . . ." It was like a fill-in-the-blank test. "What tea was served at our daughter's wedding?" The questions were not questions but an exercise of assertion. Asserting and reinforcing memories to make sure they didn't fade. And, in the process, unearthing names and dates they had forgotten, as if the missing information had been waiting patiently all along to be recovered. Like both my parents suddenly recalling the name of the U.S. adviser who had recommended my father for the Silver Star Medal.

In the end, maybe to avoid looking too long at themselves, they always circled back to America, its geopolitical cracks. If the United States had abided by the terms of the Paris Peace Accords of 1973, we would have managed. If the United States hadn't betrayed us, we would have had a chance. Once America decided to cozy up to China and we were thus no longer needed to contain the Chinese threat, we were discarded. Like lemon peel, so goes an old Vietnamese saying about people jettisoning those no longer deemed useful. The Paris treaty pledged that if South Vietnam needed military equipment to defend itself against northern aggression, America would provide replacement aid on a piece-by-piece, one-by-one basis. It never did. When the Communists gobbled up the South, we fled straight into the arms of America, which took us in and saved us, reassuring the world once again that the nation is decency, benevolence, and magnanimity incarnate. Two years later, in a redemptive finale, President Jimmy Carter sent the Seventh Fleet to pick up the hundreds of thousands of boat people bobbing around on the sea.

Forty years later, Rory Kennedy's film *Last Days in Vietnam* depicted the valiant and touching efforts of American soldiers and embassy personnel who risked much to save as many Vietnamese as possible in those final days. It was a generous portrayal of the South Vietnamese, even if it did perpetuate, understandably enough, the common trope of America as a savior.

For us America remains the country most resented and cherished at the same time.

For my father, there was always the coup. The assassination. President Ngô Đình Diệm had been shot and bayonetted to death in 1963 by coup leaders, General this, General that, encouraged and paid by the CIA. I knew them, these coup leaders—even had memory of them—before I ever met them. When I was little, whenever we drove past our neighborhood church, my father would point it out. The president had planned to escape through secret routes and tunnels from the presidential palace to this very church. From there, he was to be spirited to our house for shelter. My father thought the army should have been professional and apolitical. His airborne troops were supposed to protect the president. But President Diệm never made it. The same generals he trusted the most—especially the Buddhist generals who became Catholics in order to join the Catholic president's innermost circles—had betrayed and turned against him. There were so many enormous, unanswerable questions. What would have happened in Vietnam if he hadn't been murdered?

On a more personal level, my father himself had been imprisoned in

1963 by his best friend and, with a gun cocked against his head, ordered to support the coup against the president. He could have met the same fate as Colonel Lê Quang Tung, who had refused to cooperate and had therefore been summarily executed. But my father was also lucky. The same friend who had invited him to a pretend luncheon to capture him also decided, for the sake of friendship, to release him before the big-shot leader of the coup could order him killed.

These were the broken moments of my parents' lives. They kept breaking at the same tormented spot, even if everything looked normal and healed.

As my father reminded me and probably himself too, there is only the present. Don't trust the word *always*, which tries to fix a future into the human heart.

ONCE OUR FAMILY REALIZED THAT OUR STAY in America was going to be permanent, I knew I had to grow up fast and began to let go of what I loved most: the magic of magic, like Quách Tỉnh perfecting the art of archery in the Mongolian desert, and the magic of the quotidian. I didn't know I loved it so much until I no longer had it—the spontaneous, the meandering, the serendipitous ways of my childhood. Feeling how pure and how big and how magical the joy of living like a child can be. Because it was possible to disengage from the burn ward and the blackened bodies, the observation ward and the many amputees, and make pretend magic in your head. I could remove my first-person self from the scene and put someone else's third-person self in my stead. No one would have to know I knew this magic trick. Even the garden right behind the house could be wholly beautiful, without the metal door leading to a paratrooper encampment that was off-limits and hence interesting, scary, and strange. Like the strange howls of the soldiers at night mixing with the swells of a summer storm. A perpetual reminder that the war was nearby.

But in Falls Church, Virginia, I learned to guard the imagination and became a data-driven child, trying my hardest to take full empirical inventory of the new niceties of American life and, more often than not, failing. My first day of high school, in September 1975, my father walked with me from our house to the bus stop, which was about three blocks away. I was the only kid in flared trousers and the only one accompanied by a parent. My cousins were in middle school and took a different bus from a different spot to a different school. The bus stop, particularly its utter impersonality, became the place I dreaded the most in my life. Students from the neighborhood congregated there to wait for the school bus, which picked us up at 7:05 in the morning. They eyed us in silence. I watched my father as if through a keyhole and took in a devastating data point. For the first time, I glimpsed not what was there but what the students could see, and I allowed that image to stick with me.

A foreign man, still sturdy because his posture was always militarily erect, but foreign and neutered nonetheless. Not comfortable enough to be breezy or casual. Rigid and observant and cautious, like me. My father, like foreign men—or rather, Asian men, or more specifically East Asian men, with smooth, golden, hairless skin—carried his body differently. In one summer, I already knew that men in my family, even combat soldiers, were not considered masculine or manly in this country. The way they claimed space was different—exaggeratedly less proprietary, more courteous and self-restrained. The way women carried themselves. I soon learned the word others used to describe them: *effeminate.*

Like in *Grease,* when the Pink Ladies had their sleepover and one of them showed off an embroidered bathrobe "from Bobby in Korea." And the others screeched, in utter disbelief, "You're dating a *Korean?*"

These men, my father, brother, uncles, were not male enough. The way black men were "too" male and threatening. Thank God for Bruce Lee. My first year in college, I bought a giant poster of him in *Enter the Dragon*— one of the first Hollywood movies starring a Chinese man with equal bill-ing to a white actor. Luckily, my roommate, Annie, with whom I had been randomly assigned, was super sweet and understanding and didn't mind having a poster of a bare-chested man holding a pair of nunchaku dominating an entire wall of our dorm room.

WE WERE NOT IMMIGRANTS. We were refugees. When I think of immigrants, I think of going somewhere, maybe toward hope and faith in the future. Refugees flee. Away from. Toward nowhere. We are stateless, without an anchor in the home country. We bring memories of war with us, and by our tarnished presence, we keep that war alive in the minds of Americans who want to forget.

My American life, the biggest parcels of it, began at that unremarkable bus stop every weekday morning; it was where I staked my future. Where becoming American seemed more cryptic and complicated than ever. The dreaded and dreadful and dreary bus stop. With its mysterious nodes of power here and nattering nonsense there. A seemingly innocuous spot in front of a nondescript house on the corner of an idyllic street. There was also a big tree that drew us to it, and it became the spot where everyone congregated. It looked like it was beckoning with its branches, promising sanctuary. Trees have a way about them that evokes comfort and shelter. But for me it was a place that reflexively induced panic, incited by the impassivity and inscrutability of American youth. The vein near the back of my neck pulsed whenever I approached the area.

It was, in many ways, the same pulsing, foreboding feeling I experienced years later as a mother when my daughter herself was bullied in high school. As awful as being a child sufferer was, being the mother of a suffering child was worse. On the surface, the ostracism we each faced was very different. Harlan had classic good looks and charm, an impeccable sense of style; from her outward appearance, she did not seem to suffer. She knew how she wanted to look, and from her curated assemblage of clothes and footwear, she was able to put herself together with ease and flair. I took all that veneer to mean she was doing well because she had all the external indicators that I lacked—aesthetics, poise, native knowledge of America, friends to hang out with, teachers who liked her, good grades to seal it all together. Ipso facto, she was fine. True, there were days when she zoned out and sequestered herself in her room, but I saw that as a vintage journey of American adolescents. Sometimes she felt lonely and different, but I saw that as a universal part of being human. If it were specific to her, I told myself it was because she's stunningly different, intense in that unique combination of cerebral and emotional.

I remember showing her a photograph of Louise Bourgeois's magnificent and slightly menacing spider sculpture with its massive sticklike legs and its larger-than-life body improbably, delicately suspended high above the ground. We were leafing through an art book, and she grabbed my hand to keep it from turning to the next page. She was about eight years old and very intrigued. I told her the name of the sculpture, *Maman*. Like you, she said. Scary and always there. I wasn't sure whether to be pleased or offended. Maman the spider became our version of the helicopter parent. Sometimes, not wanting to be an overwhelming spiderlike presence, I made a point of giving her space.

Only later, in her sophomore year, when a breakup with a boyfriend resulted in her math grade plummeting and visible tears, did I discover the extent of her inner turbulence and isolation. I had compared her to me and people who had it much worse than I did—that is, the average anonymous refugee, the common foot soldier who sacrificed everything for a piece of land, and in our case a sliver of hope that is the American Dream. Only when I removed myself from the comparative picture did I realize that beneath the surface, Harlan too was the new kid, when we moved to California, and although she had made new friends by high school, those friends already had deeper relationships with others. She was not the most important person in her friends' lives. And the backlash and nastiness of cliques and factions were magnified and proliferated and broadcast to the world by Snapchat and Instagram, whose workings were mysterious to me.

I had no way of fixing her loneliness, as I'd had no way of fixing mine when I was her age, but that didn't keep me from trying. My desire to fix things generated other kinds of resentment. I'd make her go back to the house and put on a coat before going for an evening walk on the beach even when I knew she would rather feel the night chill. In fact, she told me at the time, and often after, that in my efforts to fix things—for instance, by taking away her smartphone to pluck her from smartphone-enabled gossip—I only made things worse. But my need to right the wrong was not only a rational need. It was a form of desire. A vivid and deep desire, palpable like hunger, to rewrite a high school childhood larded with unrectified wrongs, producing in the process different probable outcomes. I imagined myself with a different mother, more like me. More like an involved parent who knew how to pay attention, had the time to pay attention, and had the knowledge and know-how to fix the child's world when it went awry. In the end, however, the result was the same. My parents' inability to maneuver American life was of no use to me. And conversely, my ability was of no use to my child.

IN NINTH GRADE, I made a point of being the first one to get to the bus stop to pick my spot, not too close to where the other students congregated, for fear of being a trespasser, but not too far either, for fear of appearing aloof. Fading into the background. Making nice with Americans was key. But to this day I still wonder why, after four years of standing tactfully in the same spot, I never spoke more than two sentences to any of the students. Nor did they to me. Most had known each other since elementary school. Most lived within one or two blocks of each other. Most were interested in things I knew nothing about—Nair and Neet for hair removal, conditioner to soften hair, cream to moisturize the face, makeup to hide this or accentuate that. Most were preoccupied with and engrossed in their mutually intersecting lives. They were simply indifferent to mine.

Except on those occasions when I overheard someone spit out the word *Vietnam* as if it were a national rebuke. It was the owner of the house where the bus stopped. On rainy days, he allowed everyone but me to huddle close to his house and take shelter under his sloping roof. The slow accumulation of these bus stop incidents became but an unremarkable aspect of daily life in Virginia, where I learned to develop and perfect a hard, protracted, and unemotional stoicism. Every day for four years, before the day even started, I already wanted it to end. I wished I could return to Saigon. But the city I knew no longer existed; it had a new identity, even a new name. What I had was my New World, where myth-mongering and the gushing promise of the American Dream and the melting pot, so evocative yet so evasive, only made America seem all the more unattainable.

Although Vietnam dominated American news for years, it remained a parenthetical aside—many Americans did not know anything about us. We fled in 1975, clearly because we were on the losing side, and we fled to America because we were American allies, and yet it was not out of the ordinary to be called Vietcong. Through the thin roar of conversation and laughter, someone could still lob contempt. "That Vietcong over there" was what I heard on the bus. Or "She's a freak." I was cowed by the withering description until I consoled myself by returning to the ways of the Seven Freaks of Jiangnan from Legends of the Condor Heroes, so beloved was the book series that it was now thankfully available for rent in Vietnamese stores.

My father once told me how when the two sides were meeting to negotiate French withdrawal from Vietnam, the French had mistaken a Vietminh general for a coolie, since he was wearing sandals and white cotton sheaths to accommodate the tropical heat. That was how the French viewed us, he said, giving me a knowing look. He had joined the Vietminh, a precursor of a sort to the Vietcong, in high school, as thousands of young

Vietnamese did at the beginning. His time with them gave him something to stand against, which in turn showed him what it was he stood for.

Remembering this anecdote, always knowing it was more than an isolated story, he made a point of standing erect when commanding his troops in battle, even when enveloped by enemy gunfire. American advisers were embedded in Vietnamese units to train and evaluate the Vietnamese. He suspected the Americans were not so different from the French—both barging into our narratives (and then barging out) as if it were their natural right. In Vietnam, there were so many ways we were obliquely if not blatantly consigned to the shadows.

At one point, when my father saw that his soldiers had dropped down for cover, he swiveled left, using his right arm to summon them from their defensive crouch and charge forth. A bullet that would have hit his heart was shielded by the pivot of the right shoulder instead. His American advisers recommended him for the American Silver Star and wrote in their recommendation that he had "moved decisively, erectly and conspicuously" during the battle in Kiến Phong Province, even though he had been wounded by an enemy bullet.

Vietcong wasn't the only name I was called. There was also "moo moo moo," like a cow, in a play on my last name. I was actually grateful that I didn't have names like Phước, which means "grace" in Vietnamese but quickly morphed into a knowing wink-wink "fuck," or Dung or Dũng, which means either "beautiful" or "brave" depending on the tonal accent but certainly means neither in English.

There was no salvation, even from the established Asian Americans who wanted nothing to do with the rice-paddy self-pitiers, the mutant refugee Asians like us. Perhaps they could see through our elaborate costuming, the embellished artifice designed to create presentable, palatable selves.

Mary Ellen in biology class objected to my being her science partner because she was worried that my eyes—"They're shaped different"—would mean I could not see the microscopic specimens accurately. When the teacher chose a different partner for her, and when I was relegated to becoming the teacher's partner instead, the odd kid out whom no other student wanted to be companions with, I was, to my great surprise, overcome by a very different feeling about the Vietcong and the Vietminh. Although most of my family fought against the Vietcong, I was suddenly proud of them. So hungry was I for a win that I was thrilled they had defeated the most powerful country on earth, no matter that we were defeated and crushed in the process as well. My pride was my defiance and self-defense. I was even proud that they had dug a labyrinth of tunnels that defied American detection.

Fade to black, always fading to black. Despite the come-hither panache of America, what we had instead was Falls Church. My high school was named after the Confederate cavalry commander J. E. B. Stuart. In neighboring Springfield, we had Robert E. Lee High School. We also had Jefferson Davis Highway and Lee Highway. Virginians have always been so tragically sincere about their heritage.

I LOVED FOOD, but not at my high school cafeteria, where fifty minutes of free, unchoreographed, and unsupervised lunch was an exercise in palpable collusion and exclusion. There were tables for those deemed part of the ruling class, like athletes and cheerleaders and class officers. Next came members of clubs like the high school yearbook or the school newspaper. The out-crowd kids too had their tables. I usually paid a quarter for a pint of milk and went to a classroom to get extra help. American high school culture was not easy to procure on command. And I liked solitude, even erasure.

There were days when I felt so gossamer light and untethered to the world that it felt good to float almost weightless and invisible in an empty classroom, doing homework during lunch period while the teacher was busy in the background doing her own class preparation.

I liked being able to be my own insulated, self-contained entity at this school. I could enter it anytime, this world inside my head where I could order up, by pushing a button, color and music and poems and other beautiful things.

THE FIRST BIG SNOWFALL TO HIT FALLS CHURCH was memorable for all of us. I woke up at six in the morning to catch the bus at seven. The wind had lofted snowflakes and deposited them against the windowpanes. I had boots from Memco. Being a military man, my father had a soldier's inclination for advance planning. He had bought me nonslip straps for additional traction. I trudged from my house to the bus stop, but unlike other days, there was no one else along the road or at the stop. Still, I waited under the beautiful but oppressive tree until a woman I recognized as the mother of a brother and sister who also took the bus popped out from her house across the street and said, "No school today." Seeing my blank face, she added, "Snow day," pointing her finger at the snow falling from the sky.

Neither my parents nor I knew that we could listen to the radio to find out what to do when it snowed. We must have assumed, throughout that entire year, that only Americans had access to this uncanny proprietary information. And so I would just wake up as usual and walk the customary route to the bus stop, and if there was a schedule change, the nice lady would swing her front door open to share the news. "Two-hour delay." "No school." I looked forward to her upbeat, informative one-liners, which she sometimes imparted with a wink and a half smile.

I remember our first Thanksgiving feast in Falls Church. There was the sun's bright, round saffron eye watching our first American Thanksgiving. My mother was getting used to trees with bare branches shivering in the autumn wind. She was even taking English language classes in the evening at Northern Virginia Community College. The whole clan, in high gear, gathered at the house where my grandmother stayed—the house of

Father Six and my nine girl cousins. The grown-ups were starting over—sliding and settling in the third quarter of their lives as subsidiary characters in a new country. Clearly, the many contingency plans they might have prepared for in Vietnam didn't actually pan out. That didn't mean giving thanks was superfluous.

Shedding our alienness and renewed anxieties (as anxieties have a strange way of resurfacing) efficiently, gracefully swatting them away with the rituals of giving thanks, we imitated our neighbors and decked our houses with pumpkins and paper cutouts of turkeys. Americanize us, Americanize us, we were saying—hyperbole, yes, but also true. My parents and I had read up on Thanksgiving and its many sustaining myths. My father told me that the way he saw it, it was a holiday to remember the time when the first Americans, the Wampanoag tribes, took pity on English immigrants called the Pilgrims and took them in. To show their gratitude, the Pilgrims made a feast of thanks to share with the Wampanoag.

Our meal was meant to be versatile, aligning and merging the best bits of our old and new history. I liked that the family was working America into the system, rather than trying to get Vietnam out—at least in the universe of food. This was because none of us had tried turkey and didn't particularly love the idea of eating it.

But the Moores, directly across the street from us, gave us a turkey, which my mother was extremely grateful for. When I think of the American Dream, I think of them. Their gestures of welcoming kindness. Husband, wife, two little girls. The husband raked autumn leaves from his yard and without fail would proceed to do the same for ours. He piled them onto a giant blue tarp and let me jump on the heap. Our first Thanksgiving, he showed up in his uniform—air force, maybe—and presented what we called our gratitude turkey to my father. "We're thankful you're here," he said. "Welcome."

The turkey, unspiced and bland for our normal palate, would be treated, in our household, as more of a decorative than a culinary centerpiece.

Around it were edible manifestations of American tradition such as cranberries, baked yams with brown sugar, and deviled eggs, which were also gifts from our neighbors. Our main meat was roast beef marinated with Maggi sauce, soy sauce, fish sauce, and lemongrass. Instead of mashed potatoes, we had sticky rice, broken rice, grilled pork chops with scallions and olive oil, papaya salad, and lotus stem salad. We concocted our own stuffing of rice, pork, shiitake mushrooms, and chestnuts laced with a little bit of cognac. We dipped our spring rolls in turkey gravy, not fish sauce. Instead of pumpkin soup, we had crab and asparagus soup, which was a French soup popular in Saigon. Our desserts were French sweets, petit choux, and flan.

It was like home, except in a new country.

THAT FIRST YEAR, English class was my salvation. The readings were special and spoke to me. Reading gave me a chance to have an intimate relationship with this new language. Being alone with a book meant I had the space to feel my way through the pages and grasp the emotionally fine-grained passages, because when I spoke it, as I had to all the time, it was an alien, technical tongue, something I had only a rational relationship with. Once I learned *armpit*, then *knee pit* and *leg pit* seemed like logical words to deploy, which turned out to be all wrong. "I am mad at you." Wouldn't "I am happy at you" be similarly acceptable as a sound and sensible improvisation? "I started the car." Why did "I began the car" produce derisive laughter?

I hated how I was punished for my tentative, stuttering elocution and my inclination toward linguistic inventiveness and experimentation, which more often than not fell flat. And I hated hearing others speak it. It was, even at its colossal best, a bully language that made me cower in its shadows and kept people like me at bay.

But in soft, contemplative focus, unspoken and on the pages of a book,

English was something else altogether, linguistically smooth and gentle, strangely more modest and relaxed. Poetry and fiction were my salve and gave me a safe place to hide while my imagination took flight. I could be in my own room but in my itinerant's clothes, traveling the world in my imagination, getting to know and even at times becoming the characters dreamed up by my favorite authors, whom I studied in AP English junior and senior years—Henry James, Virginia Woolf, James Joyce, Dostoyevsky—people sputtering and flinching, carrying big satchels of love and hurt and yearning, sometimes expressed, sometimes not. My AP English teacher, Ms. Helen McBride, who was the epitome of love and devotion to teaching, opened up the world of the novel for me, especially novels by Irish writers who wrote in English, connecting me once again to the world of stories I'd loved as a child in Vietnam. I fell headfirst for *A Portrait of the Artist as a Young Man*. I liked that I could live with those characters, know them without their knowing me. It's not an escape but rather an immersion of a different kind into a different life.

I fell for the story and its moods. Everything inside Stephen's head, the sights, colors, sounds, smells, tastes, the feel of his childhood, bullying and blustering, the name-calling, pondering the meaning of the name "suck" as ascribed to him by classmates, submitting, obeying, confessing, conforming—or not—school buildings soaked in rain, the foul, slimy sewers, rotted cabbage, the dull thud of foot against soccer ball, politics and the Catholic Church and family life and family fights and how Ireland has had enough of God. Like Vietnam has had enough of war. And I have had enough of the moody, brooding reverberations of loss and betrayal replayed in our house and in every Vietnamese house I knew. And through it all, the mood of Stephen's trembling heart and soul and where it ultimately took him. In that sacred space of his inner being, he is who he is, uniquely himself, not bound by the nets of nationality, language, religion, or even family. Even family.

I am a Catholic Irishman. I am Stephen Dedalus. This was how I found magic again, in the bliss of solitude, immersing myself in the enlarged consciousness of fiction so I could live in a big way in the skin of others. The more different, the more varied the assortment of stories, the more I realized how, despite the distinct, the discrete, the dissimilar, and everything else that might define and divide countries, we are nonetheless very similar in our eternal hopes and dreams. It was as if sometimes these stories, these poems, showed me a way to proceed, other times luring me into their folds as if to sleep.

Another English teacher handed me sheets of poems that she thought would speak to me—to *me*, in particular. She brought me "Refugee Blues" by W. H. Auden. And then there was "One Art" by Elizabeth Bishop: "The art of losing isn't hard to master." And Emily Dickinson's "I'm Nobody! Who are you?"

I wanted to study English literature, but literature felt like an undeserved indulgence—too dreamy, not practical enough; it was difficult to make that choice when your refugee parents were working so hard you almost never saw them. My father approved—he had a master's in French literature. But who was I to dare? To think that I was qualified for the American Dream? American, maybe. Dream, no. Work hard, yes—dream, no.

Math classes, by contrast, were always disastrous, not because I wasn't capable but because I had the misfortune of having two of the scariest people as my teachers. Mr. Cantor was short with a tufted mustache and an outsize grin. What I noticed immediately upon meeting him was his penchant for blond models. On the wall above the oversize blackboard were posters of Cheryl Tiegs and Farrah Fawcett. No student could look at the blackboard smudged with *x* and *y* and square roots without also taking in that hair—all feathered locks and voluminous—that smile, and that famous red swimsuit that wholly defined Farrah Fawcett and the age of the supermodel. Same with Cheryl Tiegs, whose "pink bikini" poster hung directly behind the teacher's desk, inevitably attracted a rowdy, unruly, and raucous congregation of certifiably credentialed boys shoulder rubbing, backslapping, and generally hovering about with the teacher until the bell rang. The rest of us in the parade of the damned, some scrawny and gangly, others acned and plump, who came early to get help, could never squeeze ourselves through that charmed circle to even ask our questions, knowing as we did that we were already small and less worthy.

But the real bane of my existence was a different math teacher, Mr. Wendell, whom I had my junior year. After two years in high school, I was ranked number one in a class of over five hundred students. Using a ruler, my father had proudly underlined that with red ink. I had succeeded in presenting the best, most spit-shined version of myself to the school, and he was pleased.

I started my junior year with much more confidence, though still friendless. On the first day of my junior year, Mr. Wendell called the roll, and once he got to my name he widened his eyes and put on a mock expression of exaggerated confusion. "Ching chong?" he asked with swaggering theatricality.

When we turned in our application for citizenship, my father had suggested I change my name to something that approximated Lan but sounded more American, like Lana. True, Farrokh Bulsara had renamed himself Freddie Mercury and became the lead singer of the magnetic band Queen. But Lana as in blond, sex symbol, voluptuous Lana Turner? That didn't seem to fit a skinny, almost scrawny kid with black hair, a bad haircut that made me look like I was wearing a coconut shell on my head, and a flat Asian face. I was becoming a naturalized citizen, not homogenized or sanitized. Still, I imagined that with the right name, the right costume, a different constellation of rightness, I might be chosen by the tastemakers.

I ended up just modifying my name, from Cao Thị Phương Lan to Lan Cao, making it shorter and more pronounceable, reversing the Vietnamese order to the Western order, with the family name last. Phương was a quintessential Vietnamese name but it inevitably tripped people up. Thị was a filler name given to girls. It seemed redundant and Americans pronounced it biblically, as in Thy. So I got rid of both the Phương and the Thị. Now I regret having eliminated Phương from my name because there are so many with the name "Lan Cao." Without realizing it consciously, I revived Phương by including it in Harlan's Vietnamese name, resurrecting the part of my name I used to be ashamed of.

But even a truncated, simple name, Lan, became Ching Chong. Lan meant orchid, I told myself with a mythmaker's determination to be seen differently. I was named after a flower that is fussy but at the same time so adaptable that its many varieties could be found in the equatorial tropics as well as the arctic tundra. It's just a foreign name in America, but it could stand for mythical or even supernatural resilience. I looked up, throat parched, and could only stare at Mr. Wendell's stubbled head, which reminded me of the severe crew cuts worn by those great GIs I'd known in Vietnam who gave me Wrigley's gum and played rock and roll music. Some students gasped, but many others chuckled. "Ding dong?" the teacher continued. More chuckles from the class. I knew nothing about Asians, much less the Chinese, in American history, but I knew this was something that was not meant to be funny. "Chinaman," someone said from the back of the classroom.

I had no other attribute such as excelling at sports, being clever with jokes, or being a cheerleader to diffuse and dilute the gritty foreignness that was mine. I came into class every day hoping to be invisible and inconspicuous to the teacher, until my tests came back with so many points deducted for minor mistakes that I felt I had no choice but to stay after class to ask for clarification. The decisive moment came when I noticed that someone else who had made a similar mistake had fewer points deducted. I felt shaky inside, like a squeaky little gerbil, as I approached his desk, but I knew I needed to defend my grade and my grade point average.

Teachers are bestowed unwavering reverence in Vietnam, and Vietnamese parents rarely—probably never—sided with their children against teachers. If the teacher was "unfair," there must be a reason. You just are not allowed to complain about your teachers to your parents. In fact, when I became a mother years later, my daughter's complaints about her teacher seemed like a violation of a cultural tradition. Naturally I listened, feeling fine that she had unburdened herself to me, but I couldn't help but also think about the story my parents instilled in me about the Emperor who got off his horse to make way for the village teacher when both found themselves on a narrow village lane. Teachers and mandarins had higher rank than even the Emperor.

Thus, I approached my math teacher with a lot of fear and hesitation. I felt I should bow to him. I wanted to show respect. I crept into the room quietly, deferentially. He looked up, tapping his shoes like an animal tapping its hooves squaring up for a fight.

"I think there is a grading mistake on my test," I mumbled, knowing I was standing in quicksand.

He stared at me and said emphatically, "No mistake."

He issued his declaration as if it were something obvious and sensible: "No way in hell am I going to let people like you graduate first at J. E. B. Stuart High School."

I looked at him and proffered my determinedly unemotional face. Here I was in a country of second chances. But the American Dream was just like the horizon: The closer you think you're getting to it, the farther it recedes.

I came home that afternoon and locked myself in my room, cranked up the music, and screamed, but not loud enough for anyone to hear me over Frankie Valli's exuberant hit "Grease" blasting from my radio, turning scrappy Rydell into something daring and sprawling. It was true what my mother said, that pain leaves the body through music.

Aside from the nonnegotiable stricture "Study hard," my parents expected very little of me and gave me the space to do whatever I wanted. And so that afternoon, I was able to sequester myself without anyone's inquiry. Indeed, my parents were too busy nursing their own grievances to notice, until I refused to come out for dinner. Feeling hopeless and helpless, I decided the task of repair should be handed over to my parents. But then I saw my mother clearing plates from the folding table in the kitchen and putting away our assortment of plastic and tin utensils. And I saw my father's face, so eager to find out what was wrong, and yet at the same time so optimistic about the opportunities available in America, so convinced that hard work and hard work alone pays off (no need for trivializing shortcuts), always insistent on sitting with me every afternoon while I did my homework at the dining room table, even if it dealt with subjects he could hardly contribute to—and I knew I couldn't make the confession. It felt wrong. It felt wrong that I couldn't save them, as it was my faithful duty to do. And it felt wrong to flatten them further.

I wanted my father to have his dramatic simplicities. And so I kept the hurt to myself and protected him and my mother, along with their stubborn faith in the mythic trappings of all that was American.

ALL AROUND US, SLOWLY BUT SURELY, a little Vietnamese enclave was being built as an antidote to displacement and diaspora. The blueprint for it centered around memory and gratitude—memory of Vietnam, from which we fled. And gratitude for America, for taking us in. Because of course, America—sigh—did save us from Communism, after all. Even if it left us with war's debris of defeat and loss.

The little gaggle of shops, some on Wilson Boulevard, then on Leesburg Pike, then later around Seven Corners, was supposed to bestow solace, strip-mall-style, by convincing people like my parents, who wanted very much to be convinced, that Vietnam had been brought over here. Let us have a little legerdemain here and there. Even the tinniest, flimsiest pretensions would do. Plastic banana trees in planters lined against a row of windows, for example.

Our grocery store, lit with fluorescent tubes, was in an even less salubrious spot, a lone Vietnamese store in a small parking lot with two other shops of dwindling fortunes. But it sufficed, or seemed to, for my mother. American vets, many searching for ingredients for pho, came and chatted with my parents and my brother Tuấn (when he happened to be there). They started with "I was in Khe Sanh" or "I was stationed in Bien Hoa" and stayed for an hour, even more. I remembered one man in particular. Each time he came, he reintroduced himself—"My name is John"—as if we had forgotten. He looked normal, but couldn't be if he preferred being ensconced with refugees like us to being with his fellow Americans. For many GIs, our little store, like other little stores, was a haven, from a war already deemed a bad war, primed for desecration by history itself. They were in their own country, but these vets too were drowning in the wreck of their own fraught lives.

Tuấn, always the dreamer, would now sit for hours into the early morning, strumming guitar, sucking on a cigarette, blowing smoke circles, pausing to sing a few songs. Drinking beer. Nursing memories, just like my parents. My father with his battlefield ambushes and scars and the immensity of loss and failure; my mother with her own remembrances of floating among decapitated corpses and leeches sucking on flesh. And me. Our family couldn't be exceptional. And it was not. Years later, when I walked the streets of New York City and saw people I thought had been refugees from somewhere else, I knew they were carrying war's debris inside their bodies the way most of the people on earth were doing. And I thought it's those who have never seen the wreckage of war who are the exotic ones.

Because I saw what my parents didn't have—neither home nor peace within—I was determined to keep all of my school troubles from them as a way of easing them into American life.

I would have to take care of my emotional and academic burdens myself, with intellectualized calm and proportion. In full-fledged American fashion, with my orderly mind filled with knowledge, I was going to fight for my rights. I summoned up my courage to talk to the principal. Unlucky for me, the school was gripped by a teachers' strike, and the principal had no time to deal with my little problem. I got a B in my class with this teacher, bringing down my GPA and my class rank. I noticed that once it dropped from the coveted number one spot, my father stopped underlining my class rank.

The next week, another math teacher told me I was welcome to stay after school in her classroom and she would tutor me every day for as long as I needed. Her name was Mrs. Agazarian. She was my angel.

When Mr. Wendell found out I had tried to meet with the principal, he walked a few blocks from his house to mine—yes, there is supposedly no fate or destiny, only coincidences, and it was a coincidence indeed that we lived in the same neighborhood—and told me that he was going to get my family deported. We were in a small three-bedroom, two-bath split-level with a fenced-in front yard. Having the house made the country less frightening. Papa Fritz had personally guaranteed our mortgage. Mr. Wendell saw me on the front stoop and traipsed across the lawn. Flashing boldness and jabbing his finger, he warned that we were going to be deported or put in camps, just like the Japs during World War II.

"But we were on the same side in the war," I said. Faced with a choice between prudent silence and defiance, I opted meekly for equivocation—and despised myself for genuflecting. The second time he ventured by my house, he brought with him a magazine, flipped it open, and pointed to the infamous photograph of General Loan, the police chief, in all-knowing black-and-white summarily executing a Vietcong prisoner on a street during the Tet Offensive. The photographer, Eddie Adams, had captured, in a still photo, the crashing movement of death, that split-millisecond moment when the pistol recoiled and the prisoner's face contorted. For Americans, few photographs captured the epoch of the Vietnam War as that one did. For Adams, the photo got him a Pulitzer Prize and haunted him with regret for the rest of his life because according to him, that one frame had isolated the moment without telling the rest of the story—that the Viet-cong squad leader had just slashed the throats of the wife and six children of the police chief's friend.

Go back to where you come from. He also said that, but it would be inaccurate and misleading to put quotation marks around it and impute it solely to him, because it is an all-purpose phrase. At our neighborhood Giant supermarket, someone yelled "yellow nigger" at my parents. A black man, no less. But those words, though gibberish to me until I looked them up, carried a certain sound and sensation, a rock-hard specificity that lodged itself deep in me.

Go back. You dare complain to the principal? You should be grateful you're here at all.

Chink, slant, gook, yella. Words overspilling. Colloquial slurs beyond our understanding. The English we knew was a more formal English. It took us a while to even figure out that "uh-huh" was yes and "mm-mm" was no. Up until then, the only breezy, casual English I had heard was the Beatles' "She loves you yeah, yeah, yeah."

English is not my first language. It is not even my second language. I still have trouble making out lyrics in pop and rock. For years, even when I got to the point where I prided myself on my control of the English language, what I kept hearing when I listened to Cindy Lauper's song was "Girls just wanna have pho," instead of "fun." Even when I found out my mistake, I kept it and owned it. We hear what we want to hear, especially if it feels good.

And of course, we often heard "Go home." Using different words that sounded more sophisticated and palatable, the political elite felt the same about us. The now-esteemed Governor Jerry Brown of California, that most liberal of states, fought to keep the federal government from sending Vietnamese refugees—even orphans—to his state so we wouldn't overrun the place with our colliding lives. "There is something a little strange about saying, 'Let's bring in five hundred thousand more people,' when we can't take care of the one million out of work," Mr. Brown said; the governor even took the extra step of personally trying to prevent an aircraft filled with refugees from landing at Travis Air Force Base near San Francisco.

One helpful thing about the United States is that newspapers are everywhere. I no longer believed I was destined for magic-carpet flights and martial artistry. Information is freely available and I had replaced magic with research.

Others who echoed Governor Brown's opposition included Delaware's Joe Biden, the much beloved "peace" candidate George McGovern, and feminist Elizabeth Holtzman. Senator McGovern sounded just like my math teacher. "Ninety percent of the refugees would be better off going back to their own land. . . . The Communist government has already given orders that the people are not to be molested. Our program should include the highest-priority steps to facilitate their early return to Vietnam."

I knew all this because I now scavenged for data. I wanted knowledge, facts, information. I spent all my time in the library. My math teacher was not alone. He was mouthing the prevailing social and political script.

The following Saturday and Sunday (and many regularly after), when my father and brother Tuấn dropped me off at the main public library before driving to our fledgling and somewhat scruffy grocery store, I spent hours reading about the internment of Japanese Americans. I read about Fred Korematsu of Oakland, California, who, at the age of twenty-three, defied the government's order to report to the incarceration camps; and the 442nd Regimental Combat Team, composed of all Nisei second-generation Japanese Americans, who volunteered to fight and became the most decorated unit of its size in U.S. military history. When my father came to pick me up for lunch—I remember something good had happened at the grocery store, and we were going to splurge by going to Roy Rogers and ordering roast beef sandwiches—I told him what I had learned. He said he already knew about the Japanese. Can we be deported or interned? I asked. He said no.

MEANWHILE, MY MOTHER'S BUSINESS WAS STRUGGLING, bedeviled by technical regulations she didn't know or understand. The wheels of our family business were spinning without gaining traction. Customs had decided that something she was importing should be taxed at a higher tariff than what she had anticipated. The products would be held at a government warehouse and would not be released until she signed papers acknowledging mistake or fault and paying damages.

Papa Fritz came down to help. We weren't faring well in the sedate Sleepy Hollow neighborhood in Falls Church either. Pink flamingos, plastic gnomes, and trolls were fine, all in harmony with the sustaining myth of peaceful suburbia. But not my mother's emerging vegetable garden of lemongrass, bitter melon gourds, red perilla, Vietnamese basil, and coriander, an unwelcome novelty among rows of manicured lawns. She tended to the garden regularly, snipping a sprig here and there so her herbs would bush out plump and full instead of vertical, spindly, and sparse. And at night before bed, she watered them lightly, patting the damp soil down as if to tuck the plants in for the night.

It was my mother's idea that I start working somewhere, and soon. She had a good friend, a Vietnamese woman married to a rich Frenchman, who owned a jewelry store in the upscale Tysons Corner mall. Her friend introduced me to the manager of a restaurant, the Magic Pan, who agreed to hire me because my mother's friend told the manager that I was two years older than I actually was. I was to be the toilet cleaner/salad maker, which sounded like an inappropriate and disgusting job combination, but those were my two duties there. I felt sick the first few days cleaning the public bathrooms. The manager told me my job was very important. "Would you eat in a restaurant with a dirty toilet? Everything here depends on you." My father, always instilling in me an old-fashioned sense of duty and manners, told me to do the best job I could, which always started with stamina and diligence. I brought Q-tips to clean the crud and grime caked on the toilet seat hinges. The manager told me I was the best toilet cleaner she had ever hired. Every two weeks, I handed my mother a check reflecting the number of hours I had worked multiplied by the minimum wage of $2.65 an hour.

One day my parents told me we would have to move to an apartment in a complex a few miles from our house. We would have to sell the house and rent. We would no longer be within walking distance of Father Six and Mother Six and all the nine cousins, who still lived in Sleepy Hollow.

I was sad when I realized I wouldn't be able to just walk over to my cousins' house anymore. I could still feel between thumb and finger the memories of us playing together like puppies. On the plus side, our new place was closer to my high school, which meant no more bus stop, and I'd no longer have to live near the math teacher. Our new apartment had no garden, which meant I wouldn't have to pull down the shades to keep my mother from seeing a neighbor let his dog urinate on her beloved plants.

My senior year, I had the same teacher for math. I went to my guidance counselor and asked to be transferred out. She reacted with arched eyebrows and pursed lips and told me in a high-pitched officious voice that students were not allowed to select teachers. She fiddled with a ballpoint pen, pinky finger up. That was my only meeting with her that lasted more than five minutes. She was also supposed to help me with applying to colleges, but never once did she give me information about any college or applications. But for Papa Fritz and Aunt Margaret, I would not have known the intricacies of the PSAT and the SAT, or navigated the whole college application process.

One day, Aunt Margaret casually suggested something called the Seven Sisters, a group of highly regarded historically all-women colleges in the Northeast. The seven daughters of the Titan Atlas and the sea nymph

Pleione were known as the Seven Sisters. But for me, the Seven Sisters sounded just like something from the swordsmanship novels of my childhood. Like the Seven Freaks of Jiangnan. Except the Seven Sisters would be a band of all-female warriors, each well versed in different martial arts styles—the praying mantis, the white crane, the eagle claw. I could see the white crane spread its wings to unleash its surprising sideways swipe; the eagle swooping from high above to make the first, the only, the final kill. Each female warrior learning the history of motion, the need to disassemble excess and retreat into essence. Not relying on raw strength. Learning alacrity and deftness and harnessing chi to learn the way. The way of surviving. The way of being.

My parents never tried to steer me to nearby colleges. They trusted me to navigate the world of America, and they would not erect barriers that would limit my educational pursuits.

That is exactly how I feel about Harlan's impending college applications. Except unlike me, she doesn't have to chase some mythical American Dream, because Americans can make their own dreams. That kind of faith, that she has a dream and can pursue it, is already in her bones.

Because I did not have this expectation in my bones, I had no sense that I would actually get into college. I was astonished to find an actual chain of acceptances, affirmative, yeses, that arrived in thick eight-by-ten envelopes in our mailbox. I ended up at Mount Holyoke College, the oldest continuing college for women in the United States. And the amazing Emily Dickinson went there. And it was within driving distance of Papa Fritz and Aunt Margaret's house. But none of those are the reasons I chose it. I ended up there because it only required one essay on the application form. Smith College required two.

I was on the cusp of leaving Virginia, my first home in America.

Harlan

When I was still very small, in pre-K in Virginia, a boy named Ben followed me around everywhere. I distinctly remember having to shut the door in his face to discourage him from following me into the bathroom at school. During the school talent show, he even sang to me and made heavy eye contact for a good ten minutes while trying to serenade me in front of the entire class. And I remember the pink Ralph Lauren polo shirts he wore every day, because my mom took them as an opportunity to show me "there is no such thing as boy and girl colors."

One day, I bumped heads with Ben, and my mother hurried over to where both of us were on the ground clutching our foreheads and rolling around on the grass crying. My mother immediately rushed to Ben and cradled him, which angered me. Her reasoning was that Ben's forehead was actually bleeding, whereas mine was simply a bump. Eventually it made sense to me that even though my mother wanted to always comfort me, building strength was much more important in the end. You cannot just sit on the ground and cry and wait for someone to help you in life. She offered all of her love to a kid she didn't know, the way I felt she did with everyone else. Always so talkative with the rest of the world and so silent with me.

Today, I still want someone to lie down with me on the ground and hold me. I never had enough of that. Instead, I was conditioned to survive. Why can't I just be held and told I am perfect and everything will be okay?

And I am always told that words of affirmation are cheap. But to me, they have become valuable because I never hear them.

When I was about three, my mother took me to see her friend Mai, a sister figure whom she'd known since they were ten. She left me there with this at-the-time strange woman and told her that she wanted me to learn how to jump rope. The two of them used to jump rope together, and in a desperate desire to pass on her heritage to her only child, she insisted that I learn.

So there I sat, holding a mug of steamed milk, the curls of my hair tickling my cheeks. And the purple cat chewed on its tail and stared at me. I stared back. To everybody else, I was staring intensely at a blank spot on the wall; to me, I was in a very important contest with the lilac haze—a contest that would determine if I could successfully assert my dominance over the hallucination.

This woman really wouldn't give up. Upon realizing she didn't have a jump rope because she was a fully grown high school teacher, she sat there for maybe two hours knitting together a rope of rubber bands, the loops tied together to make one big line.

I guess that's what happens when you lose somebody you've known since childhood and find them again thirty years later—you become so devoted that you're willing to spend your weekend teaching an infant how to jump a rubber band rope.

The biggest shock of all came when it was time to try it out: Would I jump or would I treat it the way I treated crawling, by cheating? I couldn't jump. And I'd love to say it's because I was just a three-year-old, but I still can't do it. At age seventeen, Harlan Margaret can't snap her fingers, do a cartwheel, ride a skateboard, whistle, or jump rope.

I think Mai gave up trying to teach me after maybe fifteen minutes. She left the room and went to wash her face, probably hoping that she would drown in the sink. I would too, if I were stuck with having to teach me to do anything.

When she came back, I tugged at her arm with my fat hands, which still get dimples in them when I make half a fist.

"Did you know that I know how to jump rope?" I whispered up at her.

"Well let's see it, then."

I don't think I've ever been more proud of myself since that moment. I laid those rubber bands down on the hardwood floor and stood back a little bit, so I'd have enough room to get a running start.

And I literally hopped over the rope, which was probably lying there confused as to what would make this child so proud of herself for figuring out a way to cheat the system.

The universe had decided that she, my jump-rope teacher, would come into my life again on my sixth birthday and, with my mom and dad, help raise me as her daughter.

The co-parenting system Mai made with my mother would become torture for me in the teenage years, being raised by two Vietnamese mothers who had been so stripped of their own childhoods that they felt the need to protect mine so heavily. It was as if theirs had been shot down, so they lined mine with bullet-proof glass and put me in a snow globe by myself.

The two of them treat a yellow light as if it's a red one, and it drives me crazy. It drives me crazy how many backup plans they have, to the point where it makes me look like I'm unprepared when really they are just being over-the-top paranoid about everything that could go wrong.

My dad would see the yellow light, sometimes even the red one, and speed up. When the siren behind him began to get louder, he took it as a signal to run away from the police, underestimating the risk. Maybe I get that from him, because at least 20 percent of the fights I have with my mother are at six forty-five a.m. and start with me letting out a long sigh of exasperation when I'm late for first period and she stops the car the minute the light turns yellow.

"Yeah, go ahead and sigh. It's all my fault that you're *so oppressed*. Getting up ten minutes late and you expect *others* to accommodate your incompetence. Do you know how many people get killed from running red lights, Harlan? I mean, my god. Use your head."

"I didn't even make a single sound. It's a free country for now. Don't you have more important things to think about than if I sighed? Whatever. Honestly, Mom, I'm not doing this right now at the crack of freaking dawn."

"Yeah, let's leave everything until later, right?"

"What?"

"Have you done any of the definitions I've assigned you? No."

"Actually yes, they're in my phone."

"What does *salubrious* mean? And what's the difference between *inveigh* and *inveigle*?"

A long pause hits the car.

"What does that matter? I mean, Jesus Christ, who are people trying to impress by using words that sound like Harry Potter potions? Having a command over words is important, but you don't need to force it down my esophagus."

"I don't know *who* they're trying to impress; I know *whom* they are trying to impress."

"You can drop me off here. I'll walk the rest of the way."

Car rides when I was little were just as educational, when I spent the trip home from school reciting multiplication tables, one through thirteen.

Something I will never forget are the car rides to D.C. we took every weekend. I sat in the back seat, my head pressed against the window, breathing fog onto the windows and drawing spiderwebs with my fingers. A thick notebook had been dropped into my lap, the cover of it dominated by a picture of a Vietnamese singer, her hair up in a beehive and her eyes lined with green.

It was my long division notebook. All my notebooks were categorized. Some of them had big magenta flowers on the front; others had pictures of young Asian children with perfect skin smiling while holding pencils, clearly trying to trick me into thinking this would be fun. I remember the binder with horse stickers that had maybe a hundred loose-leaf papers in it, full of fifth-grade math that I had to do when I was just turning five.

I left that notebook on the hood of the car in the rain once—accidentally, of course. It survived, and I spent that three-hour drive working on all of the problems my mother had written out the day before. Still using a car seat at the time, I sat there, with her in the driver's seat, passing the book back and forth between us for her to check my work.

It was maybe an hour and a half into the trip. The minivan was parked in front of the Marriott that marked the halfway point, and my mother had reached the end of her thread of patience, which to me was about an inch long. She unbuckled her seat belt and climbed into the back with me, demanding that Mai drive. I had made the same mistake five times in a row on these problems, and she couldn't let it go.

"Harlan. I've told you a thousand times how to do this."

"I'm sorry."

"Are you stupid or do you just not listen?"

"I don't know."

"I know you're not stupid, so you must just not be listening; you're choosing to drive me crazy."

I wanted to tell her that nobody would choose to make her that way. Anybody in their right mind couldn't ever actually *want* to be in the position I was in.

And today, I still ask myself, "Harlan Margaret. Are you stupid or do you just not listen?"

It helps me make better choices. I see that I have to be not-stupid *and* I have to listen, or at least notice what other people are like and what triggers them, so I don't end up cornered in the back seat of a car like that again.

On the other hand, it felt absurd to me to have to walk on eggshells around my mother, the woman who was supposed to help me find myself, not make me afraid of all the ways I could make her mad. I was so little at the time that I hadn't yet discovered the link between her childhood and the way she chose to raise me.

My mother and father once got into a huge fight over which one of them should be in charge of brushing my teeth for me when I was little, as my mother felt that my father was doing a "lackadaisical" job. What's really strange, now that I'm thinking about it, is that my parents were brushing my teeth when most of my friends at that age were being entrusted to do it themselves. One of the first Vietnamese words I learned was *lè phè*, which means "lackadaisical." My mother hated anything done in a lè phè way. She used the word so much that it lost its value. Today, a Mercedes driving below the speed limit in the left lane is lè phè, as is the gardener who comes ten minutes late.

But I hated brushing my teeth and obviously took my father's side, because I knew that if he were to brush my teeth, the whole thing would only take about thirty seconds. However, if my mother were in charge of it, it would take five minutes, including the part where she pried my mouth open and watched me spit out the toothpaste.

And I never felt as though I went through the transition between toddler and teenager. I remember being tiny and scooting around town; I remember being thrown into the pool as an infant. But then it was as if one day I just woke up and found myself at age fifteen in a CVS looking for condoms. I had come clean about the fact that I was becoming sexually active, so I had to be *sure* I was protected, according to the woman who had made my rubber band jump rope for me. The term *sexually active* always bothered me because it felt like a euphemism adults would use to make me feel like I was sinning. And it made things real. When I was little, "using protection" meant wearing a helmet while riding a bike.

My mom, I'm sure, had the same experience of going straight from infancy to adulthood, but in a different sense. She went from being close to royalty and having everything done for her to having to slave away every day after high school to provide for her family. I don't work as a waitress or anything the way most kids my age do. I don't have a job because I don't want one, and my mother and I are different because I have a choice and she didn't. It's very simple for me with things like that. If I don't want to work, I don't have to. Just like if I don't want to study, there's a good chance I'll still get an A on the test because, unlike my mother, I went into high school knowing English.

My mother's parents somewhat misjudged how much time they would end up spending in Virginia, waiting for their Vietnam to experience the fall of the Communist government. They bought plastic lawn chairs as furniture, because it wouldn't make sense to buy anything else, given the fact that the Communist regime was supposed to be over soon enough, and they could go back to their tailored lifestyles.

She got a job at a restaurant, where every morning she had to take out the tomato sauce, which was kept in a huge basin in the fridge. And there it was, the cockroach, probably having a smashingly good time floating there. And the owner of the restaurant casually told her to just take it out and go on with the day. About fifty people ate sauce that had come from that container.

She also cleaned the toilets in the bathrooms. My mother, at my age, sat on the floor and cleaned the seams of the bowl with a Q-tip.

And I don't even know how to use bleach.

———————

MY MOTHER WAS A SLACKER during her childhood years in Saigon—until high school in the United States. We're talking about a girl whose mother was woken up every morning with a massage and whose father hired bodyguards to take her from her house to school and to any friend's house. He used to pay the older boys she would play soccer with to let her kick the ball into the goal (I don't know why they wouldn't just let a little girl beat them anyway).

And then she shows up in the States and spends her nights with a radio under her pillow and listens to the American news to help her learn the language. She graduates *second* or somewhere near the tip-top in her class, though not first, because a racist math teacher gave her a B and told her that he couldn't let "people like her" succeed.

The inside of her head became a box—at least the part that controls how she mothers. Inside that box are rows and rows of bins, and each of them represents a category of my flaws. One of them might read, "procrastination," or "carelessness," or "laziness," or "disrespectfulness."

The ones that bother me the most are the ones that I don't think should even exist. I'd really love to take them and put them through a wood chipper, along with the purple cat, which now comes around only to stare at me with disapproval and has become less of a companion and more of a parasite.

My whole personality is in these boxes, but the boxes are nothing to be proud of. And it makes me feel like a broken toy whose defective parts are thrown into each one.

I think my mom's parenting method is made up of three steps. First, she analyzes what I did wrong. This step is already problematic because half the time I really don't agree with her analysis. Second, she decides which box the issue belongs in. If I leave my unicorn mug on the coffee table for longer than a day, then it goes into the "carelessness" box. And third, from that one corner of the sofa that she always curls up into, she takes the persimmon out of her mouth and stops sucking on it long enough to address the issue.

"*Harlan.*"

And why does she wait until I'm upstairs to summon me, disturbing my nap?

So, because I'm not ready for my life to be turned upside down by this woman because I didn't come down and take my cup off the table, I shout back.

And she doesn't answer, which forces me to throw the blanket off and stomp downstairs, because I know I'm in trouble for something I feel I shouldn't be. The last time this happened, I came down to find my spoon in a bowl in the sink, along with a half-hour-long argument.

She places the mug incident in the bin and pulls out all the ways to fix it.

Leaving the mug there isn't just about the mug. If I can't bother to put things back where I found them (in this case, the unicorn mug belonged next to my life-size stuffed unicorn in my room), then I could get into actual deeper trouble down the road, when I potentially forget to turn off the oven and die.

I can make fun of the situation, because it deserves to be made fun of, but I see her point. And I know why she makes every situation into a teaching moment. She didn't have guidance at my age and she did fine. I can barely do fine *with* guidance, according to her.

Then again, my definition of *fine* and her definition run like two parallel tracks with trains that are racing each other and will never meet up.

When I was little, the stories she read to me the most were from *Aesop's Fables*, especially "The Ant and the Grasshopper" and "The Tortoise and the Hare." She also quotes all kinds of Vietnamese proverbs her father taught her that deal with the wisdom of hard daily work.

She put me in a public school for my elementary years, and the bus would come get me every morning at 7:48 on the corner by the lake. There were two bus routes: the one that went through Kingsmill, the gated community where I lived, and the one that picked up the kids on the other side of the city, in the trailer parks.

Kingsmill was full of families with four cars each, who lived in big brick houses with willows in the front yard and basketball hoops in the driveway. The fathers would raise their sons to become obsessed with the ultimate rich-person sport, golf. And the mothers would come every year to the oyster bake and serve food for the children, who all wore clothes from Vineyard Vines. The neighborhood was on the riverfront and there was a guard at each of the four entrances, which were just in front of the pools. There were two huge pools with waterslides and private swimming instructors and gift shops that sold outfits that resembled something a preppy frat boy might wear.

And I loved living there.

And I saw how the other side of town lived. I had friends who took the other bus route to school, but they never came over. I was always too busy practicing the violin or art or getting tutored at home in order to keep up with my advanced classes.

My mother was one of the most active parents, coming in to volunteer in class and always donating to the teachers. She filled their cabinets with the fluffy rich-people tissues that were laced with Vaseline. And she gave them Crayola boxes with all the colors.

WHEN I TURNED FOUR, I began to see the demons that lived in her. PTSD demons. Shadow selves.

The fits that she suffered from were so violent that her overall personality became erratic and unpredictable as she writhed there on the floor, holding her own throat, trying to strangle the monsters inside her to death so that she could live.

The issue was that it was impossible to hurt only the monsters and not hurt herself. And so her chest would bleed from the inside out. One second, her body was the typical olive-toned color. About twenty minutes into her seizure, the vessels above her breasts would become angry, like a volcano with its paths of fire spreading over a once-peaceful place. Another shadow would come out of her. She would say things to me that I have shoved into bins of my own. The difference is that these are bins I will never open again. How can a mommy threaten her daughter by saying she'll kill herself in front of her if she doesn't behave? Even if it really isn't mommy, but rather a shadow inside of her.

And when the dark episode was over, she would go back to chewing on her persimmon. And now I wait for it to happen again, so I can talk to all of the versions of herself that possibly exist. So I can see how our relationship will change, because it's one way in the morning and another in the afternoon.

Sometimes neither my mother nor I relate to anyone outside ourselves, and other times we hold each other and share everything, but sometimes it feels like we're sitting on opposite sides of the room mouthing words to each other desperately, trying to get any sound to come out but failing, and end up being totally deaf to each other.

In Vietnam, just before the city of Saigon fell, children's school desks began to be empty. Slowly, one by one, everyone would disappear. Everyone wanted to go before it was too late, but no one could tell anyone else that they were planning on leaving for fear of being snitched on. My mother, no matter how she chooses to present herself now, was a strange child. Perfectly tailored clothes (colored linen pants with a checkered collared shirt to match, and patent leather shoes with white lace socks) were her thing, a different color every day, along with short curly hair and an innocent gaze that makes me want to hold her every time I see her childhood pictures. But she wasn't normal. She didn't really know how to make friends. Nobody showed her; nobody taught her. I've realized from knowing her and her relationship with her father, who was one of the most important commanders of the airborne troops during the Vietnam War, that sometimes being important comes at a price.

My mother had once been this tiny girl, in patent leather shoes, going to a school of kids in sneakers who arrived every day on their parents' motorcycles, and she paid a price for living in a house with servants who woke her mother up with a massage every morning and who cooked all her food for her.

There's always that thing she tells me: "Harlan. You're a pearl. You do not give your pearls to swine."

What if I don't want to be a pearl the way she was? What do pearls do? Just sit in an oyster shell all alone, all closed up, lonely and isolated. There are so many ways to be isolated other than physically. But to feel isolated psychologically from everyone else is something she and I share. And I never realized how similar I am to my mother until now, because she and I seem so different. We are just two deaf best friends having one long conversation.

Until the age of thirteen, my mother and I actually had pretty similar lives, from what I've heard from her.

This huge house, near the battlefields of Tet, and my momma was so little. She had the same face she has today: her mother's lips and freckles and expression, her father's cheekbones and demeanor. Getting driven to school every day in a special rich-person car, being monitored by bodyguards who stood outside the schoolyard while she learned math and English and looked around at all the other kids playing. Going to important military events and spending evenings with accomplished politicians and soldiers, both American and Vietnamese. Sitting in a corner watching everything, worshipping her father and dealing with the close yet odd dynamic she had with her mother.

This huge house, in a safe neighborhood in Virginia, and I was so little. I had the same face I have today: my mother's lips and freckles and expression, my father's habits and laugh. Getting driven to school every day in a special rich-person car, being monitored by my mother, who put me on the ground with a notepad every weekend to learn long division at the age of five while I looked around at all the other kids playing. Going to important academic events and spending evenings with accomplished politicians and teachers, both American and Vietnamese. Sitting in a corner watching everything, worshipping my father and dealing with the close yet odd dynamic I had with my mother.

My mother's father, because of his position in the military, was able to pluck the entire family from the war-torn state and bring them to the East Coast of America, while other kids whose parents had normal-people jobs had to crowd onto a boat in the middle of the night and sail aimlessly away, knowing they'd never come back, knowing they could die from a pirate attack or a storm.

My grandmother, my momma's momma, had a husband before she met my grandfather. She divorced him after he beat her, and the family disowned her, because God forbid a woman should be able to leave a love-less and abusive marriage and marry for love, even if the marriage is to a nobody Vietnamese from Laos. They took her right back when that no-body rose through the ranks of the army, from sergeant to one of only two South Vietnamese four-star airborne generals in the history of the Army of the Republic of Vietnam during the war, fought in fifty-three assaults as a paratrooper, and got important medals from the U.S. Army. The fam-ily picked and chose when they wanted my grandmother in their lives.

True family doesn't always associate with blood. Family can end up being someone who notices you're lost on the first day of school and grabs your hand and leads you to safety.

In 1970, my mother, little Lan, met Mai Lê in the new American school she started going to, when Mai noticed her alone and introduced herself. Their friend, an Indian boy named Jubeer Ali, worshipped them, and pretty much did whatever my mother told him to do, including cheating on a true-or-false test with her. I think Mai was the closest thing to a sister my mother would ever have. But she left her behind when she turned thirteen. Mai never heard from her again; she stayed there through high school, enduring the new rules the Communists inflicted upon her family because they were part of the upper class and were seen as abominable poor-people-hating criminals. And then she left by boat just before her eighteenth birthday and went to college in Vancouver, British Columbia, while my mother started to attend Mount Holyoke on the opposite end of North America.

And then in 2003, a little after their fortieth birthdays, Mai was sitting in her Canadian home, surrounded by math papers she had to grade from the high school she taught at, and examined a list of Vietnamese American authors a friend had given her. And there it was: my mother's name, which had been changed from Cao Thị Phương Lan to just Lan Cao. (The reason for this was the torment my mother went through in high school when the ignorant idiot American students deliberately mispronounced her foreign name as a way to bully her.) My mother's novel *Monkey Bridge* had landed her a spot on this list, and so they reconnected.

For five years it was just my mother, my father, and me in that big house in Virginia. A nine-thousand-square-foot mansion with a circular driveway and Disney-style staircases was all I really knew. Growing up, I knew my family was different because other kids' houses were a lot smaller and the mom was always home and baked me cookies when I came over. At my house, I would take my friends up to my room and have to warn them about the possibility of witnessing the tragic death of a bird flying into my window, which covered the whole wall, floor to ceiling. The basement was behind the garage, which kept the motorcycle and cars, and behind my dad's workout room, which was the size of a hotel gym. It wasn't cozy with a pool table and TV the way I had seen in magazines. It resembled a bomb shelter.

When I was five years old, Mai moved in. There was no explanation why; she just arrived one day, and I accepted her. I was at that age where I was simply happy to be alive and was nice to everyone and never suspicious, although my mother probably wanted me to be more so. Mai was an artist and created really large paintings of beautiful colored circles and bubbles or faces or buildings, and then when they were done, she'd cover all the colors in brown and paint tree branches over it—tiny, thin, intricate lines crossing over one another like a spiderweb. Sometimes she'd put snow on the branches; other times she'd put moss and rain. We hung all the paintings on our walls. My favorite was the only one without the tree branches. It looked like a blurry Edward Hopper painting: two inscrutable faces gazing out a window at a lonely street lined with yellow glowing lampposts.

And then one night, a bit before my seventh birthday, just half an hour before we were all going to see an expensive ballet my mother had booked months before, I wandered over to Mai's wing of the house. All of her paintings leaned against the hallway wall outside her bedroom, which my parents had furnished for her with beautiful decor. A strange ripping sound emanated from inside.

My small feet padded down the corridor cautiously, and then I saw her on her knees, crouched down, leaning over a dark green piece of art, with scissors in her hand. She stabbed it to death, as the canvas bounced and twitched, bleeding out from its gruesome holes, helpless and lifeless. I looked back at several other paintings, still intact and sitting against the wall, waiting their turn to be murdered.

"What the hell?" my dad said, approaching the scene carefully, his eyebrows furrowed in confusion . . . and fear.

My mother quickly pulled Mai up by her elbows and shut the bedroom door. I heard the two of them talking in that way adults do, where they somehow shout at each other while keeping a low whisper to hide their insanity. My father took my hand and said, "You look splendid, Harlan Margaret," and I smiled back proudly and swayed back and forth, so my poofy velvet dress would twirl and my patent leather shoes would make that satisfying clicking sound on the floor. The door swung open again shortly after.

"Come on, Harlan," my mother said, tugging me by the other hand.

"What about Mai Mai?" I murmured.

"She's gonna stay home."

I pulled out of her hard grip and scurried back to Mai's room and peeked my head around the doorframe.

"Phương Mai?" I whispered. She sat there, on her knees again, clutching the scissors in one hand, their blades separated to form two knives, the other hand holding her tense forehead.

"Yes, baby?"

"Please don't kill my favorite painting, okay?" I asked her to promise me. She didn't say anything.

I came home that night and found my painting, the beautiful lonely lamppost painting, gone from its place on the wall. I could only assume it had died, and so I mourned the death of the lonely people who had been standing behind the window near the lampposts.

She was clearly deeply disturbed. It was tragic to watch, because it obviously came from a place of self-loathing, I thought. At the time, I saw it as self-hurt. I had learned about it from my father. People act out because their insides are undone. Mai would finish a painting, sometimes even hang it up, and then take it down a few months later and paint over it. I don't believe that just because someone has gone through something traumatic, that thing is the source of all the odd things about them. Mai never showed signs of having gone through whatever it was she had gone through; she didn't display the usual signs of trauma. She was calm but often easily hurt, many times by my mother. From what I had seen, she acted out in peaceful but extreme ways. When I say peaceful, I mean that her breakdowns didn't affect other people in the house, the way my mother's did. She had quit smoking but went through phases where she'd go out to the back deck and smoke for two hours. One time, she smoked and didn't talk all day. I never thought she'd take scissors to a painting, though.

That same night, upset, bordering on enraged, I stomped over to my side of the house. I was brushing my teeth with an electric toothbrush, something Mom had forced into my hands since I was tiny. I always resented having to use it for a full two minutes and tried shutting it off early, standing over the porcelain bathroom sink, still wearing my velvet poofy twirly ballet dress. My mother stood behind me. She sounded strange as she came closer.

"You know, Harlan Margaret, Cecile brushes her teeth for a full two minutes, and you should too," she said.

"Yeah. I like your freckles, Cecile," I said, and touched my mother's face, feeling the brown spots on her nose. It was my mother's body, but it wasn't my mother; it was her shadow state.

"Mm-hmmmmm, la la lalalala la la," she hummed, turning away to get her own toothbrush.

"Have you talked to No Name in there?" I asked, spitting the toothpaste out. I inquired about it because no matter how much I associated No Name with cruelty, I knew she took care of my mother's body.

"No, No Name doesn't like anyone except for herself," Cecile giggled, "but I do like *her* because she saved us, you know. When Cecile was in the bomb shelter in nineteen sixty-eight, No Name held her and made me—I mean *her*—feel better."

I nodded at her, half understanding what she was talking about. I knew my momma and her family had fled from their house to a bomb shelter that was in her father's military headquarters.

Then her whole face changed. Cecile was gone, and the expression went blank for a second. I watched her sway back and forth, as if her posture couldn't decide if it wanted to give out or stay upright. It gave out. Already fragile, already small, and now she looked so much more helpless lying on the ground like that.

"Momma?" I whispered, poking her shoulder with my big toe.

Her eyes flew open, and she began to shake. A seizure spreading from the mind to the arms, and then to the legs. And back up to the mouth: beautiful pink lips hanging open and then closing; a fish gasping for air.

"Mommy?"

I kneeled down and pulled the collar of her shirt up and back, so I could look at her neck and chest better. It was just something I knew to do.

And there it was: a crimson spiderweb spread over her chest, as if all the minute capillaries, thin and intricate, were bleeding out from the inside. I watched them get darker. Pink branches turned red. My eyes got wider, and I touched her forehead with my pinkie finger only, afraid to really touch her.

She shook harder, and I started to scream now, as her bony fingers reached up to the collar and tried to rip the shirt off. As the fabric lifted, I saw the veins and capillaries, blue turning to black, pink turning to red.

The sweet freckled face turned into one big smirk, snickering diabolically. "You think that it's *Cecile*? Cecile is gone. She ran away like the little mouse she is. You stupid little thing. I hate this . . . I should have killed everyone in here when I had the chance," she spat.

I backed up a little.

"Why do you have to say that, Mommy?"

"Mommy is gone. Mommy is *gone*."

And then I realized who I was talking to: No Name.

"How come?" I chirped, trying to draw the being out.

"She'd be dead if it weren't for me. None of you appreciate anything from me. She's weak, like you. Like that stupid *Cecile*."

"Oh," I muttered, "Cecile isn't stupid. She's my best friend."

"Because both of you are *idiots*."

I wasn't upset when she said this. I understood now, the difference between No Name and my mother. And No Name resented the idea of living.

I remained quite calm—alarmingly so. I felt some tears coming down my face, like raindrops racing down a window. Inside, however, I remained still. I understand that this isn't how other people would have felt, but even though I was a very sensitive child, I was starting to get talented at feeling numb.

"Okay, No Name. Do you feel okay?"

"Do I *feel okay*?" she spat again.

"Yeah. Can you put my mommy back now?"

She didn't say anything after that, and her eyes shut hard, the body going still. Too still for my liking.

I began to shriek, and my eardrums went numb, and all I could hear were heavy footsteps. First my daddy, and then Mai Mai.

"Should we call the police? Ambulance?" Mai asked aloud.

My dad calmly shook Mommy to get her to wake up, but she didn't. He felt for a pulse and found it, so he carried her to bed.

The next morning I woke up and Mommy was back and she was cooking breakfast downstairs.

Mai played with me a lot. She taught me how to ride a bike and how to play soccer and how to run really fast. She did it when my mom was working all day and I had no one to be with in that gigantic house.

As a child, what were my feelings about the things I had seen? I didn't know. We didn't talk about them. No one asked me if I was suffering from what I witnessed. Cecile was brought up sometimes, when I wanted someone to play with, but how was I to know what to feel when no one even clarified what had happened? It was something that happened and was quickly left behind until it happened again.

MY MOM STAYED ON THE OPPOSITE WING from Mai's with my dad, sleeping in a king-size bed. All three of us, lying there together until I was about eight and he started going in and out of hospitals. I never used my bedroom except when I wanted to impress whichever playmate from school I had convinced to come over. It had a wall of windows that overlooked the back deck and the swan lake, a gigantic bed with fluffy pillows, and custom-made embroidered beanbags.

I had one friend—my best friend in the whole wide world. Lauren was a girl I had been friends with since we were learning to walk. She had long black hair, curly, with chestnut skin and beautiful lips. We didn't talk to anyone except each other—ever. We sat side by side every morning on the school bus, my head against the window, her leg sticking out into the aisle.

We did everything together. I once even convinced her to "run away" with me, and we made it about two miles away to a nearby restaurant. My mother called the police and sent all the neighbors out to look for me. Within four hours, a policeman brought us back. It was a very big thrill for me—skipping my Wednesday piano lesson and getting to ride in a cop car. Lauren was just embarrassed and afraid.

I don't know why she's so scared, I thought to myself. *I'm the one who's gonna get a real thrashing.*

First, my mother gave me a nice warm hug, and then she inhaled a sharp breath and spanked me. And then I was forced to watch a two-and-a-half-hour movie about a little boy who wandered outside and got kidnapped by a child molester who cut off little boys' limbs.

Lauren and I never talked about our little adventure afterward, since she remained mortified by the scene we had created.

I didn't tell her anything about my mother. I wanted to tell someone, just in case Mom did end up having one of her attacks and didn't wake up like she normally did. But I knew not to tell anyone. My parents told me I couldn't ever share what happened to her sometimes. It looked bad, I was told. People would misunderstand. My family, so heavily respected and looked up to, would be hurt if anyone heard anything.

The sign hanging from the gazebo roof in the back of the house on our deck, which overlooked the neighborhood pond, read "Harlan Margaret and Cecile Only." It was a wooden sign my father had carved for my best friend and me—well, the best friend I had at home. Lauren was my best friend outside home.

I had to tell everyone that the name Cecile on the sign was my cousin. But Cecile was actually my mother from forty years ago. She was my mother at the age of six. She had been around since 1968 but was only six years old. Six forever. Cecile was her own person, self-named after my mommy's mommy. She was her own person without her own body. Her emotional maturity level was that of someone who had lived a very long time, but she still mispronounced words like an infant and stomped her feet when she didn't get what she wanted.

My mother had seen things I don't even know how to describe.

Something horrible had happened when she was six, that maybe she'd seen at the hospital that my mommy had sometimes gone to with her mother, and so a part of her forever stayed that age. Or maybe it was something she'd seen at the paratrooper armed camp behind her back garden. She grew older and managed to forget about it, but a small fraction still remembered, the fraction she'd left behind physically but still carried emotionally. Cecile was a genius and, to me, a miracle.

This is why Mai lived with us, I decided. Because the two of them, my mother and Mai, were the only ones who understood what the other had seen.

Mai, during her high school years, after the northern Communist powers had won, lost her freedom.

Every day after school, she attended a mandatory seminar where the upper class had to sit in a room and basically just listen to Communist officers lecture them about how they were disgusting thieves who committed crimes against the poor by having nice things. And if she didn't attend each day, her family wouldn't get food for the week.

In order to teach everyone from wealthy families about manual labor, Hồ Chí Minh's cadre declared that Mai's high school, an all-girls school, would have to do certain tasks, because the Communist party was an army of laborers and farmers.

She told me about the day she was sent to a cemetery to do work—not the kind of cemetery with clean tombstones and nice flowers on the graves, though. It was a dirt field, and underneath the ground lay severed body parts—feet, fingers, heads. It was a leper cemetery. The body parts had been plagued by leprosy. The class was to dig out every single limb.

Mai had told me she had tried to put on gloves, as one would, and her teacher ripped them off her hands and threw them to the ground, spitting, "Is manual labor not glorious enough for you? It's *beneath* you?"

The ten-day escape on a fishing boat was brutal. Apart from the obvious issues like the possibility of being raped and robbed by Thai pirates, getting caught and locked up by the Vietcong, or simply drowning during a hurricane, there was a pregnant woman who gave birth on the boat, and a serious shortage of fresh water.

Other boats, with other children, babies, and old ladies, didn't make it. Every day, new bodies washed up onshore. But every day, more people left Vietnam anyway.

My mother had seen men without legs and without eyelids and without skin in the war, and Mai had dug out limbs from the ground and been attacked by pirates, and so they could understand each other. No matter how perfect my father was, he couldn't understand or picture what his wife had really gone through that would cause this. I really did my best to do that for her, though.

I can't keep everything to myself all the time. Some things are too painful or stressful or confusing to be kept secret, because eventually it eats you alive like acid. But this didn't feel like a secret. If it had been treated as something the family needed to be ashamed of, then there's a good chance I would have gone to school and described the things I had seen to my classmates. But my mother was everything to me. She was my caretaker, my provider, my guardian, and also my little sister, somehow. She was everyone, all the time.

My mother and Mai were also connected because my mother's brother had dated Mai's sister, and that was all I was told. Mai lived with us in her own part of the house until I was about seven, when she bought a small home on the next street over, where she did all of her painting and hosted some of my playdates. I didn't think anything of it, even though sometimes my teachers would ask me during recess "which Asian lady" was my mother, because often they'd alternate drop-offs when Mommy had work.

So, there I was, standing in the schoolyard in my little school uniform, trying to explain to my teacher that Mai and Mommy weren't twin sisters but just really close friends, and that the man who often dropped me off in a sports car was my daddy and not my grandfather. Well, he did until I was about eight, but then one day, as I was walking home with Mai and Mom, we saw that his new Jaguar had run off the road. The car just sat there, in the ravine, and we decided he shouldn't drive anymore. I think that really broke his heart.

But if Mai was just a close friend, then how come all three of the adults showed up at Back to School Night? Lauren's mother's best friend didn't come—it was just her biological parents. So I didn't know how to answer that question when I was asked. I would look around the room, make my eyes appear bigger, and rotate my neck to appear lost, as if I didn't even hear their questions. And most of the time, people would give up on the ridiculous inquisition.

Mai's ex-husband often came up in conversation, and I had this fascination with him. I was fixated on the details of her marriage and why they had split up; she had told me it "just hadn't worked."

"But *why*?" I asked.

"Just because," she laughed.

When I was fourteen, she revealed to me that she had found herself interested in women, more so than in men, and so she and her ex peacefully went their separate ways, yet remained good friends.

Why couldn't anyone have just told me that before? I had understood the word *lesbian* since I was nearly seven, because Woody Allen's *Manhattan* depicted a confused neurotic man whose beautiful blond wife (Meryl Streep) had left him for a woman, which made him feel incredibly emasculated.

Mai was very possessive of my mother, I noticed, even though no one thought I did.

I had gone through a very strange year in fourth grade when I became unusually aggressive toward boys. Small things that had little to do with me at all suddenly enraged me to the point of violence. I once kicked this boy Jordan in the shins for calling another boy gay because he wore a pink polo.

This might have been explained by the tendency Mai had to teach me how to be "tough." Fell off your bike? Get up. Boys are being mean? Don't cry, just stand up for yourself, however you wanna do that. I did it by starting fights, but who cares? I was a happy but very easily enraged child. I was peaceful, but going through a few confusing things at home.

After we moved to California, I wasn't so tough anymore. It's hard to fight back when you know no one will back you up because they don't know you and you're new and odd.

Lan

My parents drove me to college in their blue Chevy packed full of dorm items. Before we left, one person came to say good-bye to me. It was John, one of the vets who frequented my parents' grocery store in search of safety and absolution. When I first met him, he was wearing a short-sleeved T-shirt that revealed a tattoo on his right forearm: "Highway 1A." My brother Tuấn said to him, "You were at Đông Hà." It was not a question. It was a declaration. John replied yes, emphatically, with a hint of triumph. When he hugged me farewell, he said that he wanted me to know he was proud to have served in Vietnam. "The Vietnamese are worth it for me."

I was touched by his solicitude. I always remembered those words and took them with me when I left our apartment in Virginia. College was my first true immersion in American life where Vietnam—my parents, my family, their overheard voices, the Vietnamization of Falls Church itself—was absent, gray and muted, withdrawn from the landscape. Which made my recollection of it, of the last time I was there, all the more precious because it stood alone, solitary, like an undertow in memory's play of light and shadow.

Like many affairs, mine began with a look. The first time I set foot on the campus to begin my hero's journey, I felt its single sensibility: peace. It was not just that there was a palpable absence of menace. This beloved patch of campus was a wonderland of elegant old buildings, shivering waterfalls, lakes, an outdoor amphitheater, wooded running paths—beauty that I found to be insanely addictive.

I felt I had escaped the gray conformity of high school through a quick trick of fate. My dorm, part of a coterie of buildings on the edge of campus, was a replacement of sorts for home. Here, English was my native tongue. Here I succeeded in exchanging Vietnamese for English, and only in the occasional dream did an image start in Vietnamese, only to melt midway into English. People who in real life could speak only Vietnamese spoke clear English in my dreams. Even memories of Vietnam came back not in Vietnamese but in English. The soccer field near my house in Cholon returned as an image my mind simultaneously named and labeled in English.

I had an ambivalent relationship with language. Language was always about home versus the world. When we were in Vietnam, French was our private language, a strategic language meant to keep our conversations from servants. Vietnamese, of course, was the mother language—language at home, intimate, like mother's milk. In America, it was of course our private language when we ventured out into the world of English. But as I excelled in school, Vietnamese lost its status, eclipsed by English even at home. It was English that gave me sanctuary, shielding me from my parents and their Vietnamese world when I needed to salvage myself from the crippling presence of their past.

Here at Mount Holyoke, I was as free as I had ever been.

I WAS ASSIGNED A ROOM ON THE FOURTH FLOOR, with bay windows overlooking Upper Lake and its wide openness to dreams. I had my trusted

Smith Corona typewriter, a gift from my father, always wrapped against a pillow inside a pillowcase. I even had a good-natured, good-humored roommate from a city with a funny name, Rocky River, in Ohio. Annie had flaming red hair, not too different, I imagined, from the red hair of Charlie Brown's Little Red-Haired Girl. The air was light and crisp, not weighted down by ruminations of loss or my expendable past or the dark judgmental moods of high school. Though I could tell that the darker sides, the shadow selves hiding in the crawl spaces of my heart, were still palpably with me as I tried to make my way through life's new coordinates.

On my first night alone, after my parents tearfully left, I sat on the built-in seat by the bay window and waited for the color of the night to change slowly from gray to purple to inky black.

It was indeed as promised. The time of my life! Dreamily paced. The campus beckoned, promising hope and second chances, and I happily complied. We were offered the gift of excellence, as the college motto reminded: Mount Holyoke—the Challenge to Excel.

As far as I could tell, there was no other Vietnamese at the college or in town. And no Vietnamese refugee enclave like the one in Falls Church that could threaten the racial balance of a town. American magnanimity could flourish here. And it did.

And I had food I'd never had before. The dining hall ladies knew us by name, and I in turn knew their names. I liked to watch their movement, fluid and efficient, as they circulated through the kitchen area. I had received a work-study scholarship, and my freshman year I worked in the dining hall of my dorm. One day I was on duty, along with a junior, Kris, who was also on my floor, to set up breakfast. "Let's have a bagel," she said, "before we open up."

"What's a bagel?"

"A bagel, a bagel with cream cheese," was the nonchalant reply. When I told her I'd never seen one, she exclaimed, "You've got to be kidding. Really?" She seemed incredulous.

We turned on the large industrial toaster, popped in two halves of a bagel, and waited for them to pop out. The bagel was hot to the touch, and I quickly dropped it on the plate, admiring from a place of utter wonder its shiny crust with a little bit of glaze. Kris then stuck a knife in a slab of whiteness she called cream cheese and slathered it on the toasted bagel halves. I tried it, giving it my unflinching attention. Chewy, but not doughy. Phenomenal. Magnificent. When Kris told me it was Jewish food, I loved it even more because I had heard from my parents that Jewish people were very smart and tightly knit and I was to emulate them.

I also discovered many delectable American confections. We were spoiled with the most incredible tradition ever: the nightly M&Cs, which stands for milk and cookies. But we had more than cookies. There were peach cobblers, cinnamon-sugar-dusted snickerdoodles, pecan pralines, raspberry crumble bars we called princess bars. But best of all was the carrot cake, a taste that would never leave me: dense, moist; rich, decadent cream cheese frosting. Needless to say, I gained what they called the freshman ten! I had never gained weight in my life, never even thought about weight. Annie was cognizant of her weight. She drank only Tab. Of course, the diet I'd been on all my life—rice, vegetables, canh and its clear broth with various vegetables, watercress, winter melon, or bitter melon and other variations—was all low calorie. I had never even known about the concept of dieting.

The casual, the quotidian that people knew all their lives I had never known, like the humbling, incomparable smoothness of cream cheese. From that moment, whenever I ate a bagel, I was completely "here," and finally not "there." Almost every morning, I chose a toasted bagel with cream cheese. I was newly minted, away from home, eating a bagel. Far from the perforated past. Not taking any stands about history, or, more precisely, the history that had broken us into little pieces. Not having to see refugee family after refugee family sacrificing themselves for the kids while sacrifice and suffering were normalized into yet more sacrifice and more suffering.

Our meals were served in our individual dorms with their own dining halls, and I ate with Annie and other friends on our floor and often also with our designated student adviser, Maureen, a junior, whose room was directly across from mine. Maureen's job was to make sure no one on our fourth floor was friendless and brooding and alone. Her job was to offer guidance and companionship.

It was the first time since arriving in America that I had sat down and eaten any meal with Americans my age. Or any Americans except Papa Fritz and his family.

Our dorm facilitated community, love, friendship. The common room on the ground floor, with separate spaces and seating arrangements for studying, congregating, even doing nothing, was set up to create special moments every day. We were busy because there was a lot of work to finish, but we inevitably yielded to the lure of this space. From there, enduring friendships emerged.

There was a grand piano edged gracefully in a corner, and to my surprise, one in every dorm as well. I played it in the afternoon when many students were in class. I had the space to myself. I played Vietnamese songs my mother used to sing. Some I already knew; some I figured out because I could play by ear. Two years after our arrival in Falls Church, my parents got me a Kawai upright piano, lacquered black. It was the closest approximation of what I had left behind. But I wasn't ready for a substitute.

Now that I was in college, far from home, the piano at MacGregor Hall reached out to me, inviting me to spend time with it. The songs played themselves. I was often still studying in the hours after midnight, marking the quiet beginning moments of the next day, with the piano, as lonely as it was beautiful, gorgeously lit by streetlamps. I would take breaks to visit it, or I'd study next to it.

I was fumbling along nicely enough in this new world, even if I struggled to keep up in every class. The assigned readings were unnerving in their scope and difficulty. Students and professors made casual references to notables I had never heard before, like Goya—in English class, not in art, where perhaps it was expected that we would know who he was. I turned to the piano even more for sanctuary and comfort. It also got my dorm mates to gather nearby, chins resting on palms, as I played melodious tunes. They were songs my mother loved, Vietnamese songs that were meant not to transcend loss but to be immersed in it. The others didn't know this. They knew only that the music was beautiful.

In the community of the dormitory it was easy to make friends and confide a little here and there. Down the hall around the corner was someone from Iran, whose family had fled Tehran when the Shah was overthrown by the Ayatollah. And there was an Iranian man named Hassan who was always visiting and studying in the common space on our fourth floor because he was dating one of the sophomores, who was certain she would major in Middle Eastern studies.

These were the first Iranians and the first Muslims I had ever met. It was surprising both were Iranians because their features were drastically different—one looking like she was a northern Italian heir to a Milan fashion label and the other much darker, with a deep brown sheen to his skin. She looked at him the way the Vietnamese looked at the darker tribal people of the highlands or at the Laotians. My father said he used to get those looks from the Vietnamese, who assumed he was Laotian because he was born in Vientiane. Sometimes the preambles to our social gatherings, often late at night in the cozy common space on our very own floor, with its sprawling sofas and armchairs, were heated political discussions. Hassan was ready to express, amiably but firmly, what some might consider scurrilous and bad-tempered views about American involvement in Iran, though to me they seemed factually accurate enough. Ten years before overthrowing our President in Vietnam, the CIA had overthrown the President of Iran too, although I did not know that until Hassan informed us. I began to see that I knew so little about the world that was not Vietnam, that it would take time for that world, which seemed slightly blurry, to slowly come into focus for me.

Hassan sat frozen next to the coffee table, telling us what had happened in his country.

The hostage-taking saga was still being counted down; every night we, along with the rest of America, tap-tap-tapped our feet, waiting to see how President Carter was going to flex American muscle and do something. On the radio, I heard a modification of the Beach Boys' "Barbara Ann," in which "Barb Barb Barb, Barb Barbara Ann" became full-blast "Bomb bomb bomb, bomb bomb Iran."

"It's outrageous the embassy of any country should be breached," Kris, my work-study mate and bagel-eating partner, said.

"Can I *just*—" Hassan offered but stopped when Kris shook her head.

"There's no justification," Kris said, closing her eyes.

"All right. But do you think there's justification to go into a country and get rid of its leader just because you don't like him?"

Maureen nodded obligingly.

No one told Hassan to go back to where he came from. And he even had a foreign accent. He returned Maureen's smile. Kris also smiled, apparently agreeing. The conversation meandered. It was all dizzying and uplifting and exhilarating to me, to be surrounded by ideas and arguments and debates. Someone named Kirsten said she was Norwegian, from several generations back. Maureen said she was Irish. No one declared herself American. People like me wanted to become American, but others, whose standing was never disputed, preferred to emphasize their original non-American roots instead. That too was part of the American Dream, it seemed. To go back to the past and claim it, not just to relinquish it in favor of the present and the future.

ONE MORNING, ANNIE AND I WOKE UP and opened our door to see that a sheet of newspapers had been taped over the entrance, covering it completely. It was the beginning of Elfing season. We had two secret elves, sophomores, who would be giving us, the elfees, presents for a week. Our elves mysteriously called themselves "Me & T." I'd come back to the room after class to find glorious treats to eat, a bag of apples from the local Atkins Farm, a porcelain box for mementos, sweet little notes galore. Annie and I were so curious to discover who our elves were. It turned out those beauties were our very own next-door neighbors, Barbara and Donna, and they delighted in spoiling us because they were witness to the excitement they were bringing to our first semester. Me & T referred to *The Giving Tree* by Shel Silverstein, which they gave to us the night their meticulously burnished secret identities were finally revealed. I didn't know who Shel Silverstein was, or even Mother Goose.

And then there was Mountain Day, a surprise day of no classes. The bell from Mary Lyon Hall pealed. It was a shimmery, golden day. The leaves were unflinching in their red and orange colors. We clambered out of bed and were ready for the day off. To climb Mount Holyoke itself. Or to do nothing.

The ritualized passage—M&Cs, Elfing, Mountain Day—created an atmosphere of easy collegiality. History somehow managed to relegate itself to the past, throbbing far beneath the surface of my daily life here—when I vaulted up the stairs to my room or roamed the library with its stained-glass windows and stained wood shelves and cornices or walked alone around Upper Lake, where the unpaved paths among the beautiful sap-filled New England trees inclined toward the untamed. There was almost always a breeze here—not always strong, but enough to touch the heart and open it up to life's tender moments. Like when my roommate tiptoed in and out of our room softly so as to not awaken me in the early morning or late night. Annie never turned on the light but felt her way to her bed instead.

On the subject of beauty—the college was beautiful. Its beauty, shown off every day with nonchalant ease and affecting seamlessness, was incontrovertible. There were no tamarind trees, but I began to love the reigning monarch of our campus, the majestic copper beech, a joyous tree with smooth spreading branches, a massive trunk, and protruding roots. And I didn't care that the town of South Hadley was itself little, and the Commons, also referred to as the Village Center, which we could walk to if we had the inclination and the energy, was equally minuscule.

All of it, all that beauty, was enough. The beauty extended itself further, to us. And at some point, I realized that I didn't think about beauty as it related to me. If I was beautiful. Or not. No one seemed to obsess over the various configurations of beauty here. I could just be an endearing freak like the Seven Freaks of Jiangnan. On my way to becoming an Uncommon Woman. Yes, we all knew about Wendy Wasserstein's play, which we claimed as part of our legacy.

We were uncommon women in a beautiful college in South Hadley, Massachusetts, where there was but one bookshop, the Odyssey, which I didn't even know was a reference to a Famous Poem by the Famous Homer (pity my high school education, which I'd thought was more than adequate, at least in English; it seemed to have left out Greek literature). There were a few small restaurants, and there was the Chanticleer, which specialized in carrot cake. I didn't need to go to Northampton or Amherst in search of excitement. I was happy with South Hadley, Mount Holyoke, and the beautiful, serene environment I was enveloped in.

But what was really different about college was the absence of empty chairs next to me. I felt a deep, seeping appreciation for the place where I was no longer relegated to eating alone.

BECAUSE MOUNT HOLYOKE HAD VARIOUS ACADEMIC REQUIREMENTS, we students had to choose courses from different groupings. I signed up for classes I would never have thought to take. One was listed in the politics department. The title appealed to me: Women and Work. I found myself ineluctably drawn to the description, which promised to explore the meaning of work and women's relationship to work.

We talked about a strange new idea: passion and ardor and following our hearts. Even finding ourselves.

The class was taught by a legendary professor whom students called Penny. Not Mrs. or Ms. or Professor. Just Penny. It was held in the common room of a dorm, one of the less beautiful ones on campus. The setup was circular so that no one was positionally situated to head the class, although of course Penny was our leader. I sank into one of the sofas and was face-to-face with my teacher, who was so accessible and so amiable that I was startled. Her elfin head was framed by a neat bob cut, and her clothes were streamlined for comfort. She started each class sweetly and smiled a lot and sometimes even let out an effusive jangle of laughter. She strove to affirm our answers, and when she challenged us with follow-up questions, it was with a gentle look and a slight tilt of the head. The assigned readings included Studs Terkel's *Working* and Louise Kapp Howe's *Pink Collar Workers*. Discussion was informative, provocative, evocative, and sometimes searing and raw.

There were strict rules for papers. "Two typos and I stop reading," Penny warned. "I will return your paper and you will be marked down." We can all make mistakes, but not mistakes that are easily avoided.

I was no longer meek or shy, and Penny seemed to want to hear me and listen to me, encouraging, indeed expecting me to let go of the silent role I had adopted. I relaxed my arms, releasing them from their habitually folded pose, crisscrossed against my chest. As someone who had learned to adjust behavior to changed expectations and circumstances, I quickly complied and became a regular contributor to the class. I dared and then dared more. I became gregarious, like an archetypal extrovert, even if I was not.

The most beautiful part of the class was the way we talked. My classmates were not lawyers but were steeped in the language of rights.

We have the right to lead happy lives.

Work can bring happiness.

Do what you love.

Do what makes you happy.

This prompted me to tell myself, "Lan, don't worry. Go where your mother has given you permission. The road you follow is the one your parents don't even see."

These were strange ideas to me. It wasn't surprising because the American Declaration of Independence elevated the pursuit of happiness into a founding principle. Being happy was not a foundational code in Vietnamese culture. We were taught in civics classes in school to engage in correct behavior—for example, to repay debts. Debt was not merely monetary but was understood more broadly. If someone did a kind deed, that deed generated a debt in the recipient, who was expected to do something kind for the original actor or for third parties. In fact, even relationships were viewed as debt; that is, an obligation in which a correct *behavior* was owed. Behavior should not be guided only by feelings, which were by their nature evanescent, part quirky, part dreamy, like a kitten's mewl. Behavior came from principles, and principles were not dependent on emotions or desires such as maximizing happiness and minimizing sadness.

We strove to do the right thing, not only when we felt like it, but even and especially when we didn't.

Even our songs were about not happiness but loss and sadness or the fleeting nature of life.

In college, I was introduced to happiness as a principle, not just as a feeling, which brought me back to my mother. "Lan ơi," she said. "They say do what is expected of you, but I say do what makes you happy," she used to tell me. It was a singular voice, small and soft, in a Confucian world that loudly promoted rectitude and the right balance in human relationships. She was telling me to do what she had not done. Still, over time, it was the Confucian world, not my mother's voice, that framed my dreaming.

Penny posed questions that were surprising and oftentimes shocking, and then she stepped back and let us ponder them. Her questions illuminated but never imposed. Palpating her hands and tilting her head backward, she watched our parries and thrusts, eager for us to come up with our own answers.

"What is it like for women in other countries?" one student asked.

I was the only one from another country.

"In Vietnam, women were not so discriminated against as you might assume," I said confidently, while also realizing I hadn't studied the subject rigorously by any means. Still, I felt I could speak with authority and some degree of knowledge. The personal is political, we were learning in this class, and in my personal experience, women and girls were for the most part equal to men and boys.

"My grandfather was a landlord in the Mekong Delta. He was a mandarin educated in the traditional Chinese classics," I explained. "You would assume he was not modern. But he desperately wanted a girl and my grandparents both went to a temple to pray for a daughter, as they had two sons."

By the reaction of the class, wide-eyed and attentive, I gathered that they were confusing Vietnam with China. "Girls were not snuffed out at birth in Vietnam. Their feet were not bound. My grandfather was so enamored of his firstborn daughter that he wanted to order a gold-plated jacket for her," I added preemptively. "He made sure my mother and her sister were educated and sent them to a top French boarding school."

A curious silence followed. I realized my classmates were disappointed in what they heard because they were primed to expect a different narrative, one about the cultural deficiencies of an imagined, disfigured Orient. I followed up with a sensational, more compelling story that Westerners preferred to hear about us. Something that juxtaposed Western modernity against the very non-Western backwardness and clichéd exoticism that Western feminism could remedy. These were the rules of assimilation: Difference was good, even celebrated, as long as it was intriguing and not threatening. And any difference that was bad must be salvageable by the rules of assimilation themselves. American empathy (and salvation) hinged on this.

"That's not to say women in Vietnam don't face a lot of obstacles. More than women here." I rattled off the differences. "My grandfather had many wives. The main wife, who was the first married, was called Big Wife. That was my grandmother. His other, lower-ranking wives were called Little Wives." I could see I had their attention. "My mother had to endure a virginity test after she married her first husband that was frightening and humiliating." I went on to explain what had happened to her. Her husband had placed a white cloth on their bed on their wedding night. If she didn't bleed, village tradition dictated that he and his parents would consider her not a virgin, which meant they would have lugged her on a horse-drawn wagon with a pig shamefully shorn of ears and returned her to her parents. It would have been their right to reject unwanted goods.

My friends were appropriately aghast and listened attentively and beseechingly, wanting more—more of the narrative that showed off our world as superstitious and backward. Even though the class was about work, the conversation was both personal and theoretical and could lead to other relevant topics, such as why all cultures have tried to control women's sexuality. Penny did not just let us pour out sad stories. We were indeed learning how these experiences were to be understood within a critical and historical framework that elucidated the condition of women in America and elsewhere.

I gave more details, assembling nuggets of historical and personal truths to make sense of our history. Yes, it was an arranged marriage, and my mother suffered, although she did consent and was not coerced by her parents. Her first husband was a cheater and a batterer, but her family approved of his family's social standing. Chịu đựng was what her mother had taught her. The first word means "to give in." The second word means "to contain or accommodate." She was to give in and hold within herself whatever the husband doled out.

In her second marriage, to my father, she married purely for love. And my mother worked all her adult life. I learned the right way to say it. She worked "outside the home." This gave proper acknowledgment to women who worked "inside the home"—women who had also been working all along, cleaning the house, raising children, cooking, doing the wash— but were not paid for it.

The more educated I became, the more I understood that the road my parents had let me take was one they could not even imagine.

I knew that my mother's grocery store had closed—because it did not prosper, not because she wanted to follow new dreams or pursue happiness. My parents were at the point at which they had to step back from the falls and missteps, the point at which it all had to sink in and they had to do it again, dismantling, packing and unpacking the remnants of loss and failure. She, along with Brother Six (Father Six to me), his oldest daughter, and her husband, did have one small mercy: They were starting a cleaning business. After doing some of the work themselves, they were able to get contracts to clean a few government offices and buildings because their bids were among the lowest. The business was expanding and they even needed to hire other workers, mostly other Vietnamese. Even my brother dabbled in our family's new business. The Vietnamese diaspora was beginning to form a new ethnic niche in Falls Church. This would be in addition to the now-famous nail salon niche.

The nail salon niche began when the actress Tippi Hedren sponsored a Vietnamese refugee out of Fort Pendleton in California and tried to find a vocation for her and others. She flew in her manicurist, Dusty Coots Butera, to teach twenty women how to do nails. Dusty is famous in Vietnamese circles—the first nail salon master and warrior single mom who passed her trade secrets to the first twenty Vietnamese women in California.

In the meantime, hundreds of thousands of Vietnamese were desperate to leave their mottled lives, to start again by fleeing on overcrowded boats. Like the migration of the wild geese and the monarch butterflies that opened their wings toward sun or water, theirs was perilous and arduous. The world called them the boat people, and those who survived pirate attacks and storms and even cannibalism tried to get to Malaysia, Hong Kong, the Philippines, and then from there to Australia, Europe, Canada, and the United States.

To the crushed, peace meant nothing. Many were coming to Falls Church after their escape from the twin tragedies of peace and postwar Communism. There was enough of a community being made here to beckon these newcomers, the cursed vagrants who would find jobs in these newly established niches. According to them, there was a saying popularized by those still stuck in Vietnam: "If the streetlamp had legs, it would leave too."

My mother, knowing how fond I was of Father Five, our lone Vietcong in the family, had forwarded me letters he sent to the family from Saigon after 1975. The letters came in envelopes with rows and rows of stamps, postmarked Ho Chi Minh City. Given the U.S. trade embargo against Vietnam then, the letter had to be sent to Paris to a friend who then forwarded it to us. Some letters made me sad. He needed help and asked us to send him American goods—soap, shampoo, medicine—so he could sell them on the black market to survive. What was particularly heartbreaking was his fear of our judgment.

His letters were replete with coded references. He mentioned that he sometimes thought about making the trek to a particular family friend. That seemed innocuous enough, except we all knew that friend had escaped in 1978 by boat after three years of imprisonment in a so-called reeducation camp. Father Five nonchalantly referred to his good health, comparing it to the oxlike stamina and strength of another mutual friend, but we all knew that friend had been weak and ill all his life. He told us he was living in a "spacious house" in Sóc Trăng, my mother's family's home village. But that very house had been burned down by bandits many years ago.

The condition of Vietnam after the Communist victory was, in other words, dire. Hanoi's jackbooted cadres were crossing into Cambodia, having fought a border skirmish against China.

The hallway closet with its black rotary phone was my once-a-week umbilical cord connection to my parents and Virginia, and through them, to Vietnam.

With every new book I read, I was on my way to becoming more uncommon, polishing my pedigree, taking me further and further away from the lives of my parents. This was what they wanted, except they did not realize I would stray and not find my way back.

I could become covetous, daring to find something that fired my own individual imagination. Or I could return to the core of my extended family in Falls Church, city of conflicted nostalgia, where my parents, still suspended in time, spoke English like they were singing a song. Up and down with the six Vietnamese tones.

WHEN I SAW MY PARENTS AGAIN FOR WINTER BREAK, the cleaning company had replaced the failed grocery store. I think they knew this was now their country, not just a way station. Many nights, my mother reached for her wine to help her sleep. And my father remained devoted to his Buddhist meditation. Like the famous Vietnamese song about the woman who turned into a stone as she waited hopelessly for her husband to return, my parents were like stones—petrified and sedimented. A lifetime of waiting can do that to a person.

Every day in Virginia, I forced myself to return to the mother tongue, to reenter their world, loving them and knowing, as an adult, who they were, not projecting who I imagined them to be, the way I had when I was a child. Sometimes just my mother and I and sometimes my cousins too went for breakfast or lunch at Phở Hoà, a nondescript, humble restaurant that made only pho. It served as a place where the garrulous and the lonely came to exchange confidences and gossip. There was comfort there, with its cauldrons of bubbling pho broth. It was also rumored that the owner was a leader of resistance forces based in Thailand, organized to infiltrate Vietnam to fight the Communist regime. No one knew for sure, but the possibility was enough for most of the Northern Virginia refugees to go to the restaurant and indirectly support this cause.

After lunch, my older cousins left for work. I watched my mother tackle paperwork associated with the cleaning business. She had never been good at math. In her French Catholic school, she used to tutor classmates in French in exchange for lessons in math. But in Virginia, she was the company's bookkeeper and responsible for the payroll, which was an immense source of stress for her.

I watched in silence as her body bent over the book of numbers.

For no particular reason, being home—home being wherever my parents were—made me cry, and it would take all my effort to stop.

I had overheard Annie's conversation with her parents and was surprised how often she told her parents, "I love you too." It was not just that she said it but that she did it with so much ease. My parents had never told me they loved me, nor I them. I used to think it was because of us, our fraught particularities. But it was more than that. Our language was a language of silence, or at least of few words. The language of sacrifice, after all, had to be wordless. My parents had left everything to start over for us. The language of gratitude was similarly silent. We children recognized this and acknowledged it, repaying their sacrifice with our own hard work, even if everything about our embattled but quiet parents, who had so many other worries that they sometimes forgot to act like loving parents, enraged us. We still recognized this language of darkness and depth and brooding silence. It's our mother tongue, after all.

The last sentence of the most well-known proverb in Vietnam instructs children to honor their parents by including them inside a perfect circle of reverence and gratitude, expressed with almost religious overtones. The phrase is hard to explain in English, replete as it is with lexicons and syntax that exist only in Vietnamese. But roughly translated, it instructs the child to pursue this singular, undivided path toward the way—almost like a faith, a life breath, for the child to follow and practice. We breathed in honor and gratitude and reverence by following the advice of our parents.

The beauty of the Vietnamese proverb was best appreciated when we said it out loud. The flow, the rhyme, the artistry, words layered one over the other not just by the choice of the words themselves but by the tone of each word when placed next to the other.

The most vulnerable, exhausting, and burdensome part of our lives in this new country was the part touched by our parents' sacrifice. Which was everywhere.

We don't say "I love you" or "thank you" to our parents because it would feel contrived to say those words to ourselves. Our parents and we are one and the same.

And so when I came home and saw my parents in their gloomy, anxious ways, I could only buckle down and try to round the misshapen circle of our lives in a way that would please them. I studied hard. I renounced everything that could get in the way. I destroyed the handwritten journal I'd begun in 1975. Years after I first sent them, the letters I'd written in Connecticut to my parents when they were still in Vietnam had been returned to Papa Fritz's address. Apparently, they were undeliverable to a country on the verge of collapse. Papa Fritz and Aunt Margaret, believing they were precious mementos, had sent them in a package to our address in Virginia. I destroyed those too.

Why shouldn't I? Shedding skin. Starting over.

Maybe I did not want my story in America to begin with these letters.

The key to survival, my father once said, is to forget what is essential to remember.

APRIL 1980 WAS THE MIDPOINT OF THE SECOND HALF of my freshman year. For me, the campus changed for the worse when 1979 slid into 1980, which marked five years after the end of the war. With every five-year interval, the country reckoned with the weight of the war, and I had to reckon with the weight of where we had been. Vietnam, unfortunately, was once again on the front page. History returned to remind me it had been there all along—even here, on the campus I loved.

On a bulletin board in the campus post office, I saw a flyer advertising a two-day conference to be held at the University of Massachusetts called "Five Years After the End of the Vietnam War," free admission. I could venture to the precipice, stand on its edge, and just look.

The UMass campus was a mini city of tall concrete buildings. Big streets with traffic lights ran through it. I ran from the bus stop to the designated room to get there on time.

A man stood front and center at the podium, introducing the program like he was launching an inquest into history. He could have been in his late thirties, but with white people, I found it hard to tell. He wore denim that was faded and almost razor thin, threads and rags showing flesh underneath. I looked at the conference brochure and its episodic collection of expository panels: some on American foreign policy focusing on the ignominy and illegitimacy of U.S. involvement and South Vietnamese complicity; some on the depredations of war and American war crimes; some on the war on the home front—that is, the antiwar movement; others on notable battles fought by American soldiers. He welcomed everyone in a coarse voice, issuing other generic antiwar imperatives that polished and tweaked his particular version of Vietnam.

What followed I will never forget. "Today we gather to celebrate the courage and victory of Vietnam and the Vietnamese people." I turned around to gauge the audience's reaction to this declaration. Applause and operatic rage were synchronized with rhetorical markers that the crowd collectively recognized. Kent State. Woodstock. Freedom Summer. The man on the podium continued about how the Vietnamese people had persevered and prevailed against overwhelming odds. The atmosphere was festive and jovial amid hand-wringing over America and self-congratulation over flower power bringing about victory.

Victory of the Vietnamese people? The war had gone wrong and we were here, seeing it again from the back, not the front side of things.

I thought we had lost. And fled. And the country was jagged and fractured. And hundreds of thousands were risking everything to flee by boat to anywhere, including the unknown.

But don't worry about that. Call it peace and what happened after the war will be okay.

On the podium, people had emotion in their voices. I heard Mỹ Lai. Massacre. There was a slide show and a photograph trapping the infamous image of a Vietcong prisoner being executed during Tet. The same photograph my math teacher had thrust in my face. Agent Orange. Napalm.

My father was the one who had seen war firsthand but my mother and I had seen how the shadows fell after. The horrors of war's aftermath, like those visceral flashes of the Cộng Hòa hospital. Here was Vietnam and my childhood hewn and pared down to a single picture. My mother applying compresses to shrapnel wounds and torn flesh, cleaning them, bandaging them. A man with intestines peeking from his abdomen, black eyes stilled like glass, body stiff like a corpse, lying on a stretcher. Silently, I used to wonder how old each wounded or dead person was. When I asked, my mother would just say, "Young."

The woman sitting on a chair a few seats away moved closer to me, probably sensing my anguish. "It was a terrible war," she said, giving me a quick up-and-down.

"Yes," I answered, sitting still instead of edging away.

"Where are you from? Are you from Vietnam?"

I stalled, nodding reluctantly.

"Excellent conference. I'm so sorry what we did to your beautiful country. We bombed the hell out of it. But your people hung in there." She leaned in toward me even more, gripping the arm of my chair, her voice sounding earnest. Her veins were bright green against white freckled skin. "What you need is peace. I marched to protest that war," she added proudly. "Our generation did."

She turned around, looking for someone. "Wait a bit here," she said.

"Actually, no, I don't . . ." I wasn't confrontational, keeping my voice soft and judicious. I knew nobody here liked our kind of Vietnamese and our provisional existence in this country.

"But I want my friend to meet you. He's always wanted to go there." She grasped my wrist and continued craning her neck in search of the friend, showing mild irritation at his absence.

My head was wobbly as I tried to find a way to deflect and duck. I was an impostor, plagiarizing my life, ingratiating myself to Americans by keeping my silence. I am not the kind of Vietnamese you like or admire, I wanted to tell her. The victims of American imperialism. Rather, I'm the kind you snub. But I didn't say anything. I was an agreeable pleaser in a long line of cringingly agreeable pleasers, avoiding battle with Americans just like Hollywood's bucktoothed houseboys did, taking whatever Chinaman roles America stingily gave them.

Sometimes you are erased because you let it happen. And sometimes what you long for is not to be seen but to be effaced.

I extricated myself with an excuse that I had to return to my college to study. And when I made it back to the shuttle bus, I again felt the weight of memories contested, storylines interrupted and disrupted. If America was so bad, and we were allied with America, what did that say about our alliance? If America was trying to save us and then stopped, what did that say about American policy, its trustworthiness? How to quiet the arguments inside the head? Sometimes the stories that need to be told are the hardest ones to tell.

I MADE SEVERAL ATTEMPTS AT DECLARING A MAJOR. I was drawn to courses in politics because they inevitably touched on war and history and the arrogation of power.

Almost all my teachers in the department saw Vietnam as their experience, their rite of passage, the trigger to their disillusionment, the portal to their identity and worldview. They wanted their Vietnam to be my inheritance. I already had my own inheritance of loss, which came from my parents. My teachers told me those who do not remember the past are condemned to repeat it. But what they wanted was for me to remember their past, to accept and ventriloquize their memories, even though I was still trying to make sense of mine.

Like always remembering that my father had taken part in fifty-three airborne assault landings in Long An Province, almost all of which he commanded. I did not know this from him; my father did not talk to me about the war unless I asked him very specific questions. I knew this only because I found his Legion of Merit documents in a box that Papa Fritz gave me. Like remembering my mother's multiple lives, each one sifted and rebuilt from the ashes of the prior ones: first, life in a village risen from the emerald fields of Sóc Trăng, burned down by insurgents; then fleeing from another hamlet pillaged by Japanese soldiers; and then escaping the French by floating corpselike, eyes closed, arms and legs outstretched, down a river bloated with decapitated heads and swollen bodies. Moving to the North before partition and then fleeing back to the South after 1954. Building a life in Saigon and then leaving in 1975.

Like asking myself how it felt to watch your family carry on like nothing had happened, like when Tuấn climbed on a roof in his flannel shirt our first year in Virginia, pretending that he and his cousin had installed cedar roofs in Vietnam all his life so a foreman would keep them on the job.

I remembered and hoarded my own memories, keeping quiet, deciding to take the easier path of capturing bliss and immersing myself in the quotidian wonder of life here, the glory of fall foliage, the pristine beauty of a snowstorm. The splendor that covered up the abyss below.

MY STORY WAS TAME, IN FACT, when compared with the charged world of other Vietnamese refugees. One small life in one small country in one war that most people around me considered an American, not a Vietnamese, experience.

I liked the courses offered in politics, but often I felt small, just like in high school. Because I wasn't willing to speak hard truths. Because I was juggling lies, secrets, and silence. I hung on to my generic smile, my manufactured excellence, and my seal of silence on everything about the war that I knew would be considered heretic. I learned to navigate the collision of all that was fraught and dire.

I told myself I was maintaining what my parents valued so much: self-control, strength, and reserve. I tried to think of it as avoiding weakness. I used martial arts principles, particularly aikido, to justify my position. Avoid the onslaught of force head-on and step to the side instead. Engage only if necessary and use the opponent's force against himself.

I went along with their story, the collective memoir Americans had been writing for years.

Perhaps I could leave the embattled world of politics and experiment with English novels and poetry and plays. Did I dare give myself the gift of language and come home to the wild and grandiose world of Scheherazade? But for a refugee alien, even one who had picked up a lot of English, to major in English meant being trapped in the shadow of the classical world, reading *Beowulf* and incomprehensible works by Chaucer, laced with words like *forsooth, lyre, erstwhile, verily, oft*, and even stranger words from the world of courtiers and nobles and peasants that look like they come from some other language. *Uhtceare, mumpsimus, quagswag, rawgabbit.* I fled Shattuck Hall promptly and never contemplated a major in English again.

Back to the politics department and the charged spectacle of the Vietnam War and its Americanized version of history, the torment of internal monologue and the many vehemently held opinions. But Vietnam already lurked everywhere, not just in this or that department, especially in the age of the five-year retrospective. It was already waiting, with me deep inside its tight-turning radius. I know that before it was a war it was a country, even if one of little interest to the superpowers.

But America's Vietnam, pitiless and punishing, was, in 1980, a recurring cinematic spectacle of surreal interludes projected on a screen in the main auditorium. My floor mates and most of my dorm mates trekked up the road, across the wooden bridge by the waterfall, and up a hill to watch the films. I cowered in my seat when *Hearts and Minds* was shown, squinting to understand what I was supposed to accept as the takeaway. The authorial voice was clear and direct and the visual choices were meant to make a point, which was that everything was pointless. Red explosions. Green rice fields. There was so much pain beneath so much beauty. The real Vietnam was not photographable. And the metaphorical Vietnam had become nothing less than an occupation. In *The War at Home*, the eternal dynamic of American salvation was in full swing: protesters protested supposedly not because they were drafted but because they were trying to save the Vietnamese, yellow people Americans were sent to kill in a distant land. I comforted myself, knowing that soon enough, Vietnam and its blighted lives would fade again, until the ten-year restoration.

There were question-and-answer sessions after. Joan Baez, a pacifist, had broken ranks with her antiwar cohorts, having written a letter to the new, victorious government of Vietnam denouncing its brutality and thereby daring to trifle with the orthodoxies of the movement. She had sent an open letter to other comrades in arms for their signatures and then had the letter published in various newspapers, prompting instant condemnation from 1960s notables such as Jane Fonda, David Dellinger, Abbie Hoffman, and Tom Hayden. Jane Fonda had refused to join, rejecting the plainspoken ironies of Baez, dispatching instead a snappy retort that accused Baez of playing into "the most narrow and negative elements in our country who continue to believe that Communism is worse than death." He held up what presumably was a copy of the letter itself. The audience snickered.

Americans were concerned about Vietnamese suffering only if they believed it was caused by America. This way, the Vietnamese remained perpetual victims and Americans perpetual holders of power—power to inflict and power to save.

As I looked around to gauge the audience's reaction, I saw Phượng sitting in the back row. We gave each other sad, knowing looks. We were both well-versed in the art of making split-second adjustments. We knew there was nothing to salvage here for us at this forum. She was the one other Vietnamese on campus. Phượng understood the place, station, and duty of an immigrant child and so she obeyed her parents and leaned toward the hard sciences—chemistry, physics. My parents, especially my mother, wanted me to have the freedom to choose whatever I wanted, which meant for most of my first two years, I was flailing about looking for an interest, if not a passion. She wanted me to be the person I imagined myself to be.

I quietly left before the program ended. I should have wanted to stay. I wanted to want it. But I did not.

When someone caught me crying quietly after, she thought it was because I was upset that the United States had invaded Vietnam. She put her arm around me as a gesture of empathy. I slunk inward.

I wished for a lullaby, maybe even one of the broody ones sung so wistfully by Joan Baez on *Diamonds and Rust*. As I walked back to my room, I felt caught between two feelings. I knew I should have the right to forget Vietnam even if Vietnam deserves to be remembered. Vietnam was both my private tragedy and my private salvation.

President Carter had dispatched the Seventh Fleet in 1979 to pick up refugees at sea. South Vietnamese antiwar activists, once filled with hope and faith in 1975, were also fleeing the country, heading to Paris, Washington, D.C., Toronto. I read a book by Đoàn Văn Toại, a pro-Vietcong— or maybe he was just an antigovernment university student whose protests in the 1960s in Saigon had made him a darling of the American antiwar movement. Like my own Vietcong Father Five, he felt it his patriotic duty to stay in Vietnam when the war ended. In 1975, secure in his belief that there was no reason to be afraid of the Vietnamese Communists, whom he saw as nationalists first and foremost, he stayed behind to pursue national reconciliation, only to be thrown into prison for asking too many questions about Hanoi's political and economic policies, especially those that involved land confiscation masquerading as land reform.

I read his book, *The Vietnamese Gulag*, in two days, astounded that it had been published by a major American publishing company. I was moved enough to search for his phone number through an operator in California and make a call. I began a conversation with him one evening in my dorm room that continued, metaphorically speaking, until his death more than thirty-five years later.

He had been thrown in a prison, hands manacled to feet, given rice, sand, and water to eat and drink. A scoop of sand was always mixed in the bowl of rice to symbolize the prisoner's sinful life of exploitation and oppression of workers. Confess, the guards ordered. Then you get rice. He did not know what to confess but began to make a list. The guards toyed with him. Wrong answer, or almost but not quite. Sometimes he got two scoops of sand in response to an errant confession.

The gate to the prison was blandly garlanded with a large sign that proclaimed Hồ Chí Minh's famous slogan: Nothing Is More Precious Than Liberty and Independence. Paradoxically, portraits of Soviet leaders adorned the iconic post office, city hall, and other public buildings.

I called him anh Toại—older brother Toại—because he was older.

Mai Chí Thọ, a top Central Committee party member, visited the prison and delivered a chilling speech to his fellow prisoners: "Hồ Chí Minh may have been an evil man; Nixon may have been a great man. The Americans may have had the just cause; we may not have had the just cause. But we won and the Americans were defeated because we convinced the people that Hồ Chí Minh is the great man, that Nixon is a murderer and the Americans are the invaders. . . . The key factor is how to control people and their opinions. Only Marxism and Leninism can do that." The empty words stayed with him and kept him up many nights thinking about the fakery of his postwar world.

Toại was more than willing to reckon with the weight of our history. He was not particularly well liked, to put it mildly, by the Vietnamese refugees, who distrusted his prior antiwar, antigovernment stance. Our weekly conversations pleased both of us, I could tell. He used an endearing term when talking to me. "Em ơi, come to California for a visit."

When Western reporters and human rights groups came to monitor, he and other prisoners were transferred out and Vietcong soldiers were put in their cells instead.

But in class, in my liminal, precarious state, my heart refused to speak anything of this. Why should I? I kept my double consciousness to myself and shared nothing about the country I'd lost. The Vietnam I knew receded even as the one America made up loomed over the future.

I WANTED TO BLOOM WHEREVER I WAS PLANTED, in this present tense where I had found myself, like a lotus flower that grows in mud and turns to face the sunlight. I was reminded of both the Buddhist perspective on the lotus and the inscription on Sylvia Plath's gravestone: "Even amidst fierce flames the golden lotus can be planted." But even in college, where I was busy, busy, busy as much as possible, in quiet moments alone, the non-lotus-like feeling persisted. Unstrung, undone, psychologically unruly. I had good-enough English, good grades, better clothes conveying serious-ness of purpose and apparent success. But what I wanted was the courage to cut myself open and see what was inside, a canny melding of strange, resonant memories from the seemingly waning past—limbless beggars, army hospitals, amputee soldiers, Tet Offensive bomb shelters, soldier en-campments in my back garden, young men howling—with a droll sense of discombobulation, brooding, and alienation in this furious present.

Some memories I did not even remember. But I knew them intimately.

I had my nightmares and daymares, an overlap of images and counter-images that trapped me in a recurring dream. In Vietnam, people were thrown in prison for ten, thirteen, fifteen or more years. Boat people were drowning. What was I upset about? I could not even pinpoint my anxiety. Free-floating stuff that haunted. But it was bad enough that one of my professors, Joan, ignored strict conventional boundaries and brought me to her house, tucking me into the bed in her guest bedroom, so she could watch over me. What did she see? What would it take for me to step out of character, almost fantastically, like in a Woody Allen movie, and stop the narrative—to watch each small part in me, broken off and detached, spin its own reality scandalously separate from mine? As it turned out, I was disturbed enough to be unable to continue with school. And after holding it all together, I suddenly no longer wanted to. I wanted instead to let go and let things split and fall apart. And with the permission of a beneficent dean of studies, I took a semester off and returned to Virginia, back to the home I had once wanted to flee. And just waited.

My semester at home made me realize that by virtue of having left—or rather, merely by having had the deepest desire to leave, wandering about in a floating sense of restlessness—I had become an even more minor character at home, mysterious to myself as much as to others. I had disrupted the social order of our lives, unsettled Confucian boundaries, collapsed family hierarchy and dynamics. I was just waiting for the time to pass, to feel better, to realize that much of life is about stamina, and to eventually return to college, as soon as I could. Whereupon my professor Joan pressed me to go to the college counseling center for help.

It was the beginning of my time in therapy. Progress was lumbering and nonlinear. Sometimes it felt like burning through layers of skin and flesh to get to the wound, without anesthesia—because it wouldn't work if one were numbed. The author Thomas Hardy wrote, "If a way to the Better there be, it exacts a full look at the Worst." There are built-in paradoxes. It's a compartmentalized hour, but it's in that precisely packaged therapy compartment that the shadows can emerge from their private fates to be safely, magically unboxed. The shadow sides can have names. Like No Name. Cecile. Sometimes they are happy and other times they are angry. It was hard to explain these shadow selves because they come from the dark corners of the night sky and seem alien and mysterious, even to me. But to put it simply, they are really just me passing through my sometimes angry, sometimes happy childlike states of being.

Then I came across the famous Frida Kahlo painting, *The Two Fridas*, a double self-portrait I first saw in an art book in the library my senior year. There is a traditional Frida and a modern Frida. Both have hearts that are visible, etched on their clothes. The heart of the traditional Frida is broken and cut open, with an artery severed by surgical scissors, blood dripping down her white dress. The heart of the second Frida, unbroken and whole, is connected to the first heart by a blood vessel that winds from their arms to connect their two hearts. Their faces don't show pain because the pain has splintered and is separate from them.

Frida claimed that the painting was for an imaginary childhood friend. She later said it came from loneliness. When I saw it, I thought of Frida creating, in a moment of wonderment, an imaginary self who could magically hold her hand and to whom she could transfer some of her troubles. I have No Name and Cecile to do that for me. I've learned in clarifying moments to integrate and assimilate them, like e pluribus unum, in therapy.

"There's no coming to consciousness without pain," the psychiatrist Carl Jung said. But he also said, "Who looks outside, dreams. Who looks inside, awakes."

"NIHAO"—HELLO—STRANGERS, USUALLY WHITE, but of all races as well, would call out when I passed by. Instead of the catcalls women got, I braced for nihao from strangers instead. They thought I was Chinese. They smiled. They might have meant to be nice, but I only wanted to be spared. The smooth banality of this slovenly uttered but combustible greeting upset me more than it probably should have.

America made me Asian. I became by fits and starts conspicuously and hence self-consciously Asian only in America, and Asian meant Chinese, according to the movement and compression of American history. The Chinese were historically the most established Asian group here. I could accept it and use Chinese to showcase exoticism, which Americans always appreciate. Having grown up in Cholon, Saigon's twin city of mostly ethnic Chinese, I know the Chinese have an old, venerable civilization. Their food is world renowned. Still, being considered Chinese was a shock to the system. It wasn't because the Chinese had invaded and occupied Vietnam for one thousand years.

I did not see historical grudges in personal terms. Sure, in school the Vietnamese kids called the Chinese ones ba tàu, meaning "three boats," which was a somewhat derogatory term, referencing the Chinese coming to Vietnam by boat, moving their wares by boat, and being restricted to settlement in only three communities in Vietnam.

Maybe my overall irritation with the question had something to do with what happened to Vincent Chin, a Chinese American engineer who was bludgeoned to death by two white laid-off auto workers who blamed Japan for the demise of Detroit's auto industry. A Chinese man was killed because the killers thought he was Japanese. In a world of ambivalent calculus, which one was safe harbor, Chinese or Japanese?

"I'm not Chinese," I replied, irritated.

"Where are you from?"

Having tapped into America's id, I understood the conundrum. Americanness is part performance, part declaration, part assumption, part provocation. If I said, "I am American," the questioner was not willing to let that go. I knew what was waiting for me as I anticipated the follow-up question, which was so predictable that it was almost boring. "No, I mean, where are you *really* from?" asked with a mix of curiosity and complacency but always deployed to devastating effect. There has always been at least two sides to the American Dream: the shiny, bright, "come here" side and the darker, "go away" side.

To irritate the person, as if I were clueless about what he was really asking, I would answer, "Virginia." Sometimes I enjoyed such moments. Sometimes I was irked. Because the questioner would proceed with monochrome persistence. "No, I mean, what about your parents?"

At this point, if I insisted on making my point, I would have to prevaricate or outright lie. "They're also from Virginia," I'd say, at which point the stranger would predictably become impatient, sometimes even pugnacious, hanging on and refusing to let go of his entitlement to, after all, purely innocent curiosity. The questions continued in rapid succession. "No, I mean, originally, where were your ancestors from?" Or alternatively, I could just give in and admit I'm actually not from here at all. At which point the stranger would predictably settle down with a satisfied look, thinking, "Yes, of course."

We may have Americanness officially documented in birth certificates, passports, or naturalization papers. But despite the seductive panache of the American Dream, the message that we can never really be American has curiously been passed down from generation to generation.

Whenever I experimented and turned the tables on the just-curious stranger, asking, "And where are *you* from?" I would watch his face carefully. He would turn notably coy. His face would show surprise. No one has ever pondered his ancestry before, even though it was by no means a certainty that Italians, Greeks, or even Germans were deemed white. Their whiteness was granted and conceded only much later, to distinguish them from the more unpalatable, darker immigrants.

When pressed, I sometimes conceded with the fake "My parents are from China." What then? I would be an ABC, American Born Chinese. The chic kind of Asian Americans who were the so-called model minority, the same ones who had ignored me and other shabby newcomers when they encountered us in high school.

Or I'd say, "They're from Japan." My answer would depend on my mood or on nothing discernible at all. But however recalibrated, however curated, it was almost never "They're from Vietnam." I was fine with self-effacement as long as it was on my terms.

After all, from a cultural standpoint, we never emphasized the self anyway. The English "I"—stand-alone, capitalized, individual, independent of others—cannot be expressed in Vietnamese. The Vietnamese "I" could be conceived of only in relation to another, constantly shifting depending on the party on the other side of the conversation. So minute was this distinction that we have a different word for uncle or aunt or uncle-in-law or aunt-in-law on the mother's side versus the father's side. In Vietnamese, you and I are relational only. The English "I" sounds so brash.

IT WAS STRANGE HOW A SINGLE OCCURRENCE changed the rest of my time at Mount Holyoke. At the end of my freshman year, I found out that Annie had decided to get a new roommate. Perhaps it's expected that people separate and branch out. Still, I felt a gaping wound. It was just like in high school, when I remained unpaired in lab work or PE. But I too had developed the ability to walk away.

I became Vicki's roommate. I said yes because she asked me.

Because of our luck in drawing the lottery, we were able to select one of the more desirable dorms, Wilder Hall, an older one filled with charm at the center of campus. So beautiful.

Vicki was also majoring in politics, and we began to make friends with other students in the department. Lori, from New Orleans, was skinny, her body tight and compact, and her skin was dark. I found my thinking pulled toward a different kind of universe, rocky and slippery and difficult in its own ways, like a deep plunge into a terrifying underbelly of history. Since our arrival in America, my world had been one marked by Americans versus Vietnamese, war and peace, white and Asian. Not black. Even in Vietnam, the American soldiers who played the Rolling Stones for me were white.

In Vietnam, we knew a few ethnic Chams, whose country Vietnam had wiped out sometime in ancient history. They were darker, with jet-black eyes, long lashes, a brownish sheen to the skin. Growing up, it was not unusual to hear people clear their throats and mutter something about the Chams in an intonation and inflection that suggested what was being said was to be kept entre nous. A famous and beloved male singer, Chế Linh, was Cham, but he was deemed an exception. And then there were the famous Hynos toothpaste advertising billboards all over the city, which prominently featured a black shiny face beaming an exaggerated mouthful of shiny white teeth. There were also Cambodians in Saigon, whose darkness was a few shades deeper and hence deemed less respectable than ours.

Still, color was not part of my historical or personal metrics until I met Lori in college. "What do you mean the black national anthem?" I asked when she first casually mentioned it. Scratch the annals of the New World and find its roots in the forbearance and grace of black history. It's one thing to have watched *Roots* or read about the Freedom Riders; it's another thing to be friends with someone whose entire being has been shaped by this immense history. I wanted to know my friend's family history and its connective tissue to us, the new refugees. Slave ships. Branding irons. Beatings. Lynchings. Sharecroppers. Great Migration. Jim Crow. Separate schools. Separate water fountains. Separate everything. Police dogs. Church bombings. And then it occurred to me that the America I was welcomed into and benefited from had in no small part been changed by the herculean efforts of the black civil rights movement.

Seeing things somewhat differently from your own community makes you strange to them, like the village eccentric perched on the perimeter, neither out nor in. The nicest people who themselves have been hurt by anti-immigrant stereotypes will easily peddle stereotypes about blacks. Like the time when a family friend, citing more knowledge of America because he had worked for South Vietnam's ambassador to the United States before 1975, warned me in a soft, uninflected voice to emulate Jews and stay away from blacks, as if blackness were contagion itself. Prejudice is the mother's milk of so many of us newcomers, fragile and fractured and filled with curiosity and yearning but keen and uninhibited in our knee-jerk, gut-deep need to fasten ourselves to whiteness, to look down on some and look up to others, to celebrate individual triumphalism as if we have done everything our own lonesome selves. With curt finality and brusque efficiency, some people I had known all my life, themselves disembodied, disfigured ghosts, would declare about African Americans when they were in their own racialized bubble, "They're lazy."

God help us.

The American past remained occluded to most of us refugees.

It sounded eerily like what the Americans had lobbed at us: "They're incompetent." "No wonder they lost their own bloody war." Repeat this tall tale steadily, evenly, over and over and it would become, soon enough, a historical fact, releasing America from the yoke of history.

Harlan

I didn't care about moving away from my birthplace when I was ten, because I had this idea of what California was, and it would be great. I didn't think I would feel so lonely, like that one weird-looking pigeon you see in New York among all the normal ones. Next to the girls wearing white Vans and light blue tiny dresses, I stood with my Frye winter boots and leather jacket.

Nothing in California worked out the way I had imagined it would.

In Virginia, it was considered cool to wear all black and to be intelligent. In California, my black made me look goth and my intelligence made me look like a know-it-all.

And we had driven across the entire country in a gray Honda Odyssey, with my dog at my feet in the back seat.

We listened to Khánh Ly, a Vietnamese singer whose beautiful voice was clouded by cigarettes. Her voice was velvet, but blue like the sky with no clouds in it.

My dad was going to join us in a few days. It had been a year since his retirement, which I can see now as the hardest day of his life. I had only seen him cry that one day. He spent the whole time before his last day at work downstairs in his office, smoking a pipe through the night. My mom had bought this special long, insulated pillow full of little beans to help block the smoke. It was placed at the bottom of the door, where the crack above the floor would release the gray puffs of tobacco.

A year later, he had surgery that was supposed to cure his scoliosis and stenosis and other spinal issues, but it only made it impossible for him to walk on his own. He went to a rehabilitation center with a name like Happy Meadows, or Meadowlark. Every sad place always has a happy name, as if they're trying to trick people into thinking it's a preschool.

My mother left behind a lot more than I did. The difference between the two of us was that it was her *third* time leaving a home. It was my first.

Her second time was when she left her Wall Street job in New York for my dad and moved to Virginia to teach with him and have his baby. My mother didn't see why they needed a government license for their relationship, but after I was born, she changed her mind. She wanted to make sure I would have a real dad.

She had a friend from William and Mary who had a son two years older than I was. She had convinced her to push him into Tae Kwon Do lessons with me, and they bonded by talking about their similarities; both of them had much older husbands who were slowly becoming less husband and more harsh responsibility.

Her son, who was also my friend, was the pickiest eater I had ever seen. His mother would make four trips to the kitchen to fix the amount of butter on his pasta, to chop up his meat a little more, etc. The first time eating dinner at their house was just a recipe for a lecture I'd get on the way home.

"Nancy is a good mother, but could you enable a child's behavior any more?" she went on, turning around for just a second to make sure I was actually sitting in the booster seat, not sitting *next* to it, the way I often tried to do.

"What does *enable* mean?" I chirped.

"Well, Harlan, *enable* means to allow somebody to—" my dad began to explain, only to be cut off. He probably knew my mom thought he enabled some of my bad behaviors.

"Please, Bill. In Saigon, you were lucky if you could find even a cricket to eat in your cell in a concentration camp."

"What's a concentration camp?" I chirped again.

"I understand that Nancy wants him to grow, you know, because he is small and light for his age, so she wants to make sure he eats . . . but—"

"Okay, Lan," my dad tried again.

"And you know that friend I told you about, Bill? When the government outlawed all private property, they had to sell every little thing. Even the goddamn window shutters. And the children were scraping bugs from the ground for food."

"What does *outlaw* mean?" I asked, determined to include myself in the adult conversation.

"And now her kid complains about food and she has to literally sit on her hands to keep from lashing out at him."

The only friend I made the first year in California was Taylor. She was tall and skinny and had long blond hair and fifteen guinea pigs. When she was ten, she turned her roof into a quail farm. Her bedroom was the house for five generations of guinea pigs. And her bird sat in the cage with a plastic wife whose name I've forgotten. She rode a pale yellow bike and wore a crooked white helmet and blue high-tops.

"You're strange," she'd tell me.

"Says you."

"You talk to my guinea pigs like they're your best friend."

"At least I'm not carelessly throwing them out of windows."

"Harlan, that was one time! It was an accident."

Taylor had taken a pipe from the side of the street and placed it in the pigs' box. Every day she had to clean it from the inside, dangling it over the side of the balcony, emptying it out. Taylor's issue was she never remembered to check the inside to make sure no pigs were left.

And one day, after insisting she had checked, she began to tip the tube over the edge of the balcony. And we were met with the sound of claws scraping against the plastic, along with a desperate squealing noise. Earl the baby guinea pig nearly lost his life that day. It made me wonder how Taylor still managed to be so perfect.

She took me all over school with her like a baby dragging its blanket behind. She tried teaching me how to throw a football, how to skateboard, how to do a cartwheel. I failed at all of them. So as she began to train for a heptathlon, I went home each day to a violin lesson or a piano lesson, leaving my boots at the door. I spent my evenings downstairs playing the three minuets by Bach, with my mother's voice in the background each time I played a wrong note: "It's G-sharp!"

And I spent my days writing essays for school, which my teachers would often use as an example for the whole class. It's no wonder the girls in California hated me. I was the teachers' pet, and I spoke differently and dressed differently than everybody else. It probably didn't help that I wasn't ugly either.

I was still awkward, though. I had quit Tae Kwon Do upon moving, which meant I would lose any chance of getting that black belt my mother could never get. Because of this, it became imperative that I follow through in music.

"You'll regret quitting later," she told me every day when she saw how my face would drop upon being reminded to practice. The idea of me not honoring my commitments was almost like the thought of me murdering someone. In a house that had walls covered in the Bill of Rights, which emphasizes the freedom to make one's own choices, it seemed strange that I also lived in a family where my mom shamed me when I told her I was unhappy with something.

Violin was just like school. I didn't have to practice to be good at it. I could skim a whole book once and write an entire essay on it, just like I could go over a piece once with the violin teacher and improve somehow overnight. Once I discovered I was a "natural," practice and interest dwindled.

When I began high school, I quit classical music. The guilt I felt over quitting violin didn't come out of thin air, though. There were reasons I hadn't quit sooner. First of all, my mother had always wanted to play violin. And she loved when I played for her. She had collected all the sizes of violin I had ever played and kept them hidden around the house, like tiny gems.

But history doesn't equal love. Sometimes you have to break up with your history when you see it isn't real.

To my mother, loyalty can be broken anytime I don't take her side right away. She doesn't want to be told she's being unreasonable; she wants me to support her as, for example, she spits profanities at drivers. Pointing out that it doesn't mean a driver is racist toward her just because he cuts her off is like suicide.

It begins with a car, usually a big one, like an Escalade. Maybe the Escalade driver is on his way to the hospital because his wife is in labor. But the scenarios don't matter, really, because the point is that the Escalade cut off my mother's orange Mini Cooper. So I curl into a little ball and make myself invisible to anybody outside the car, preparing for her to roll down the window, pull up next to them, and scream over my body.

"Do you realize how absurd you look when you do that?" I ask.

"They cut me off!" she screams, trying to justify her rage, which is clearly a result of some serious childhood trauma. Well, it's clear to everybody except her.

Everything is taken to the next level. It isn't just another traffic annoyance; it's a hate crime. It's a personal offense. This is because all the times during her teenage years when she was kicked to the floor, it actually *was* a personal offense, a hate crime.

The only result of me trying to show her the difference between then and now is a colossal fight every day. I am "disloyal" for asking her not to bring such a negative energy to the car on the way to my swim meet.

I can't tell if she even likes the Vietnamese community that much, which is what confuses me. She'll bring me to a pho restaurant, but only if we won't be sitting in a room lined with fridges full of flan wrapped in saran wrap and xôi (sticky rice) in Styrofoam boxes.

It was ironic to us that the restaurant owners in Vietnam were more conscious of aesthetics than those who lived here, where a lot of white people ate. Most "low-class" restaurants are covered in flat screens showing live performances of reality stars dancing to corny romantic music about the love between a flower girl and her soldier. And it isn't even as if the music matches the video. You could be hearing a song about the death of the wind and be seeing a lady with purple eyeshadow and her grandson dramatically dancing on a gigantic melon.

The tension entering high school rained onto me like acid, as we had to face the reality that Taylor was moving to Oregon and I would be left with nothing but my isolating reputation.

And I came home every day to my mother and her moods, which seemed to exist like a cold fish out of water, flopping this way and that, never easy to catch.

WHEN I WAS SIX YEARS OLD, my mother took me to live in Vietnam for two months in the summer. The air was wet and smelled of durian. And the buildings, even the new ones, looked proud, but also sad. The ones that were older than forty had seen the pain of the people, and their sadness rubbed off onto all of the new government's efforts to modernize the city. I took all my prior understanding of who my mother was and where she came from and shoved it into a tiny box to leave in the middle of Saigon, waiting for the wind to take away what was wrong and bring only what was right.

It was summer, so there was no school, and I was put in a daycare with kids who didn't speak a word of English, with a bathroom with no doors, with an outdoor sink with toothbrushes assigned to each of us hanging there, and with nap times that I couldn't sleep during because of the weird bamboo mat that hurt my tiny little back.

I came to school that first day wearing a skirt that was more like a tent, and a backpack shaped like the head of a cat. In Vietnamese, the word for cat is *con mèo*, from the sound the cat makes, "meow." I picked out who I liked and who I didn't. The boy who threw rocks at birds went onto the kill list, but the girl with long braids and glasses who showed me where my toothbrush was went on the keep-around list. Every day after school I watched her put on a poncho to keep the rain off her—which, now that I'm thinking about it, was basically just a trash bag—and hop on the back of her dad's motorcycle.

The kids who didn't finish their food were publicly shamed as ingrates. The same teachers who would later comb through our hair and kiss us on the forehead showed up in the middle of the courtyard and slapped these kids' palms with rulers. After witnessing that, I realized that I'd have to eat every last drop of this cold egg porridge that brought out a gag reflex I didn't even know I had.

There was no trash can; they did this to make sure that when the kids washed their dishes, they had to be empty. No one would be showing disrespect by throwing away peppers they didn't want. I couldn't understand most of the lecture we received after a boy attempted to rid himself of what he didn't want by tossing it in the bushes, but I saw him return to nap time clutching his red little palm in his other hand.

Every teacher watched us wash our hands. They made sure we saw them see us, so no one would even try not to clean under a fingernail or not put the soap back where we found it, or run off without brushing our teeth for two and a half minutes. I felt embarrassed even to be alive at that school; I find that's what happens when one is scrutinized constantly, even if it is out of love. My embarrassment grew when one teacher felt the need to escort me to the bathroom and watch every move I made to make sure I cleaned up after myself and respected the toilet, I guess.

My most vivid memory at that daycare is perhaps the most unfortunate one. It was about my tenth day there, and I lay on my side at nap time, listening to the buzzing of the only fan in the entire school, avoiding eye contact with the teacher as she said, "Đi ngủ."

Maybe I could sleep if you didn't put us on the floor, I remember muttering inside my head.

I felt a tap on my shoulder and ignored it. I felt another one and turned my entire body around to face my classmate, who also couldn't sleep. It was a boy, with his black hair buzzed short. He looked at me and blinked a few times, and then suddenly, there it was: the first penis I'd ever seen.

I didn't pay it any attention, because to be honest, the only emotion I felt was confusion. I turned right back around and just stared at the floor, where a tiny baby dragonfly fluttered along the edges of the baseboard, desperately trying to teach itself how to fly.

"It has no mama," I muttered to myself. *Like Little Orphan Annie.*

That day, I sat outside for about ten minutes, watching the dragonfly struggle on the ground, putting all of its tiny effort into trying to lift itself off the ground. My heart throbbed for it, because it was clear it was an orphan, like in that movie *Annie*, and didn't have anyone to teach it how to fly or live on its own. The other kids watched me watch it, talking among themselves about what I could possibly be doing, and after a while, one of the boys came up to me.

I remember what he was wearing very clearly, because I'm pretty sure he was the first person I ever truly loathed to the point where I thought about all the ways I could painfully murder him. His black linen pants and blue T-shirt were all a blur as his foot came down onto the baby dragonfly without a second thought. I watched this minute little being get its life snatched from it, simply because this boy's mother hadn't raised him well enough to have compassion for things even if they seemed insignificant because of their size. What's wrong with people?

That was the first and last time I ever beat someone up, other than the minor bursts of aggression from my younger years, like when I kicked Jordan in the shin. I stood a few inches shorter than this little Vietnamese boy, and from a distance, one would only see some weird white girl with long brown hair banging her fists into the skull of a helpless scrawny Asian boy. But from where I stood, every time I pounded my fist into his torso, another little dragonfly would be saved.

I turned seven on the last day of daycare, and they brought me a cake and all sang for me, even the little boy whose face I'd bashed in. He stood quite far away from me, and looked at me only when he had to.

I never saw the daycare again. I never entered its walls, which were green like the color of mint chip ice cream, and I never again saw the doorless bathroom, which at the time seemed violating but now seems like my ticket to feeling grateful for what I was given.

I HAD A VIOLIN TEACHER IN VIETNAM, whom my mom hired to come twice a week and enforce what my old white teacher had given me to do back at home. I had been forced to drag my violin through customs, through security, and onto every airplane my entire life. The teacher had long black hair and round glasses, like Harry Potter, and I never paid her much attention until the day she left, when I followed her in my bare feet to the elevator of the apartment building I had been staying in and hugged her, my elbows barely reaching her waist. After she had gone, I chased after her into the street, the hot rain drizzling down, her black hair gleaming. She had never seemed so angelic as the time she was leaving. Her dimples pressed into her pale smooth skin as she gave me a final smile and kissed my wet forehead, saying nothing that I would be able to understand. Now, ten years later, I resent the fact that I was given only a short time to stay there in Saigon. I wish I had been given more of a chance to learn the language. I had just begun to understand conversation, and I could form phrases and listen to sorrowful Vietnamese melodies.

There was a song that I hummed every day about a girl who misses her soldier.

Nếu em không là người yêu của lính
Em sẽ nhớ ai Chủ Nhật trời xinh

If I were not the lover of a soldier, whom would I miss on pretty Sundays . . . whom would I think of on lonely cold nights . . . who would bring me flowers?

La la la la la la la la la . . .

Much of the music we had in America was a bit odd compared to Vietnamese melodies, which were lugubrious yet addicting. I listened to them when I was already sad and wanted to be sadder; when I was teary-eyed but wanted to break down into a pitiful sob. It wasn't because I could always understand every word, but because I understood every feeling. The women cried out, and behind their voices I heard the echo of the rain, and the heart-shattering losses. I lost with them.

I find now that many of those songs foreshadowed things I'd later truly feel in my teenage years—missing men, feeling trust toward only my mother, experiencing the loss of a father.

WE WENT BACK THERE THE WEEK I TURNED FIFTEEN, my mother and Mai and three other friends. In Hội An, my moms put me on a motorcycle and gave me a ten-minute run-through on how to use it, and then sent me off into traffic, riding behind them. I wasn't scared. We rode all the way to the beach that day, beyond the city, and on the way back a monsoon hit and we rode on the side of the street against the pounding, heavy bullets of water. I found a playing card that day in a puddle of rainwater and picked it out. It was the nine of diamonds, and in Vietnam, the number nine is the luckiest, for some stupid reason that only superstitious people believe.

I take that playing card everywhere in my wallet. If I don't, my day will end up being a mess.

Our friends loved the culture but were curious to do touristy things that, at least to them, don't count as touristy. I ended up sitting in a chair while being pulled by a man on a bike. Out of everyone in the group, I got the oldest man as my guide. He was adorable, don't get me wrong, but I'm pretty sure he wasn't exactly the sharpest tool in the shed at that point, because he wandered completely off course and led me away from the rest of the women I was with. While they went down this long, pretty boulevard, I was being towed down a random alley, and to make matters worse, it began to rain.

The old cyclo drivers were all veterans of South Vietnam's army. It seemed as though they had never mentally left the time they were soldiers. My moms tipped them a huge amount of money—well, huge for tips.

People ask me if I feel any sort of connection or magnetic pull toward the country because of my family history or because of my closeness to Lan Cao. The answer is sometimes. I didn't feel any kind of connection when I was six, but when I went back the second time, I did. It wasn't in any kind of ridiculous clichéd way, but I did feel an attachment to the streets and the people and the stray dogs and the lampposts. I think that's because of that phrase my mom told me about the war when I was a baby, something like: "If the lampposts could have walked, they would've left too."

She had her fifty-sixth birthday there a week after my fifteenth, and it was her first time turning a new age in Vietnam since she was thirteen.

I didn't want to go home. Saigon made California look ugly. I couldn't go back and face my high school. I felt like I had spent the first year there unwisely. I had given out trust like it was pennies, and all the little copper bits added up to form this gigantic weight that had been tied to me, pulling me down and drowning me. A part of me, the part filled with sorrow and embarrassment, hoped I would finally actually run out of air and just give out.

The sad part of me went away and was replaced with a part that didn't care at all. I knew that going back into that school meant I needed to learn indifference. I needed to feel numb instead of absorbing all the pain that was coming my way.

And as I grew, I adopted this more modern and diluted version of my mother's personality.

I was Harlan, Lan, and everyone else.

Lan

I knew I was not fully in my family or my clan when I was called by my name instead of my number. I was by implication outside the large-hearted expanse of family and community. Third in birth, I would have been called Sister Four, which would have situated or embedded me in an enumerated fold, like a litter. My brother Tuấn was called Anh Ba, Brother Three.

We think family is gorgeously layered in familiarity and goodwill, which in turn alleviates loneliness. But its power of comfort is often over-played and constantly repurposed. In reality, it bulges and buckles and makes its own loneliness, teaching us to direct blame inward. Expulsion gave me freedom and reinforced my ability to detach. Through a conjunction of circumstances—continued cluelessness about American life and the continuing call of family—I crossed the border and returned after college to Falls Church, where we continued to see everything through the blurring brushstroke of nostalgia.

In the little community that spanned several blocks, the now defunct yellow flag with three red stripes of South Vietnam, bereft and lonesome, continued to fly high. Vietnam was a country that had split itself in half at the 17th parallel in 1954. In 1975, the broken-off southern half of which we were a part officially died off. But not in Falls Church.

And not just in Falls Church but in many cities in America—certainly the huge sprawling enclaves in San Jose, Westminster, and Garden Grove, all in California; Houston, Texas; New Orleans, Louisiana—we Vietnamese were staking our presence in this country the old-fashioned, American way, by owning real estate, by etching ourselves into the American landscape, building ethnic havens like the Italians, Jews, Irish, and Chinese before us, owning a part of America, showing off city by city, block by block, Vietnamese cuisine, making pho and banh mi culinary gems that appeal even to middle America, and in the process reviving what had been dilapidated neighborhoods.

Do you have any outsize dreams you'd like to sell? Because every immigrant group careening from the old country into America will buy into this hungry American agenda, this normal process we casually call assimilation, as if it were innocuous and trouble-free and to be achieved with a modicum of disciplined ease. The imperatives are the same for each group: Start out separate and then melt in.

At times, I could be intensely proud of this intimate Falls Church sanctuary. A little economic, social, and cultural enclave of small mom-and-pop stores; restaurants; doctors', dentists', lawyers', and accountants' offices. At times, I was incredibly frustrated with the endless box-ticking exercises in assimilation where the world was full of people like me. And not. Doctor, engineer, lawyer? Yes. Something else? Maybe not. You can only triumph. You are not allowed to crash and burn. Your success is your parents' American Dream.

The frustrations are many. Like how our parents sneaked in only the shimmering version of the American Dream and sold it to us as the way to be in America, seducing us to put our hopes in this American Dream and go for it. And then they got mad and hurt when we acted too American with them. You can be American outside, but not in the house.

What I did when I was actually in the house was merely sit in the tiny common room and watch whatever interpersonal tangles might have been going on from a corner. Most nights it was just my dad and me basking in the shaggy parochialism of our little enclave. A place that for me exuded finality and hopelessness. But we were masters of misdirection. My father and I said little. We read. We knew that the deepest feelings were shared in the complicity of silence and withholding. He said nothing about history to me, both the big-H history and the small-h history. Unless I asked. And sometimes I did ask. And took notes. Just to have, in case.

He had become a beekeeper, which meant he kept a hive of bees in the tiny garden in our new town house—yet another time-jumbling move that had happened while I was away. His body ached with pain radiating from the wounded shoulder out toward mid- and lower back and even knees. The pain was alleviated by bee venom. He would pry five or six bees with bare hands and squish them against his arms and legs, provoking them to sting him. Afterward, I'd gather their carcasses into a tissue and throw them away. Sometimes he would make himself a cup of tea and plop two codeine tablets into the cup.

Each day passed through the predictable tedium of time. Tomorrow arrived and became today, and today became yesterday. Sometimes it felt like a sad little life, the days redoubling in monochromatic fashion. I was not the character I wanted to be when I was at home. Although Vietnamese was my mother tongue, my vocabulary was stunted. It stopped growing and atrophied after 1975. English had eclipsed it and I felt bad that I had engineered this development. My father seemed stuck, along with the entire Vietnamese enclave still steeped in nostalgia over past victories. We too have a heroic history and a "greatest generation" that we genuflect to—the history of the Trưng sisters and Madame Triệu and General Trần

Hưng Đạo, and others, who vanquished Chinese and French invaders. But we were living with defeat bobbing and spinning always through our lives. One time, when it was dark and quiet, my father casually mentioned that in April 1975 he had received from Dr. Thanh, the chief of Cộng Hòa military hospital, the same hospital I'd frequented as a child, several fresh and presumably potent cyanide pills for him and my mother to take. A Communist victory was already inevitable, my father said. They were on the verge of taking the pills. But when he heard that the coup leader who'd had him arrested and threatened with execution in 1963 was now planning to have him arrested again, he submitted his resignation to the President, who signed it. And that was why he didn't take the pills and how he came to arrive in Virginia. I had never heard this story before, although I did read this exact account in a book written twenty years later by a South Vietnamese officer who had been told this story by the doctor himself.

Looking at him, I couldn't tell if my father regretted not taking the pills. And I couldn't tell why he had shared this with me at that particular moment. I gave him a knowing nod, but I tried not to think about any of it much because the entire Vietnamese refugee community is swollen with even more tragic stories, and whenever I see a Vietnamese family in a restaurant or going about their daily life, with grandparents and parents and their 1.5-generation kids like me or the second generation, born here, I think they look normal but wonder what fractured lives and worse would spill out of the older-generation folks if they were willing to be cracked open.

I knew only that my parents were lost. Their loss showed once they made themselves known to the outside world; that is, in even the mildest, most everyday moments when they opened their mouths and spoke English. Their Vietnameseness peeked through every syllable. I thought of the term *all-American*. What did it mean? The dictionary said it meant "having qualities that are thought to be typical of people in the U.S. or that are widely admired in the U.S." But in real life it was applicable only to white

Americans like Robert Redford, whose beauty was noted by *People* maga-zine: "the golden thatch, the ice-blue eyes, the all-American jaw."

One of my most prized possessions from college was Maya Angelou's autograph on my calendar book. I loved the idea of a caged bird singing about freedom; of Maya and her brother reading voraciously and being saved, like Scheherazade, by language and literature. My year after college was a year of in-between. I used it to return to reading for pleasure and to pursue freedom, not status. Not résumé building. My mother saw this time as a waste. I was working in an utterly unremarkable job as a clerk at a video store, one that my mother bemoaned because I could have gotten that job without a college degree, without going away, without excellent grades. This was true, and neither of us attempted a conversation about my postcollege choices. Except I knew that when she brought up someone's child who was now working for a big American corporation like Coca-Cola, the reference was meant for me.

But this job gave me freedom, without pressure, from having to strat-egize or even to aspire toward anything—which felt anti-Confucian and sneakily attractive. I even grew fond of the orderly rows of red VHS tapes and black Beta tapes repeating themselves from one shelf to another. I saw how far I had come, from Vietnam to here, to this ordinary store with its humble storefront in a depopulated, inauspicious-looking strip mall filled with discount stores. This was a truth that my mother bemoaned, but one that I celebrated quietly. All I had to do was drive to work, smile at custom-ers, alphabetize tapes; I even had free time to watch music videos blaring from mounted TV sets around the store.

Because the job was easy, I was able to return to my closest companion, books, especially those that told stories about an America I still did not know, by Americans who, by their otherness and estrangement, were more like me even if our stories were on different frequencies. My first few years in Virginia, when I read novels, I used to copy down passages I liked; hold-ing a pencil felt intimate and personal. It was also practical because I would switch to diagramming sentences to understand structure and grammar, and it was like taking in chaos and reordering it.

The books I read during this in-between year were almost all by African Americans and about pain hidden inside the puckers and pleats and seams of history, the messy intersection between internal and external struggles, the searing effect of race on identity. Eldridge Cleaver, *Soul on Ice*. Ralph Ellison, *Invisible Man*. Toni Morrison, *The Bluest Eye*. Reading these books changed me. The year in between was not a digression at all. Sometimes, it felt like almost being hit by a falling tree. You are not dead, but you are shocked. And even as you walk away, along the path, you are not the same because you have been touched by the inextinguishable light of their lives. These were people who survived when life, bleak and unjust, conspired to diminish and even erase them. They were my American heroes.

I was developing and creating, from my fine-tuned blend of many divided selves, a persona that was bigger and different from my original Vietnamese self.

WHILE I WAS WORKING AT THE VIDEO STORE, there was a three-day holiday weekend because of Presidents' Day. My parents told me to show my enthusiasm by volunteering to work all three days—Saturday, Sunday, and Monday. A few days after, I was called into the manager's office. Money was missing from each of the three days, and the company was questioning everyone—there were not many—who had worked all three days. I found myself walking the length of a hallway until it narrowed. At the end was a room devoid of windows in the back of the store. I stood gazing at the people there, managers, assistant managers, and security guards. The language used to emphasize what the meeting was not frightened me. "*Not* an accusation." "Just because you were here all three days does *not* mean . . ." It felt like high school again. Later, I found myself hooked up to a polygraph, which sounded less scary than a lie detector, but that was what it was. Just tell the truth, my parents said. No, I didn't take the money, I answered. No, I don't know who did.

The result apparently showed I spoke the truth for the first question but was inconclusive as to the second. My parents wanted to know if I was covering up for someone else.

Later, I received a subpoena to testify as a witness in a trial against one of the managers for embezzlement. I stepped into the courtroom, and I remembered how it felt to enter the courtroom years before to be sworn in as an American citizen.

And just like that, in the flitter-flutter of the moment, I decided to go to law school, a decision that pleased me because it pleased my parents so much. My father had enumerated all the logical, rational reasons why law would be a good career choice—solid and firm and thus especially attractive to "people like us." A good legal system protects the weak, the outsiders. And of course, it's better to turn to law rather than to war to resolve disputes. I knew about the lawyer jokes. But my father didn't.

One of my college professors said the best thing an unjust society can do to perpetuate itself is to allow minorities and women to become lawyers. They become co-opted into the system, taught to see both sides of every argument and able to nimbly defend either side, taking into account only the small-picture interest of their client and not the societal big picture. Doctors can make mistakes, but no one suspects doctors of being on the side of the cancer. Not so with lawyers. And change, if any at all, is likely to be slow and incremental and cautious. Law accommodates and does not threaten. So it was said.

My father didn't know about this side of the law either. I did, but being an immigrant, I didn't need to become a lawyer to be sympathetic to multiple sides of any situation. I didn't see it as a question of selling out, but rather a question of give-and-take.

MY FIRST SEMESTER IN LAW SCHOOL, there was a strike of clerical workers, mostly women, at Yale University. My professors supported their secretarial assistants and did not cross the picket lines. So we held classes in a church basement, a movie theater, an ice cream store. Some classes had no fixed meeting place. What made Yale stand out to me was its small entering class, a relatively supportive and cohesive community, which was also linked to the grading system of credit, no credit the first semester and pass, low pass, and honors thereafter. But the strike meant the promised land of closely knit community was hard to forge because we were dispersed. There was no common area in the law school to congregate in. At the time, there was no internet; research could not be done online. We needed a library, and I had to drive to Bridgeport to find research materials for class.

But I did have one consolation: our core group of about fifteen students, referred to as "small group," which moved from class to class together because we had the same mandatory first-year curriculum—torts, constitutional law, civil procedure, and contracts. Our small group would be together in each of these large classes. It was the one continuity in a first semester of chaos and fragmentation.

"Mr. Smith, please state the facts of *Goldberg v. Kelly*," our civil procedure professor directed. I discovered quickly that in law school, one must expect to be "cold-called," an exercise in which the primitive language of feeling would be abandoned in favor of quick, rational retorts. It was the way of law school, this threatening occurrence in which the professor scanned the classroom while we students looked down to avoid making eye contact. The professor's eyes would return to the seating chart, where our pictures and names were listed, then for no rational or predictable reason, he would pounce upon a name. That person would either be expected to answer one question, or would be responsible to tango with the professor for the entire class period. Questions, one after the next, would be launched; the student or students would attempt an answer. There was rarely a confirmation that the answer was right or wrong because inevitably one answer would merely yield another question. We were to figure out this process ourselves.

It was for us mere students to discover the truth from the problem, which was to be elicited from vague, indeterminate questions posed by the professor. This so-called Socratic method reminded me of martial arts, especially the drunken-monkey style, the style of no style, in which the master was so unpredictable and enigmatic that an effective opposing strategy was hard to come by. In the world of relative truth and falsehood—that is, the world of a Yale Law School class—there was no right answer, but there was strangely but surely a wrong answer: the answer provided by us students. To ask, "What's the ruling?" or "What's the law?" or "What's the takeaway?" only showed how superficial you were. How could you only care about what the ruling was? The ruling was so obvious! Think instead about the more hard-hitting questions: how the judge came to that ruling. Think about the legal process. Think about the theory of law that led to that result. Think about the policy implications, the normative choices embedded in the issues and in the ultimate holding of the case. And what if there was no answer, like a Zen koan? Scary, sacred, sacrosanct stuff.

But as it turned out, there were indeed ways to escape riddles and find answers: commercial outlines. Of course, after hours of the Socratic method, we flocked to the bookstore to buy these indispensable shortcuts to learning so derided by our professors.

While the other section of the civil procedure class, taught by another professor, had moved on to other rules of civil procedure and certainly other cases, our class stuck with *Goldberg v. Kelly*. Our professor adored this case and nudged, coaxed, pushed, shoved us into embracing its ruling and reasoning as well.

The hapless Mr. Smith (or whoever) would trip and stumble, becoming ever more ensnarled in the case. He would be interrupted by the professor,

who seemed gleefully impatient with the recapitulation of apparently ir-
relevant facts. But by now, the professor knew who Mr. Smith was and
would greet him in the hall even if he had been dismissed in class for lack-
ing intellectual rigor. Another student would raise his hand. The professor
would glance at him and proceed to cold-call another student. I saw he had
a pattern. Usually he chose people whose names he could pronounce. Relief for me. Next question. "What is the responsibility of the administrative state?" "Do you see any relationship between this case and a landmark
case like *Brown v. Board of Education*?" Clearly, the question alone implied
you're supposed to see it. I quickly tried to make analogies in my head and
looked down, hiding.

So many hours and days spent on one case? Even though we were newcomers to the law, we knew that *Goldberg v. Kelly* was not a case that was
usually accorded a seat in the pantheon of major court decisions. John
Kelly was a disabled welfare recipient. His benefit was eliminated when he
moved out of a welfare hotel that his case worker had assigned to him. As
our professor unwound and untangled each strand of the case, we saw its
beauty, however. As it turned out, the ruling as to what due process required was quite simple. In the context of the case, constitutional due
process means that welfare and other public benefits recipients are entitled
to a fair hearing before the government can terminate their benefits. The
law made a big difference in the lives of millions of people. To me, this
seemingly technocratic case stood for the proposition that the administrative, bureaucratic state had responsibilities to its citizens. Justice William
J. Brennan, who wrote the decision, quoted the preamble to the Constitution: "Public assistance, then, is not mere charity, but a means to 'promote
the general Welfare, and secure the Blessings of Liberty to ourselves and
our Posterity.'" In Vietnam, dissidents were scrawling "Trả tự do cho tự
do" on walls and sidewalks: "Free freedom." I was falling in love with
the law.

We had other classes, of course, but this one met in a movie theater, which made it particularly memorable because in the twilight darkness of the room, I felt like I was in Plato's cave. The professor was a moving shadow, walking back and forth, his voice a disembodied echo that stalked his silhouette. He could be talking to himself, to us, to some of us—he made eye contact with some students. He was sometimes excited, even spiteful, at times nostalgic, other times rueful about the state of the law. He once grabbed a thick book, *The Federal Rules of Civil Procedure*, the rules that determine the practical how and when and where of federal court practice, and flung it across the room. "Garbage. This is garbage," he said. Who cares about stupid, formalistic rules? Where's the justice? The equity in the case? The questions he asked were rapid-fire quick. And he expected succinct, sharp answers with equal alacrity in return. He was quick to dismiss students who spoke more slowly, contemplatively, or tentatively. That meant he was quick to dismiss most of us women, who were inclined less toward braggadocio and more toward cogitation and rumination. He called on students who volunteered aggressively, their hands thrust straight up with confidence, remaining up even after another student had been called upon. That meant he missed many women who volunteered in a more inconspicuous, modest way. Many of the men called on also tended to be those who congregated around the professor after class, a gathering replete with jovial patter. And when a female student did get called on and made her point, perhaps too softly or diffidently, the professor rarely, if ever, commented on her contribution, moving quickly to the next, usually male student, whose similar comment would in fact elicit a reaction, whether approving or disapproving, from the professor. Humility and modesty were second-class traits here.

This went on day after day. It was startling to watch in real time how invisibility was produced and reproduced and reinforced right before my very eyes. Three women in particular were consistently trying to speak and were regularly silenced, their remarks greeted with nonchalance and indifference. They were not in my small group, but within a few weeks I got to know them and other women in our first-year class. We entered into a pact, promising that any comment made by one of us would not fall into a void, because someone from our group would offer a reaction, any reaction, to engage with the initial comment.

It worked. And it encouraged even me to raise my hand. Courage can be gathered, slowly accumulated, like my beloved stamp collection. My friend Jane from my small group told me it was important to know how to talk in public, even to interrupt. Especially if you wanted to be a lawyer. I was deeply conflicted. I didn't want to be seen, but I was in law school to be a lawyer.

OUR SMALL GROUP PROFESSOR was a constitutional law professor with a thick mass of wavy white hair. He was avuncular and his raspy voice made him sound like Rod Stewart. Of course, we had to read the landmark case *Marbury v. Madison*, considered the single most important decision in American constitutional law because it established the principle of judicial review. To navigate through the complexities of the difficult case, I read a famous classic interpretation of it that had appeared in one of the most cited law review articles of the previous fifty years: "A Critical Guide to *Marbury v. Madison*," written by a law professor at Duke Law School, William Van Alstyne.

In America, we live by choice, not by chance. But it was chance that led to my meeting him fifteen years later when I accepted fate's help and took a teaching stint at Duke. Although it was indeed by choice that we decided to have a child together.

The first paper I was assigned to write in law school was on the free exercise and establishment clauses of the First Amendment. I sat on my futon, which was lying on the floor in the corner of the bedroom, and typed out the paper on the Smith Corona. The ideas were incredibly exciting to ponder. But I had no idea how to write a law school paper. I just started thinking and typed out my thoughts, tying the reasoning and rulings of the relevant cases together to come up with my own ideas. Should the Amish by virtue of their status as religious adherents be allowed to opt out of Wisconsin's public school system? The Supreme Court held yes because of the parents' religious freedom. Could any group claim religiosity and get opt-outs? Must the air force create an exemption allowing a Jewish officer the right to wear a yarmulke when in uniform as an accommodation of his free exercise of religion? The officer had argued that there was no compelling state interest to restrict his right. The Supreme Court held that the First Amendment did not apply to the military the way it did to the nonmilitary sphere and that the military had the right to enact rules to foster unity, obedience, and esprit de corps. Could a crèche be placed in a public park? The Supreme Court held that government action doesn't violate the establishment clause when it has a significant secular or nonreligious purpose, does not have the primary effect of advancing or inhibiting religion, and doesn't foster excessive entanglement between government and religion. Is a crèche a secular or religious exhibit? Is it denigrating to religion if one categorizes a crèche representing a moment in the birth of Jesus as secular? What if it's part of a mixed display and includes reindeer and Santa Claus? If there are lots of reindeer, the display will survive constitutional scrutiny. This is informally referred to as the reindeer rule.

Our small group TA selected my paper as a model to put on reserve in the library. Astonishing. One of his comments was that my logic was impeccable and my sentences fell together like "manna from heaven." I had to look up the word *manna*. My small group friends were effusive in praising me. On our first day of school, the dean told us to look to our left and right and instead of warning us that many of us would drop out or fail, he reassured us that all of us would do well. This was a community, and we were encouraged to support and cooperate with one another.

I loved law school. When Vietnam did come up, it was in the context of law—separation of power, the War Powers Act, the tug-of-war between the legislative and the executive branches. Not politics. Nor the rubbishing of the South. There was no need to call forth guilt or complicity, and there was no need to turn away. It was all legal, constitutional, and manageable.

To my delight, there were even funny and memorable characters in case law, as droll and magical as those in *One Thousand and One Nights*. We learned about officious intermeddlers—those who, despite having no legal obligation, nonetheless do something to benefit others and then demand compensation. They are entitled to none! Naked trespassers are not really naked. They are referred to as naked to signal the fact that they are owed little or no duty at all from the property holder. They are but mere intruders, different from those with higher status, like invitees.

Then there was the hairy hand case in contracts law, the only course in my first year taught by a woman professor and one with tenure. The case's nickname alone was intriguing. The first paragraph of the case had terms I didn't understand, and neither did others in my small group. *Assumpsit. Nonsuit. Writ.* I quickly got a ride to the law library in Bridgeport to access *Black's Law Dictionary.* In the case, a doctor was supposed to repair a hand marred by scar tissue, promising to make it a "one hundred percent good hand." But because of a skin graft from his chest, the patient's newly restored hand grew a lot of hair. There is something funny about a hairy hand and we couldn't help but have a few good laughs. How much is a perfect hand worth, in monetary terms? And how much is a scarred and hairy hand worth? The patient got what we learned was called "expectancy damages"— the difference in value between the promise and the actual outcome.

These characters compensated for the bizarre language of law, which was replete with and encumbered by stultifying phrases like "said plaintiff," "said contract," "heretofore," "aforementioned," and "hereinafter." It was amusing to me, and I saw it as similar to learning any new language. Law school had its own world of rituals, customs, language, and culture. Besides the Socratic method, there was the dreary, dreadful, dreaded Bluebook, a book with a blue cover containing all the most ludicrous rules in the world about how to cite everything, from a book to an article to an interview to a television show. The requirements are dizzyingly detailed, down to when a word should be in italics, underlined, or bolded, when the author's first name could be included, and when it was prohibited. I was going to try to get on the prestigious *Yale Law Journal*, and knowing the Bluebook was a must to ace the Bluebook exam. Almost every similar journal at other law schools is called a law review. Except at Yale, where it is called a law journal, probably because at Yale it's important to just be different. And as there was no grade point average at the school, one became a law journal member by a process called "writing on," submitting a paper on a novel legal topic. So learning the rules of citation was crucial, and I approached it the way I approached learning English grammar in high school—with complete devotion.

I wrote my paper, which was called a "note" because only professors and scholars were allowed to call their writing an "article." My note was on trafficking in women and how the law, not the law generally but a particular law called Racketeer Influenced and Corrupt Organizations (RICO), could address this problem. I wasn't sure the note would be good enough to get me on the *Yale Law Journal*. I had heard that at Yale, theoretical writing with a normative bent—abstract, amorphous, bewilderingly philosophical, and definitely not practical—was preferred. Mine seemed ordinary and mundane and proposed a pragmatic resolution. But my little note was deemed good enough by the editorial board and I made it onto the *Yale Law Journal*. Somehow I managed to meet the standard metrics of success, and in an even more astonishing twist, the note was selected for publication in the journal itself.

I immersed myself in the *Law Journal* culture, relishing being with other students who loved to read and write, while those who loved to make legal arguments in a courtroom did moot court. I could hide behind reams of papers and be among the stacks of the Yale Law library, with its archways, its giant wooden bookcases, its intricately carved ceilings, its enormous chandeliers dangling in two parallel rows that ran from one end of the main reading room to the next.

To be accepted as an editor of the *Law Journal* felt unreal. Professors, some I didn't even know, congratulated me. As I discovered, prestige in legal academia is measured by scholarship and publication in law reviews. Not so much by teaching.

Indeed, one of the first jokes second- and third-year students told us first-years was about choosing which professors to take the following year, when we were done with mandatory and assigned classes. "Take professors whose offices are on the third floor," they said with a chuckle.

"Why?"

"Because they will be better prepared for class than those on the second floor. They have to walk three flights down and that means at least a few minutes extra of prep time."

Professors don't have time to prepare for class. The joke is they have to publish constantly or they perish. In a curious twist, the editors of law reviews are students, not professors. So we students, second-year law journal editors, were given the task of judging the writing of our own professors and those from other law schools, deciding whether to accept or reject a submission sometimes on subjects we hadn't even studied yet. How strange. Students too did the work of editing and source citing. Being on the *Law Journal* was a full-time commitment. It had its own office, where we editors had our own respective cubicles, and a lounge where we could meet with our various committees and hang out.

Most of the work for us second-year editors was non-substantive, but we were told we should never let that description make us think our assigned work was not important. We were assured and reassured it was. We might not have known enough law yet to know whether an article had brilliant legal insight—that job was for the third-years. We were given packets that contained portions of an article our journal would publish, and we were to read them carefully to make sure all rules, spelling, styles, grammar, and Bluebook were faithfully correct. The implication was that if you failed to catch these mistakes, you were either lazy or not careful. Neither was acceptable.

It felt like a dream community, an oasis within an oasis.

BUT I COULDN'T STRIKE A TRUCE WITH MYSELF. The argument inside me, a deeper Socratic method that I could have only with myself, continued. I was not triumphant by any means, nor was there a definitive moment, the fortissimo before and after, in which the after could be celebrated as progress. There was no crisis, just a nagging and gnawing absence that reminded me I was ungrateful and spoiled to even dare feel absence, when others were so much worse off on planet Earth.

One day, for no discernible reason, my Ford Escort hit a lamppost on Interstate 95 at more than seventy miles per hour. It was a sunny day; I couldn't blame bad weather. I was tired. Perhaps it was exhaustion.

The car was destroyed. I was hurt, but surprisingly not dead. It was after my first year in law school, and I recuperated over the summer, allowing me to start my second year when school resumed in the fall.

I IMMERSED MYSELF IN THE WORK OF THE LAW JOURNAL, evading everything that was extraneous to the work at hand. Finally, I understood what my father had taught, which was, essentially, don't brood. Forget everything. There is nothing to excavate. There is only the present, thinly drawn, where I could be completely poised, posed, and scrupulous in my studies.

This was how my life as a law student, law journal editor, law graduate, and lawyer would settle into itself. The way a house and its component parts—walls, cabinets, foundation—settle. Or how a transplanted tree settles into new soil. It takes time for the tree to become familiar with the soil, the climate. It is only a matter of time.

But being invisible meant I didn't have any close relationships with my professors that would garner me glowing reference letters to take me to the next notch of recognition. I realized, belatedly, that the absence of real grades also meant those letters were more important at Yale than at other schools. The West likes to reference guanxi, which means "relationship" in Chinese, but the reference is not merely a definitional one but rather judgmental. It's meant to show that we in the West operate in a climate of transparency governed by the rule of law, but elsewhere, such as China, people operate in a more murky, enigmatic environment, on the basis of relationships. Benefits are gained when one is embedded in close and extended networks of interpersonal relations.

Of course, the law school taught us law, but in no way was it devoid of guanxi. It was probably just better at masking it. Without grade competition, references, which required meticulous cultivation, mattered supremely. Yes, there were endless recruiters for corporate firms, but jobs in academia and clerkship require connections and mentoring, something you don't realize unless you know the unstated norms of law school. My classmates had parents who were investment bankers, hedge fund managers, partners at major law firms, and law professors. They probably started connection building the first week of school. In retrospect, the building blocks were as follows: Make yourself known and become a frequent visitor of the professor during his or her office hours. Take black-letter law classes that had a paper option, which required regular meetings. Work toward becoming a research assistant or teaching assistant, but only to a famous professor with access to federal judges and the rarefied world of academia. Join a club, like the American Constitution Society or the Federalist Society (law school's version of secret societies), as early as possible and work your way up to become a board member, because the club will host very important speakers with whom you can dine if you are a board member. While I got summer jobs at law firms that paid well, many of my classmates interned without pay or with minimal pay at the Assistant United

States Attorney's office, which paved the way for landing a job there after graduation, which then paved the way for a coveted position at a top law firm, and with that credentialed history, a likely spot eventually as a partner at said firm.

I had no mentor who held the key to the kingdom, who would pick up the phone, call a federal judge, and advocate for me. I didn't know about the secret watering holes where the inner functioning of law was revealed. But it didn't matter because I couldn't imagine aiming for federal clerkships, especially the most desirable ones in New York, D.C., L.A., and San Francisco. With more than a hundred thousand dollars in law school debt, I couldn't afford a government job anyway.

But a Yale law degree was still useful. There are only two hundred of us in every entering class, so any of us could get a job at a huge law firm. With equal parts consideration and chance, I ended up at one of the big firms in New York City, which translated into a permanent job offer with a startling starting salary of almost ninety thousand dollars—in 1987. Plus a minimum of a ten-thousand-dollar signing bonus for those who had clerked for a federal judge.

I loved New York City, with its skyward reach, its compressed turbulence, restlessness, expansiveness. A city that would always be there, giving us an intimation of immortality. For the first time since losing Vietnam, I'd found a new home—unlike a lotus flower that, though open and beautiful, floats in a swamp and has no deep roots. The city became my roots. I had a lovely apartment on the Upper East Side, but it was not the apartment that was home. It was the city. I was a citizen of the city, with pride of place, and what a place it was—the accelerated pulse, the flickering beats of welcome, for me and all the other Americans, New York–born as well as foreigners and aliens, refugees and immigrants and misfits, all mixing and mingling and claiming our American home, being alone in teeming togetherness, or being together in our searing aloneness. New York City gave me the gift of being seamlessly part of and separate from. It was mischievously bighearted, allowing me to choose which one I wanted at any moment in time: togetherness and belonging, or aloneness and solitude. This was not thrust on me. Rather, it was mine to choose.

I also opted for a Wall Street law firm, to get a sense of the hyperkinetic, high-stakes intensity of law firm practice. Maybe I would fall for the irresistible charm of Wall Street, alive and turbulent in the midst of concrete, and become a lawyer in the greatest city in the world. But actually, this fantasy did not last very long. Big law firm life experienced as a summer associate was starkly different from big law firm life as a regular, permanent associate. When we were summer associates, we were auditioning for real jobs, but the law firm was also in recruiting mode. This meant there were lunches at exclusive and expensive restaurants such as Le Bernardin, where I mingled with the partners and the clients, which provided incredible opportunities to network. There were Broadway tickets, sunset cruises in the harbor past Ellis Island and the Statue of Liberty, cocktails at the Central Park Zoo. Success meant getting an offer at the end of the summer.

It wasn't all just bait, though. Later, a partner I became close to told me that sometimes when he took the summer associates to expensive lunches he asked the waitstaff to make sure something was wrong with their food order. And he watched how the associates reacted, which would be a determining factor in whether they got an offer or not. I assumed the partner would consider being discombobulated or flustered disqualifying.

Believing in the essential goodness of the rule of law, I chose litigation and joined the law firm I had summered for. Having barely survived J. E. B. Stuart High School, I wanted to show myself I could survive even Wall Street–style litigation in the global commercial center that is New York City. Every morning: pantyhose—itchy, easy to rip, but necessary because bare legs were anathema; heels; skirts—not too long, not too short. Despite a sharp haircut, expensive designer suits, and for the men a splash of something different, perhaps colorful even, in the form of designer ties, we were

all basically in uniform, distinguishing ourselves as attorneys in a pyra-
midal, multitiered, multi-rank system of partners, associates, paralegals,
mail-room, and other support staff. Despite the constraints of rules of
evidence and civil procedure, much of litigation—the scouring assault of
motions, such as motions to dismiss, motions for summary judgment,
motions to exclude, and research memos on contingent and marginally
peripheral issues—was chaotic, ragged, messy, and mysterious. Perhaps I
also wanted to go against stereotype, me versus the menagerie of big male
litigators who were more than willing to forgo niceties in order to bill, bill,
bill, and win. Here, at one of the top law firms in the country, life is not
meant to be well proportioned for any lawyer, and neither men nor women
can have the genteel balance between family and work. Despite the veneer
of professionalism cloaked in disclaimers that law isn't a business, the Wall
Street law firm culture, especially in the high-stakes world of litigation, is
a growling, ranting world where the meek will never inherit the earth and
a pioneer lust for billable hours and winning reigns supreme. In gleaming
offices that scrape the sky, there is always that snarl behind the smile. It's as
much about the law as about asserting and bragging and making a show of
it. Night after night we associates were routinely shipwrecked as we looked
forward to another day of jittery hand-wringing and fearmongering.

When the firm's clients were truly global, their needs, whether high
stakes or trivial or capricious, at nine a.m. Munich or Tokyo or London
time, must be met by us at whatever time it might be in New York City. It
was expected that no lawyer and certainly no junior associate would flinch
at the hour of night they were to work to further the client's interest. In
one transaction, I stayed at the firm for a span of three days and nights
without sleep. After forty-eight hours, I felt like time had folded into itself,
and even the desire to sleep in the wake of temporal dissonance faded. But
it was important not to draw any conclusion about willingness to work
hard or hours devoted to a case. Your even-keeled emotional temperatures
and your ever-spiking billable hours were not sufficient indicators of

anything. Because there was no such thing as a reassuring sense of progress or promise of membership in the labyrinth of the firm and its culture of opacity. We might have had our eye on the prize, but the road to that prize remained slyly, artfully hard to find without, of course, a little bit of guanxi and mentorship. The trick was that mentors were not easy to find either. Everything was moving at a fast pace and everything was static at the same time. These incongruities became corrosive for the heart and mind.

Our clients were of course big companies doing what big companies do, always audaciously: merge, acquire, expand, buy, sell, make money for their shareholders, lose money, declare bankruptcy, start all over, creating, destroying, and creating. This was capitalism doing what it did best: creative destruction followed by creation and growth and then creative destruction again. Every month I gave my parents a thousand dollars. That felt good and right. They had reconnected with ethnic Chinese friends from our hometown of Cholon, who had helped them buy a dry-cleaning business in New Jersey. My parents were now like me, away from the Falls Church enclave and off on their own. My father learned the intricacies of the dry-cleaning business. My brother Tuấn was too isolated mentally and emotionally to help. We didn't even know where he was. As the family forged forward in America, my brother was left behind, a silent wanderer with an unknown life separate from us. My father bemoaned his son's instability. My mother blamed his instability on the terror that had surrounded her when she was pregnant with him.

But I also knew I did not have the single-minded stamina and dedication to a professionally frenzied life needed to survive more than a few years of the golden handcuff that tied me to law firm life. Your law degree only meant that for the first few years, you were entrusted with ensuring that the thousands of pages of documents were stapled correctly, that no page was missing or out of sequence, that there were no spelling or grammar issues, and that everything, even those things worked on by a chain of people from paralegals to secretaries to photocopiers, be perfect, because if one thing was wrong, it was your fault.

It was important to remind myself that everything that occurred there was to be taken with a measure of wry detachment.

More than once, when I signed out of the law firm at two or later in the morning, I saw the impersonality of another signature right above mine, five minutes before, at 1:55 a.m. or some other stratified slice of time. It was a partner, and right away, I thought of Gertrude Stein's "There is no there there." I did not want a life of working until two a.m., being available to serve clients in London and Tokyo and Beijing in live London, Tokyo, and Beijing time. When I first started, FedEx stopped picking up packages at eight p.m., which meant if we couldn't finish the work to send out to clients with FedEx, we would go home for the night and start early the next morning. But once the fax was invented, there was no excuse for a cutoff time. We had to stay to finish the work at whatever hour and then fax it to our international client.

When an initial public offering was ready to be launched, our legal team headed to Varick Street, where all the printers were, so the forms and securities prospectuses could be printed and submitted to the SEC. This meant an all-nighter, amid a buffet spread of lobster, shrimp, steak, artichoke hearts, and ice cream to fuel us all through the night. Sometimes deals required seventy-six hours straight of no sleep, the usual dulling repetition of endurance quelling even the desire to slog on long enough to get to the presumably truly creative aspects of lawyering or litigating. On the surface, it might seem like law and creativity don't mesh. Do you want your pleading to be creative? No. You want it to be straightforward, and if a judge comments, "Counselor, that's very creative," that is hardly a compliment. Nonetheless, I did see creativity in the top partners, as in those who got to make opening statements, which involved the craft of storytelling. Lawyers have also used words to construct new language or interpret existing language, in the process infusing such words and phrases with the force of law. Phrases such as "sexual harassment," "marketplace of ideas," "poison pill," "golden parachute," and "junk bond" are legal creations that changed the landscape in multiple areas of law—women's rights, First Amendment, corporate law.

But in my case, our all-nighters were required not because we were doing indispensably significant work that involved sharp analytical skills or even logical thinking. I couldn't even remember what I was doing those three days and nights beyond mechanically shepherding the commas into the right spot in a sentence or ensuring the decimal point was correctly placed. With a salary of almost ninety thousand dollars a year the first year out of law school, it was expected that we would be available any time of the day. The ninety thousand sounded great, especially when juxtaposed against the mound of law school debt, but not after it was broken down per hour.

There was no escape. In the bathroom, you could still hear your name being paged. I was a word among disembodied words. "Ms. Cao, Ms. Lan Cao, please call so-and-so." Like Herman Melville's Bartleby, who exhibited classic symptoms of depression such as feelings of entrapment and passivity, when I was asked to do a task required of me, I longed to answer, "I would prefer not to." Of course, that did not happen except in my imagination. Of course, in reality, I would rush out and dial the four-digit extension of the caller, who wondered why the task hadn't been done yet. Anything less than enthusiasm for new, interesting work assigned on a Friday to be completed over the weekend would be a career-ending move.

When I became stealthily envious of the guys working in the basement photocopying massive documents, music blasting while they worked, when I grew tired of the weary ruminations about what all this meant, enthusiasm was hard to feign.

To give myself a shot at serenity, I left without any real plan. And then, although I was not actively seeking a clerkship, I discovered by chance that a federal judge who had been my hero in law school was looking for a law clerk. Her name was Constance Baker Motley, the first African American female judge appointed to the federal bench; her amazing life corresponded with every significant moment of the civil rights movement. She had initially been appointed to the U.S. Court of Appeals for the Second Circuit, but ferocious opposition from southern Democrats forced a compromise, and President Lyndon Johnson appointed her to the federal trial court for the Southern District of New York instead.

She was also confessor, interpreter, and changer of American history. Many people who knew Thurgood Marshall might not have heard of her, but she was the singular voice who changed how I saw the law. The daughter of immigrant parents from Nevis, in the West Indies, she was the first female attorney at the NAACP and the first African American to argue before the U.S. Supreme Court, in a win that forced the University of Mississippi in 1962 to admit James Meredith as its first black student. During her two-decade career at the NAACP Legal Defense Fund, she won nine of the ten cases she argued before the Supreme Court and was a key legal strategist in efforts to desegregate southern schools, buses, and lunch counters. She represented Martin Luther King in Birmingham. Her imposing presence as a black woman lawyer was deemed transgressive enough that in Alabama she had to be guarded at night by men with machine guns. Doing desegregation work was hard. The judge even referred to her litigation to integrate Ole Miss as the last battle of the American Civil War. I could hear a little chuckle when she talked about how she lost weight traveling through the South because the restaurants were all white owned and she couldn't find one that would agree to serve her.

Judge Motley was physically imposing and could be intimidating. But through her experience in the civil rights movement, or what I think of as the second American Revolution, I understood, in a new and urgent way that no history lesson could teach, the grainy dualities of win and loss, up and down, give and take, dreamer and realist. Law would always involve both sides of dichotomies. Judge Motley was alive and emphatic and full of stories, and my clerkship was as much a lesson in law as a deep dive into American history. With a twinkle in her eye, she told me and my co-clerk Scott that while working as a domestic employee in the shadow of Yale University in New Haven, Connecticut, she met a white philanthropist who offered to pay for her college and, later, law school education. When she took the train from the North to her college in Nashville, she encountered Jim Crow for the first time in her life. Standing on the train platform during one of the scheduled stops, she watched a decrepit, rusty train being hitched onto the existing cars and was blocked by the porter when she tried to enter one of the newer cars. He ordered her to get into the older car, pointing to the "colored only" sign, which she promptly stole to show her parents.

When she decided to go to law school, her mother thought she should opt to be a beautician instead. And her father was astonished she had such a thought in her head. He was a cook for the infamous secret society at Yale known as the Skull and Bones. The family was filled with gratitude for what Yale bestowed. Just like mine was for the promise of the American Dream.

When the judge applied for a position at the NAACP, Thurgood Marshall had hired her on the spot, even as law firms hesitated, citing client reluctance to engage with women lawyers as the reason for their hesitation. My co-clerk and I had lunch with her several times a week at one of the many restaurants in Little Italy and Chinatown near the federal courthouse. We were like two ducklings following behind her. She always handed her huge purse to Scott, who happily swung it on his shoulder, ignoring the amused looks of passersby, as he and I tried to keep up with her. She was strong in her opinions, such as her refusal to refer to black people as Blacks, which was the term in the 1980s, and insisting on the historical but to us antiquated term Negro instead. When I asked her about using Ms. instead of Mrs., she adamantly rejected the former, telling me that while she was growing up, white women were always called Mrs.

as a sign of respect, and she was referred to as "girl" or "that Motley woman." She insisted on the Mrs. now that she had the power to insist.

But she was no antifeminist. In 1978, when she was a federal judge, she ruled that Major League Baseball must allow a female reporter into the players' locker room.

The judge was an inextricable part of the black civil rights movement. But her family also had what we now call the immigrant experience. It was clearly legible to me in her very identity. In that special wistfully nostalgic way, she and I bonded. Nevis was a British colony. Sugar and slavery developed hand in hand on that island. The judge's parents were from Nevis and spoke English with a British accent honed from their education at the English Standard Schools on the island, and her mother even played "God Save the Queen" on their little upright piano in the parlor. The family's New Haven church was St. Luke's Episcopal Church, which had been founded by free blacks. Their Anglican roots and their perceived British heritage were used by the family to shield them from racism, but she imagined that others probably thought of them and other immigrants from the West Indies as arrogant. The men in the family wore jackets and ties and crisp white shirts with starched collars.

The judge carried herself in a manner that suggested certainly not victimization but rather superiority. Her posture was aristocratic, almost regal, and in the privacy of her chambers, involving no counsel, just us clerks, she presided even when we were engaged in mere chitchat while she sucked on her favorite chewy mint, Mentos. I understood her stories, the pinpoint provocations and uneasy settlement of race and identity. Her father, she said, did not see himself as a black American, meaning he did not see himself as part of the unresolved history of black America.

Judge Motley was sometimes like a mother to me, telling me to stand up straight and act like I was comfortable in my body, like I had the right to take up space, like I didn't have to miniaturize myself. One morning when I was worried about my brother, who seemed increasingly isolated and depressed, she gave me a hug, the heart-to-heart kind, where I could feel her heartbeat against mine. She hugged until I was ready to let go. The judge never initiated a conversation about my immigrant experience or about Vietnam or the war. The right to forget where you come from was a right that was accepted and unquestioned when I worked in her chambers. In many ways, it was a relief. Vietnam came up only if I brought it up.

As a law clerk at the federal trial level exposed to a wide range of civil and criminal matters, I was immersed in the intricacies of real trial practice and doing tasks that have immediate and important consequences. I was not going through mountains of paper for document review or proofreading or rushing to complete "legal research." I saw the law in action, not just on paper. What happens when a motion is made by the parties? How do judges rule? Sometimes, it was straight from the bench. Unless the underlying issue was novel or complex, there was no time to delegate to us clerks to do the research. Other times, we were required to review motions submitted by both parties, listen to their oral arguments, research the law, and draft an order for the judge to review and, hopefully, approve. We were manically busy all day, one of us taking turns staying in our office, doing research, writing memos to guide the judge on the more complicated motions, dealing with the backlog of mostly prisoners' pro se motions ourselves because those rarely got to the judge's desk. The other would be down in the courtroom with her.

The highlight of our clerkship was the opportunity to work on an eleven-week jury trial based on RICO charges that included murder, extortion, conspiracy, and interstate wiretapping. The defendants were members of the Genovese crime family, charged with the murder of a New York City detective and attempted murder of his partner in connection with the operation of the family's gambling and loan-sharking operations. After two state court trials that ended in hung juries, the federal government stepped in and instituted the RICO case. Most murder cases would be heard in state court, not federal court, but because the underlying murder and attempted murder were allegedly committed as part of a racketeering organization that had interstate implications, they were embedded in our case and the federal court had jurisdiction.

Scott and I had drafted jury instructions for the judge, who told us, "Best RICO jury instructions I've ever seen!"

The third attempt in federal court yielded convictions.

WE HAD PRIVATE SPACE AND TIME TOGETHER, the judge and I, even outside the workweek. Toward the end of my one-year clerkship, she invited me to spend a weekend at her vacation home in Chester, Connecticut. Her husband cooked us pancakes and waffles, which reminded me of the first time I had them, along with T-bone steaks, at the American PX in Saigon. Our personal moments together were often hitched to historical ones about America, as she told me stories about the America I had not yet experienced. For example, there was once a beautiful, rich city in Oklahoma where black people were free and owned their own businesses, ran their own schools, looked after their own neighborhoods. A black enclave, like a Vietnamese enclave.

The judge then told me about Dick Rowland, a nineteen-year-old black shoeshine man who in 1921 had been accused of assaulting seventeen-year-old Sarah Page. The shoeshiner was arrested, angry whites congregated outside the courthouse, and rumors of lynching spread. Violence erupted. Whites burned a thirty-five-square-block section of Greenwood, a black district within the city of Tulsa that at the time was the wealthiest black community in America, referred to as the Black Wall Street. Greenwood had an illustrious history—formed and established with the support of and following the model exhorted by Booker T. Washington, who favored black economic independence and separation over assimilation. In this thriving black enclave were black-owned businesses including movie theaters, nightclubs, grocery stores, newspapers, and medical, dental, and legal establishments. The Oklahoma National Guard and the KKK were called in to protect the white districts. Black neighborhoods were scorched. Planes dropped turpentine bombs. White families who employed black workers were also accosted and attacked by white rioters. After the riot, ten thousand blacks were homeless. The enclave was torched and destroyed.

It was usually in the solitude of chambers after the chaos of daily tasks, with her husband sitting patiently on the sofa nearby, that we had our moments together. She indulged my questions. "What do you make of America's brutal beginnings, its continuing struggles, and its promise of inclusion and equality and citizenship?" I asked her. The judge believed in the goodness of America. Her life story and work reminded me of what Bill Clinton said years later in his 1991 inaugural address: "There is nothing wrong with America that cannot be cured by what is right with America." It sounded almost like a proverb that stated a general but profound truth. Any refugee looking at the Statue of Liberty could have said it. Anyone in general could have said it; it almost didn't need to be said. Like a thought without a thinker, or a work without an author. There was a sense of working for change and waiting for it to happen—and knowing that it would.

What good is a promise if it is not kept? In wushu stories, the worth of a person—a revered master, an obedient disciple, a sage of good repute—is measured by the promise they made and kept. But is a promise not kept the same as a betrayal?

No. Because sometimes a promise takes time to be fulfilled. Give a promise the time it needs to make itself right. Because a beautiful promise is still worth more than no promise at all. Because you can remind a country you love of its own professed ideals and promises. You love it because it took you in and offered you sanctuary. You love it because its dreams are your dreams too, its history your history, however complicated, and after more years here than in Vietnam, it has become your home. America is my home, and there is nowhere I want to "go back" to.

AFTER MY CLERKSHIP WAS OVER, I returned to my law firm grudgingly—and somewhat gratefully. The dreamer part of me (hi) who thinks life should be about pursuing your dreams might be disappointed. But my law school debt had not been paid off, and the interest on that debt was almost 12 percent. I needed a good and stable salary, which a huge Wall Street law firm could bestow. Thank you, sort of. For taking me back and casting me into a life of long hours, anxiety, and drudgery. Which I knew I would need to leave soon after returning and feeling my body signal its forecast of dread. Coming and going and returning. A few years here. A few years away. Soon, it had its own rhythm, an internal and quiet play with its own feel of rightness and equilibrium. I was fortunate that the firm allowed it.

I would spend the next year shuttling back and forth from New York City to Virginia to visit my mother, who had suffered a stroke, then another, and finally a debilitating one that left her paralyzed. My parents had themselves returned to Virginia after a move to New Jersey to run a laundromat/dry-cleaning business. The closure of their newest business venture was prompted by the burns my father suffered because of a steam press accident. It was enough. No more pressing, steaming, or ironing.

Loss after loss, financial and physical, diminished my mother, exacerbated her anxiety, and finally paralyzed her. Not long before the stroke, she was almost gleefully scolding me for refusing to accept her gift of gold and diamond jewelry that she'd had Papa Fritz and me squirrel out of Vietnam in 1975. It had been kept in the closet, placed inside a velvet sleeve with little slots, some for bracelets, others for rings and necklaces. But I was never someone who liked to wear jewelry. So I thanked her but said no. You are silly, a silly child, she half chastised, half laughed. And then the next moment, in an almost ghostlike encounter, I received a call from my father telling me my mother was paralyzed from a stroke.

And so the broken last words hanging between us were about how silly I was. After the stroke, she could not speak. She went to rehab and learned how to pick up a peg with a round end and insert it into a round hole. She couldn't tell which way to turn when told to go left or right. And then she could no longer move and lost consciousness until her death a year later.

At that point, it was impossible to tell if she knew I or anyone else was in the room. Visitors were kept to a minimum—only the closest friends and family could visit. In a most moving, memorable, and meaningful gesture of love, an old friend of my mother's from California quit her job, flew to Virginia, and took care of her for almost a year. To be closer to the family, I broke my lease in New York City to move to Washington, D.C., after my request to be transferred to the firm's D.C. office was approved. The only thing I did that felt like it was good for her was sitting by her bed and holding ice cubes to her lips.

Slowly, day by day, she vanished, weighing less and less, her body consuming its own flesh, until she died at the age of sixty-six. I was thirty.

I fled from home soon after my mother's death, avoiding my brother's slow disintegration and consoling myself with the belief that my father was in the middle of an established Vietnamese niche with fifty-plus extended family members nearby. Tuấn had always been the one closest to my mother. She was carrying him when grenades blew apart her bus, and his most profound memories were twinned with hers. She was probably his second self. After her death, he carried her clothes with him wherever he found himself for the week or the month. He lived an itinerant life until he died at age forty.

My father wanted to gift me my mother's jewelry after her death, but the entire velvet sleeve had mysteriously vanished forever. Neither my father nor I had any inkling what happened to it.

WITHIN A YEAR, I took another unpaid leave from the law firm. With the help of a partner who was an American expert on China, I got a modest grant from the Ford Foundation to study emerging market economies and transitional economies—those shedding the strictures of Communist central planning to experiment with the market. History has shown that governmental control of the economy has meant not just economic inefficiency and hence poverty but also a diminishment of individual liberty. I was reminded of a popular saying: In the Soviet Union, everything is prohibited, including that which is permitted.

What rule of law was needed to facilitate the move from central planning to market? The Iron Curtain had fallen and the Soviet Union and its former satellite countries were following the big bang approach, dismantling the state economy and privatizing—that is, selling off—state-owned assets and shares in state-owned enterprises to private individuals. Alas, those private individuals with money to buy national gems were foreigners. All this was done quickly, presumably to prevent Communist apparatchiks from regaining power, but speed, alacrity, and foreign money had also led to other foreseeable problems, like illegitimacy, fire sales, and corruption. Other countries, such as Vietnam and China, were tentatively experimenting with the market, making sure to liberalize only the economic and not the political sphere. State-owned enterprises were privatized, but only so much, to make sure majority shares and thus control remained with the government.

Researching the process of how law can facilitate or impede economic development of poor countries seemed a glorious way to bridge my two selves—the law self, heady and cerebral and rational; and the Vietnam self, heartfelt and messy and emotional. Now I could work from the center out, starting from the depth and unruliness of my personal self and going outward toward rules and logic. For most of the year I spent my days at

New York University School of Law doing the research to prepare for that big event. My goal was to visit law schools and meet and talk with lawyers from the bar association.

Return to Vietnam for scholarly research. Stoking the past forevermore into the present, but this time within the safe parameters of law and logic. And this time, with the death of my mother still raw inside me.

WHEN THE PLANE LANDED IN BANGKOK, it was nighttime and I couldn't afford a hotel room, so I slept sitting up in the transit area after immigration control. I found a corner chair in a nonsmoking section of the airport, which was nonetheless defiantly filled with smokers.

When the plane landed in Saigon, I was afraid. It was my father's fear I was carrying with me. He was worried that something bad would happen to me in Vietnam, now that it had become a complete mystery to us. Saigon was called Ho Chi Minh City, a menacing name pixelated with imminent threat. I saw that at least the airport code was still SGN, for Saigon, which bestowed comfort. In some secret ways, I had begun not to love Saigon, for my own sake, starting in 1975.

I told myself I had never loved it anyway, and it had never loved me. It was not the place that would heal all my little wounds.

We had fled, turning away from it, compensating for the absence with emotional feints by creating fake versions of it in America. Soothing our shame by telling ourselves how the old Vietnam had been beautiful and would be again. Didn't we tell stories about its beauty?

Still, the city had not forgotten me, slyly drawing me by the elbow and pulling me toward it. We were like two gnarled trees—tamarind trees, maybe even banyan trees, the huge, spreading ones—growing twisted beside each other. Here I was, following the city as it coaxed and steered me, step by step, down old streets and boulevards and alleys until my voice, my Vietnamese voice, stripped of English, heard its own echo again, my heart coming out of my body as if it had a life of its own. I saw that I had never gotten away—and I will never get away—from the sounds of this city that loved me and haunted me and taunted me. The fire crickets chirping in the evening. The abrasive, blaring horns of tuk tuks, cars, and motorcycles daring pedestrians to cross into the unyielding flow of nonstop, warring, churning traffic. The mournful-sounding foghorn by Bạch Đằng harbor pulling the evening into itself. The constant, seething begging and badgering for money money money everywhere we went.

Through the crosscut layers of nostalgia and homesickness, I also felt resentment (they won), pity (so many people suffering), remorse (I left), and maybe other simmering emotions I couldn't even name. I only knew I felt the punch of a lot of compacted feelings that I couldn't untangle. I would love to love this city in a simple, straightforward way.

Sometimes lost in my own ramshackle head, I would think, at last, these are my people. I am among them. I felt the inner and outer moments of recognition and acknowledgment and familiarity. Other times, more often than not, I would ask myself, Who are these people with their golden, sunbaked skin? Wanting, grabbing, despairing, shuffling, beseeching, maneuvering. Enduring. And they probably thought the same about me. Who are these people returning to Vietnam? Are you returning to reclaim property you left behind? How much money did you bring back with you? What is your salary in America? How much does your house cost? Questions that were intrusive to me but apparently ordinary to them as they eyed me and other returning Vietnamese.

In Saigon, I stayed with my mother's good friend, Aunt Three, an entrepreneurial ethnic Chinese-Vietnamese woman who once, before 1975, owned a factory that made liquid herbal balms, similar to Tiger Balm, under the well-known brand Nhị Thiên Đường, with its mix of peppermint, myrrh, camellia, and gardenia fruit oils. The factory had been confiscated by the government—not by any single decree but by creeping, incremental action. One day, she said, her general manager was booted out and a new manager was installed, one with no business experience. He had been a buffalo herder in a small village in North Vietnam. Another day, the lock was unceremoniously changed.

Despite my many attempts to refuse, Aunt Three gave me her own bedroom, with its gray blistered walls, as it was the only one with a functioning air conditioner. This was a generous and inordinately unnecessary gesture, especially in the Vietnamese tradition—she was around my mother's age and thus way above my rank. I discovered that my nanny, who was also ethnic Chinese and had not wanted to leave Vietnam, had been living with Aunt Three since 1975.

I was hesitant to cross the boundary and enter, much less take over her bedroom. But I was reminded that what in America we consider boundaries are much more blurred in a country like Vietnam. It isn't that the Vietnamese don't have boundaries, but the line between public and private was different in Saigon. Everything—cooking, washing, eating, playing—spilled from houses onto sidewalks. The outdoor space was connected to the indoor space. Maybe that is why everyone is called Uncle and Aunt, even if not biologically related. Everyone is connected; everything is conditional and contextual, not bounded and impermeable. Even opposites interpenetrate, as in the yin-yang symbol.

So when Aunt Three persisted, I succumbed and, in the end, happily so. I spent most of my time in her bedroom, and the air conditioner became indispensable to happiness in a country so hot. I did then, in 1991, what I had done as a child before 1975. Tapping into a secret place outside the time-bound perplexities of the world, I reverted easily to childhood, taking naps with my old nanny and sometimes even with Aunt Three, thrusting my face gleefully into the cold blast of the air conditioner; even so, I could still feel the glowering heat outside trespass inside. They wanted to hear stories about our life in America, especially my mother's.

Too much stress, they said when I told them about my mother's stroke. The air-conditioned room was where we congregated to lift the siege of heat. How could I have played ping-pong and soccer in this heat after school? How could I not have remembered the laughing, crying, living, and dying that I had seen and experienced in this city?

My nanny wanted to hear about our adventures. Peeling off the layers of my provisional sense of self, I reordered, reimagined, and minimized the tentative paths we followed in America. The outward show of solutions. I told her life had been fine.

So far. For now.

I could tell she wanted to be told that it was worth it for me to be there even if I had become untethered. She wanted to send me off with a blessing. Still, each time I told her about something good that had happened, like my good grades, or the delicious bagel and cream cheese, she closed her eyes and said, "But it could not have been easy."

My first morning in the house, I woke up and saw a bathtub in the master bathroom already filled almost to the brim. It was so hot outside, and the water, though room temperature, looked incredibly enticing. I slipped my body in, careful not to splash or spill any water onto the bathroom floor. After discovering that neither the right nor the left faucet worked, I had no other way of wetting my hair except dunking my head, shampooing it, and then dunking again to wash off the soap.

I later discovered that the tub of water was a reservoir, a storage container for a week's worth of water for the entire household. People washing themselves were supposed to stand on the tile floor outside the tub, scoop water from the bathtub, and pour it on themselves, precious scoop by precious scoop. No one was supposed to jump full-body into the tub. The pump or pressure wasn't strong enough, and so there was no water flowing out of the faucets. To replenish the water supply, Aunt Three had to dispatch a few young men to carry full buckets from the ground floor up to the fourth floor, where the master bathroom was.

There were other awkward moments. For breakfast, Aunt Three had special Vietnamese coffee brought in for me, the kind made with individual filters and filled with condensed milk. I couldn't drink it. It was too sweet. The coffee tasted too bitter. I was no longer used to the concoction. But I couldn't refuse the drink; it would be considered impolite and ungrateful. So I took the sneaky way out—I drank as much as I could and poured the prized drink down the toilet, not realizing that the water problem was not just in the bathtub upstairs. Water flow and pressure were weak for the toilet too. I couldn't flush all of the coffee down, and traces of it remained, requiring me to skulk around so I could flush and flush until everything went down. For days after, I worried that the lingering aroma, the particular mixture of intensely brewed coarse dark roast and the thick glossy sweetness, would give away my secret.

Throughout my time there, to protect against the imminent threat of becoming sick, I took care to eat only fully cooked food and fruits that I peeled myself. I now carried with me the echo of foreignness; my system and its internal biome were no longer accustomed to the local bacteria. But get sick I did, despite all the precautions. I traced my stomach bug to the time when I sipped coconut juice from a chilled coconut bought at a street stand. There was nothing wrong with the coconut. It was probably the straw, which Aunt Three told me later had likely been reused.

The bug kept me home for several days. One evening, Aunt Three hovered near my bed and then squatted down on the floor, prying a tile from the floor and pulling from the hole a portable radio tuned to the BBC. "Ever since the government allowed us to do business, everything looked good, but we still have to be careful. We find out what's happening in the world only secretly," she said, pointing to the radio. She gave me other warnings. "Never say anything about the government to anyone. Good or bad. And if a taxi driver complains about the government, or curses a leader, you keep quiet. Don't make any expression at all, with your body or your face."

Things looked on the surface to be better, she warned. Now people could open their own business; private enterprise was no longer illegal. No one in the countryside was killing their farm animals such as water buffalo for meat to evade government orders to turn them over to the state as part of the campaign to nationalize private property.

I spent most of my days in meetings with lawyers in the Vietnamese bar association, studying the various aspects of economic and legal reform the government called Đổi Mới. The fax had been recently invented, and I would write my father reassuring letters, which were then dispatched by Aunt Three to a corner store.

But the most important, inescapable moment was meeting with Father Five again, the Vietcong uncle who of course had opted to stay behind in Vietnam. The side he was on was the victor's side. He was a family secret—my first portal into the world of secrecy—and we could talk about him only when we were alone. For my father, he was a conundrum, someone who was in name the enemy but who was also family, close enough to my father to warn him of various Vietcong plans to assassinate him.

He looked gaunt and tired, maybe because he had to travel to the city from the little village in Sóc Trăng. And he wore a "Pepsi Cola Welcomes You" cap when we met. Through the puzzling permeability of time, I could see him and his son, someone my daughter later called Ba Hai, almost as two conjoined shadows, walking side by side through the rawness of war that both fought on opposite sides of, one against the other.

I hesitated but in the end went with him to look for my old house. This trip was about seeing and not seeing, looking and not looking. Street names had changed—or more precisely, they had been changed. The only names that survived were names of historical warriors who were considered incontrovertible national heroes. Like the Trưng sisters, who led an insurrection against the first of many Chinese occupations of Vietnam. Otherwise the new names were of Vietnamese Communist figures. Tự Do Street, or Freedom Street, which I'd visited often as a child because it was a main artery in downtown Saigon, became Đồng Khởi Street—Total Uprising.

We found a taxi driver who knew the former names. He took us to my old street, now completely unrecognizable despite its gravitational pull. The tamarind tree that I had carved my initials on was gone. So was the soccer field across from my house, the national police headquarters, the noodle house nearby. I couldn't take Father Five's hand and walk him to any of these places anymore. But I could hug their shadows. From the inside, I recognized everything, the visceral, winking mix of joy, nostalgia, disappointment, and sadness among the churning humanity of the neighborhood. Through the heady mix of suppressed memory and nostalgia, I could point to the corner where my first dollop of ice cream fell from the cone and melted, even if the usual markers had all vanished.

WHEN MY PLANE TOOK OFF, I looked down through the treetops and balconies and pitchfork antennas and took in the aerial view of Saigon. I could see the snaking path of the Saigon River and venture to guess where my neighborhood was among the gossamer tangle of crisscrossing streets.

I felt the urge to rummage for a pen in my knapsack. It was the beginning of a story, unfolding sentence by overlapping sentence. The first line and the last line of an imagined book spilling over me, as if waiting all along to be unblocked and released in nonchronological time. I didn't realize until much later that what I'd felt and done that moment on the plane was actually called writing.

I will never get away from this place. In fact, I returned a few years later, even venturing to Hanoi, for more research on the rule of law and legal education. But it's not about venturing into this or that city. Because it's not the sight or the sound that haunted me and could be consciously sloughed off. It's the feeling that appears, disappears, and reappears, softly floating, sometimes ambushing, suffocating and salvaging at the same time. I still look up whenever I hear the word *Vietnam*—in ordinary conversation, in a wisp of a whisper, or loudly in the news.

Harlan

I am as stable as a dead person's heart rate. I'm not afraid of anything now, at seventeen years old; I wait for Ubers while leaning against suspicious white vans that my mother would call the vehicle of rapists. I have also grown to be very paranoid, but not in an erratic way—more so in an unreasonably accepting way. Not only did I have an incredibly persistent case of hypochondria, but I was convinced that I would have a very violent death at a very young age; somebody would either stab me viciously and enjoy doing it, or I would be put through a wood chipper and all my body pulp would be found in a lake. Once I had decided that this would happen, I calmly accepted it. This might have been because my mother had forced me to watch a movie about little boys being kidnapped and having their feet cut off after I ran away from home at age five. Or maybe I was just a weird kid. Who's to say?

The music inside my head is silent, a symphony of thoughts muffled by an eternal mute button. The cluelessness to my surroundings is apparent in the way it takes me half an hour to notice I'm being followed by that weird homeless guy on the street.

Yet, I could be sitting in traffic on the crowded 405 and look out my window into a patch of bushes and notice the smallest chipmunk, gently maneuvering the ins and outs of a plant's tiny branches. I'll watch it incredibly closely for ten minutes until it finally scurries away. For the rest of the day, I'll wonder what that chipmunk is up to.

And I somehow tune out the fact that I'm not stable at all. My emotions on a graph would look like the sound waves of an ambulance, but my anxiety has manifested itself in a way that stifles my consciousness of the ambulance; the Harlan inside turns up the silent music and pretends the sirens are nonexistent.

But I was not always this way. I used to be apprehensive and frantic inside. I think it was high school that changed that. By the end of all my internal and social confusion during those years, I saw that worrying about what people thought was such a waste of time because it wouldn't change anything—so eventually I just didn't.

I PREFER ANIMALS TO PEOPLE. In order to cope with the situations around me that were caused by classic human resentment, I sometimes turned people into creatures. To me, people were either wolves, bears, or panthers.

My mother was a bear, while I was a panther. I've never met a wolf I got along with.

Wolves are not selective about whom they choose, but once they choose, they form a pack that is impossible to break. Wolves are cruel and only loving to one another.

Bears are strong, but they do not go in packs. They survive hard times like the winter by planning ahead for hibernation—very thoughtful creatures. But they do not understand the other animals because they are in their own world.

Panthers are brooding and for the most part alone. They, to me, are a mix of wolves and bears. They survive by themselves because they feel different.

The very first time I rejected a boy's invitation for a date, he sent me a vicious video of him murdering a bird. There was no context; it was just this eleven-second monstrosity in which he snuck up behind a pigeon sitting on the ground just as it began to spread its wings to take flight. And he shot it. The video ended as the feathers began to gracefully descend to the ground, the corpse lying there. He was definitely a wolf.

The very first time I loved a boy, he did not love me back. I was fourteen years old—just a small, awkward freshman who wore black a lot. He was conceited, rude, obnoxious, and oblivious to what it meant to show care, even though he pretended to. The mistake that I had made of putting all my eggs into one basket, the basket being this boy, was one I had to pay for within weeks of loving him. He betrayed me in more ways than one.

I didn't take very good care of myself after that. I remember thinking to myself every few days, *I've had a horrible week and somebody's gonna pay.* And somebody did pay: I did. I intentionally self-sabotaged. I could go for days thinking so highly of myself: *I hope whoever falls in love with me will be the one I marry because I don't wanna put anyone through the pain of losing me. I'm amazing.* And just hours later, I would have an urge to sit down in the middle of the street and wait for a semi to hit me.

To walk into a room and have all eyes on me is something that I thought I wanted. Since my fourth birthday, I'd wanted to be in the public eye. I danced and I sang in public and begged everybody for attention. But this was different.

I SAW THE WOLVES EVERYWHERE. Every morning as my mom dropped me off at school at eight in the morning, they circled the front entrance. I used to go to the top floor, where there was a balcony outside the library, and when I looked down onto the courtyard, I saw them. Some of them wore baseball uniforms; some of them wore dresses.

Slut-shaming has always fascinated me. There is this common misconception that it is boys who lead the slut-shaming, but it is actually girls. For me, it was the girls who posed naked on Instagram and whose mothers all sat at home doing nothing who would judge me, and I genuinely never knew why. The only thing I had done to them was ignore them. It was like that since the start of high school, and it will be that way until I'm out.

I didn't go to their parties. I didn't gossip behind their backs. I didn't see a reason why loving someone and it not working out was anybody's business but my own.

I knew that I couldn't stay at that school, and that the only way for me to move forward was to transfer. I left in the middle of sophomore year. When I'd finally left, I had a huge epiphany: The less I cared, the more they did. In the beginning, I trusted everybody. I kept to myself, but I was blissfully clueless about the cruelty of jealousy and would sometimes be overly kind: easy prey. To walk into a room and feel embarrassed to simply be alive is something I did for the first two years of high school. I had blundered miserably, and I had to face the fact that loving the wrong person was unfixable. After giving myself to Justin, I was a whore. Before I left that school, I had cut my body, running a razor up and down my thighs a few times every month, and I couldn't even tell myself why; I didn't even cry once. I wanted to feel something. I did not tell my mother until a couple of years after, and even then I downplayed everything.

I remember apologizing to myself and telling myself I'd take better care of myself and I'd stop giving myself away so easily. But an apology without change is just manipulation. Friends who know me well say they find me to be a very good manipulator ("good" doesn't mean the manipulation itself is okay to do). I had so much practice on myself because doing so would protect me from reality, and so I became good at doing it to other people.

RING, RING, RING.

"Yes, Harlan? Is everything okay? How's the new school?"

I had just transferred, and now it was time to face the consequences of the choice I had made to leave midsemester.

"Yeah so everything's good, but um—Mommy? I was just wondering if it's normal for when you get to a new place to suddenly start thinking about suicide for the first time in your life."

"What?!"

I held my face in my hands and whispered, "I'm all alone, Mom."

"Harlan. We need to be strong. I know this past year has been hard, but you need to think about how strong you've been."

"I don't think I can." My voice got even lower as I murmured, "Oh god," and held my chest because I was startled. The lilac cat, whom I still hadn't named, sat inside the white sink in front of me, which was backed by a graffitied mirror. Its eyes were squinting at me, its ears twitching.

I wasn't crazy. I didn't spend my free time petting the air, thinking that I was actually petting a cat. I had never attempted to touch it or chase it or speak to it. It and I both knew it wasn't real.

But in that moment, I saw my reflection in its eyes.

"You know what? I'm good. I'll see you later."

"Harlan, it is normal to be apprehensive the first day anywhere new. Life is about circumventing those feelings."

"Mhm-hmm." I hung up the phone and turned the tap on, pushing down on the faucet. In that moment, I wanted that cat to drown.

"Leave, would you?" I said to it. It wasn't wet. Its ears simply pressed themselves against its head.

The high school I'd attended my freshman and sophomore years was full of wealthy people. They vaped in the bathroom and exhaled into their sweatshirts so a passing guard wouldn't smell the vapor. A small bag of pot dangled under the sink, and it made a reappearance every few weeks, after inspections had been done.

Tampon boxes in the girls' bathroom were disgusting, but they were never more disgusting than the day I found a used condom, torn in half, sitting under the lid. The only time I had seen one opened up like that was when I was eight, at a park. Then again, I had assumed it was a balloon. I'm just lucky I didn't try to blow it up.

Certain sports teams were frats—they practically hazed new boys who joined a team, and they were the epitome of rape culture. Although half of my sophomore class was two grades ahead of the rest of the schools in the district when it came to math, I will never meet a dumber group of people.

And now I was here, in a new school on the other end of the city, with kids whose parents had dropped out of high school, who didn't know the difference between *your* and *you're*. But at least here I could walk down the hallways and be left to myself. No one slut-shamed me for no reason; no one gossiped about me while I stood ten feet away.

But by the time I had escaped the toxicity of the first school, my personality was already completely changed and twisted; I hated everybody.

But I still wasn't suspicious of everybody, the way my mother was. I wasn't paranoid.

Since I was around nine or ten, Cecile had insisted that every phone in the house was tapped, and that even while we were in a locked room, the Vietcong were listening somehow. I had to speak to Mom/Cecile in the third person each time a sensitive topic was discussed. Throwing Communists off track would be the key to survival, according to her, and so we could never refer to each other in the second person, or to ourselves in the first person. I think she pictured all these Vietcong sitting around listening to our supposedly tapped phone conversations, confused and muddled as to who "she" was. She thought that referring to herself as "she" would detach herself from all possible dangers.

Watching her scream, "Don't say *you!*" in the middle of a supermarket after I asked, "Do you think we should get bananas even though they're green?" was horrifying. I felt another part of me just run away, and I watched it scurry out the door in embarrassment. I wasn't sure what to do when she acted that way in public. But unfortunately, my physical self was still standing there in the organic produce section holding bunches of green and yellow bananas, one in each hand, as the entire grocery store watched.

"Shh!" I hissed at her, only to get an "I'll scream again" back.

It got to the point where referring to myself as "Harlan" in daily conversation was more natural than simply saying "me" or "I."

And I was bullied at the first school for it. In a rush, I might have said, "Can you get Harlan's pencil for her?" or "Harlan isn't ready yet." And people who were supposedly my friends treated me as if they were spitting in my face and told everybody I was crazy. I was a crazy slut.

And I think that since the start of adolescence, I'd been waiting to wake up and love myself enough to find the self-control to stop accepting a few moments of thrill in exchange for later heartbreak in a relationship.

In order to reach that point, I had to go through multiple relationships, often abusive ones, and my mother sat there and watched the entire time. She watched me slam the door in her face because I was in a bad mood from being cheated on and not even having the courage to confront the cheater about it; she advised me on how to handle receiving a total of twenty-three love letters from an ex-boyfriend; she held me when I broke down like a dandelion in the rain.

High school relationships sit between that awkward seventh-grade stage where dating is a joke and actual adult love. Everybody is confused and everybody wants to have sex but won't admit that they don't know how. Ninth-grade dating means that you actually have to talk to your significant other, and Bobby can't send his friend over to tell you he thinks you're cute. Bobby has to tell you to your face that he wants to date you, and you have to do more than giggle about him to your friends.

The girls who don't date at all stay close through high school. The ones who are pretty enough to be approached by baseball and soccer and football players grow more and more fake in their friendships. And it isn't their fault. It's just that they and their priorities change, and they soon begin to all look like one another. They all start smiling the same in pictures. They all start dating the same kind of guy.

And when those guys started to like me, I don't think the girls liked that very much.

I was still drawing attention, even though I didn't talk to anyone and continued to dress like a widow in mourning. The reason why I think boys began sending me unwanted pictures of themselves was that my breasts had started to come in. They weren't just these weird lopsided lumps on my chest anymore; they started to take an actual geometric shape.

I wouldn't tell my mother about how uncomfortable I felt walking down the hallway, knowing that as I passed a group of fifteen-year-old boys, my butt would be stared at relentlessly. With all the porn they had started to watch, every girl was fair game. I chose to keep to myself the constant unwanted influx of pictures from random boys who thought they were men. And it wasn't that I wasn't curious about sex or about dating—but the boys were so obnoxious about *their* curiosity that it turned me off of the idea of it completely, at least at that time.

My mother would never forbid me to do something. She doesn't believe in forcefully eliminating anything from my life, except things like cocaine and violence; she knows that taking candy away from a child only results in the child bingeing on it later when there are no rules around. The exception to this was when I was fourteen.

November 8, 2016: The day Trump was elected; also the day my phone was taken away.

February 19, 2018: The day I got my phone back.

These dates are very important, because they mark the start and finish of my downward spiral. The intent of the phone confiscation was for me to have motivation to get my trig grades up—I had a 79 percent at the time, and I was told that if I got it up to an A by the end of the semester, January 20, 2017, then I would get it back.

I ended that semester with an 89.1 percent—only 0.4 percent away from an A.

My mother and Mai thought that not having a smartphone would keep me from "being distracted," but during that year and a half, I got into the most trouble I'd ever been in before, socially. And I blamed the phone—or lack thereof. And I knew it wouldn't get any better. Every time it looked as though my mom was going to come around and give it back, Mai changed her mind.

And my mom was no help whatsoever when it came to my relationship with the male species.

My mother was a woman who spent her high school years completely by herself. She used to call her house phone and talk to her parents in different voices and ask to talk to herself, so they'd think she had friends. How could she ever understand or give advice?

THE PROBLEM WITH MY HAPPINESS IS THAT, to me, total contentment is defined by pure numbness—being 100 percent impervious to pain. I am happiest when I can think of memories that torment me, such as my dad's death—but only *think* of them, without feeling the side effects of those memories. It was like watching a stranger's montage—I could analyze the pictures, but I couldn't feel the agony.

I once told myself that if I stressed about something before or after it happened, I'd pretty much be putting myself through it twice.

When I was fourteen, at the first school, I met Justin, and it was absurd how rapidly the situation progressed, only to rewind itself, like an elevator going up to the sky and then dropping down again. My relationship with him felt like this precious little box swinging from a solid rope, but as the box was pulled up higher, the rope became a thread, and then it became dental floss, and then it became nothing. And the box shattered on the concrete. Justin was my basket, and I put all of my emotions, my eggs, into the relationship with him.

One day I was convinced that he was my first love, and the next day he forced me to shout at him, "I don't want to lecture you, I'd just like for you to see that this is not okay behavior for a friend, or just for a person in general! And I'd love for you to verbally acknowledge that to me! Because there is no need to create drama. I'm not interested in sitting here and crying over you; I'd much rather go home and even do my SAT practice tests than look at your two faces."

He had allowed all my secrets to be unveiled, all our private moments to become public . . . and he had done it all on purpose, because it was what would make him look better. And I wiped away my tears and forgot about his voice because if I remembered it and allowed it to linger in my head, my heart would throb. And it would throb harder thinking he had already forgotten about me and my neurotic self. And I would hate myself even more for wanting him to care about me.

And his only strategy was deflection: "You're acting fucking crazy, Harlan. This is an incredibly immature side of you. Like, what the hell? All you do is blame me when I haven't done shit."

What he didn't understand, and what made him the immature one, is that doing nothing is the same as doing something. When he heard his friends calling me a whore, when he saw a picture of me graffitied with the word *slut*, he should have used the shards of our broken relationship to cut up my bullies, to cut up my slut-shamers.

He just did nothing.

I screamed and I cried. And it wasn't because I had been thrown out of my own feelings, but because I didn't know whether he was genuinely stupid and incapable of taking blame, or whether he knew he was wrong but didn't want to admit it.

I was just a little girl who had convinced herself she was a woman, but after the box dropped back down and shattered, it was as if I was slammed back to earth. And I felt smaller than ever; not even a little girl, but a baby.

I saw him one more time after that. I came over and put my shoes by the front door of his house the way I always had. I climbed up the staircase and giggled at his dog yapping at the bottoms of my feet. I sat on the edge of his bed and looked at the model airplanes on the shelf; I observed every fold in each sweatshirt hanging there. His friend came over, someone from a neighboring school who distantly knew him from soccer. And then more people came over; a small party formed. The friend spoke to me very kindly with a sweet voice and seemed to have smoked a little bit of weed, which relaxed him and made him appear smaller to me.

He picked me up and cradled me in his arms like a baby. He carried my body away from the party and toward another room at the end of the hallway. It had a spare bed in it and a large wardrobe with a full-length mirror on the front of it. He set me down on the bed, which was a lot taller and higher than any other bed I'd been on.

He started to kiss me on the mouth and then took off my shirt. That was fine.

But then he began to push my head down. He grabbed me by the neck and took his palm and shoved me as hard as he could farther south. That wasn't so fine.

I began to realize what was happening and frantically tried to push him off. He was six foot two, and I was five foot three, sitting there vulnerably in front of him while he stood over me and yanked me by the hair.

I pushed him off as hard as I could and ran off toward the door, grabbing for the doorknob clumsily. He soon followed behind, snatching me by the waist and putting me on my knees on the hardwood floor. His hand around my throat caused me to struggle to breathe. I felt dazed, weak, and very small as he forced me back down. I had no choice: I bit it. He screamed and let me go. I remember after that, I slowly got up and returned to the other room, calmly taking a seat on the edge of Justin's bed. Until my mother came back to get me, I sat next to Justin, watching a movie on his computer. I said nothing. Both of those boys had swallowed my spirit and my soul, split open my heart and shared it with each other. Wrecked me. This wasn't how boys were, right?

It took me eight months to realize what had actually happened. The *r*-word had never once crossed my mind. In fact, it didn't sink in until I was lying in my bed the next year watching *The Vampire Diaries*, my favorite TV show. A sex scene came on, and, as odd as this sounds, watching consensual sex on the screen made me realize I had been forced. And no one else knew about it. I felt incredibly detached. I wasn't angry at him so much as at everyone around me who had judged me for being sexual yet had no idea what had actually happened.

After that, I trusted nobody, not even those who begged me to. I knew I was different from others, but it didn't look like that from the outside. For the most part, my behavior seemed the same as that of most, but I found myself working quite hard to appear normal. I now know that if someone appears "normal," you probably don't know them.

My grade went from a 92.4 percent to 90.1, which was close enough to a B that an alarm was rung through the family. I watched my mom fight with Mai almost once a week about what they were going to do with me— how should they parent? How should they deal with this "catastrophe"? My mom had convinced herself that her daughter's heartbreak was ruining her ability to calculate trig solutions and the only way to fix it would be to do *more* trig problems. She had no idea how much deeper this was than simple heartbreak. So, every day, after I got out of third-period English, she stood outside the classroom and took me home. The timing behind this made sense, because the next class I had was with Justin, and there was no way she would allow me to become even more eroded. The rumors just kept going. Some began saying that the reason I went home every day before fourth period was because I had an STD and had to get it fixed.

The most memorable wolf was my best friend, Jocelyn. She and I were inseparable, and my mother loved her because she was basically fluent in Vietnamese, and I think my mom had this idea in her head that if I spent enough time with Jocelyn, I'd come home respectful and fluent also. She probably pictured the two of us standing in front of a stove making pho while doing math homework and talking in Vietnamese about how wonderful our mothers were.

One day someone took a picture of me and wrote WHORE on my face and posted it. Jocelyn was nowhere to be found when I went into the stairwell and cried. In fact, she and I never said good-bye. I just stopped contacting her when I found out she had begun seeing the boy who'd posted it.

Within a month, a girl had claimed to have fallen in love with me. She was someone I had gone to middle school with, but we were only acquaintances until I gave up on Jocelyn. I began to enjoy the feeling of always being wanted, and being inaccessible, just the way my mother was with everybody around her—isolated. The difference was that she, by nature, was like a hermit crab hiding in a shell, whereas I was naturally social but ended up hiding to protect myself later. I had given myself away very easily before and had been torn to pieces. I had kneeled in front of a wolf and offered it food and it bit my hand off and shared it with its pack. I refused to do that ever again.

Nobody truly left my life, because I either wanted someone and couldn't have them, or it was the other way around. I enjoyed being chased, just as I actually enjoyed the agony of being ignored. It was very rare for me to experience a relationship of equal effort, of balanced commitment—of mutual love. I'm sure many other people my age felt the same.

This girl and I were very much equal in terms of caring for each other. But I was incapable of telling her that I wanted to be with her, and also incapable of telling her that I didn't. I was simply silent. I kissed her. But I still don't know if I did that because in a way, I wanted to be fluid, or because I actually wanted to. That year, 2018, everybody was suddenly bisexual. I thought I'd give it a try.

I am not bisexual, though. And she was. And so we both moved on. I very quickly found somebody to be with, a boy who sacrificed everything for me. I left her behind and yet also took her with me.

"I'm really beginning to feel like you're the hardest thing to deal with. Sometimes you can be really disgustingly cruel and even perhaps possibly mentally ill, but regardless of that you're probably the love of my life and my fucking soul mate. So thanks a lot for that," the girl once said to me. And all I could do was stare at her.

I am nobody's soul mate, I thought.

Mentally ill *is a strong term.*

Each of my friendships was like an unfinished project. My mother had never taught me how to make friends or how to keep them. Instead, I noticed how loyalty was too important to her to be forgiving of those who didn't love her as much as she did them.

But she did like the girl who claimed to be in love with me.

And I became just like my mother. One by one my friends began to fail to meet my expectations, and I had to come to terms with the fact that maybe my expectations were too adult, too high for people my age.

In the end, I wasn't kicking them out. They were running away. And if the lampposts could've walked, then they would've left me too.

I expected people to have adult relationships that resembled those in a beautiful Woody Allen movie, but these people were just kids. Half of us couldn't even drive yet.

I would focus on one person, one single relationship, for three months. I would think of only them, until the fabric of my head and my mind turned from velvet to silk. And they would do the same, until they disappointed me in some way or another. Somehow, nobody was good enough and nobody could keep up with my intensity.

The only people who didn't leave were the ones I didn't pay attention to. This girl loved me, and I put my energy into somebody else. As my devotion to a new boy began, her devotion to me grew. As I entered new relationships, she waited.

I was just like my mother now. I loved people *because* they loved me. And my mother had taught me to value myself, because she was the first person I had loved other than myself.

My mother and I were never closer than during that year, between freshman and sophomore, despite how hopelessly tumultuous and disastrous my personal life was, and how awkward our own relationship might have been at times.

"Do these jeans make my butt look okay?" I asked her once.

"Yes, Harlan," she said in a huff.

"Well, don't look at me like that as if you're thinking, 'Oh my god, my daughter cares too much about what people think. Who is she trying to impress?'"

"Well, I wouldn't say 'who,' I'd say 'whom.'"

My vanity had reached an all-time high, but in hindsight, it was all just compensation for the fact that I had fallen so deep into a lull of depression that I didn't even care anymore who used me and who didn't.

My most vivid memory is of the day I lost my virginity. It wasn't something I lost, but something I totally gave away. And it was not given to Justin, thank God, but a boy a bit older. Even then, while lying there on my back experiencing this transition into something that was foreign and monumental, I thought, *He's definitely a bear.*

And afterward, he leaned in very softly and murmured, "I just wanna make sure you know that I care about you very deeply, and I mean that." Any other girl would have breathed an internal sigh of relief, grateful for the fact that the boy had at least cared enough to reassure her she wasn't being used. But I could not have cared less at the time. I dismissed him quickly, saying, "You really don't have to say that. I know you feel like you might have to, but you don't."

"I'm very much aware you have emotional intimacy issues, Harlan Margaret Van Cao, but I won't allow you to push my feelings for you away. Now, put on your damn seat belt," is all he said.

I didn't have the energy to entertain such an intense partnership when I barely had the energy or common sense to take care of myself. I was a mess. My emotions resembled a ball of yarn unraveled and mauled by the purple cat that had followed me my entire life, for reasons I'd never know.

By junior year, I wasn't even capable of knowing what a healthy relationship was. A lot of girls look for their fathers in boyfriends and measure relationship health according to that, but what did I really have to go off of? How well did I really know my father?

After changing schools, I began seeing a boy named Michael. Before him, I don't think I really understood what it meant to be more than simply infatuated with someone and mistaking it for love. There was no mistaking my love for Michael, and he was the only one who took that and preserved it and kept my love safe and sound. He had curly hair the color of chestnuts, green eyes, and nice lips. He was obsessed with sports cars and had way too many pairs of shoes. Michael was the safe space.

But my happiness was short-lived.

My father was dying. The week leading up to his death was when I felt the numbest. My mother slept on the floor next to his bed for ten days before he died in his sleep.

He was in a coma, yet completely awake. He couldn't physically move but his brain was running at all times, as if it were spelling out lines in the sand, drawing a beautiful pattern as an indentation in my own life. Sitting next to him, waiting for it to be over, was a long-distance relationship— loving someone and never being able to reach them.

"I'm sorry I didn't tell you how proud I was of you every day the way you did for me, even when you didn't know enough about what I was doing to say it. You were proud of me even when you found out about my mistakes."

By the time I told him I loved him, all he could do for me was squeeze my hand.

January 29, 2019, I woke up for school to catch zero period at seven o'clock. Every day I would do this, and every day I would see my father lying there, asleep, the red color rushing up into his cheeks and through his body, keeping him alive and full of the passion that had made him so successful. That day, he was just white. No color.

To see a corpse, white and cold, a marble counter of death, is a perplexing sensation. When the corpse was my father, there was no sensation. There was nothing. I felt the pain behind my eyes, the water going down my face, but nothing in my heart. That day, I felt both of us die, one before the other; one physically, and one emotionally.

That day, Michael and I listened to the Beatles and he watched me weep and began to weep too.

MY MOTHER USED TO CHOOSE WHEN I GOT TO BE AN ADULT. When I fed my dad pills at night when I was eleven, I was an adult. When I watched Mai viciously murder her artwork and stab her paintings to death in the hallway of my home when I was six, I was an adult. When I carried my mother's body away from a tree to keep her from climbing it and possibly falling and put my hand over her mouth to keep people from hearing her say, "Put her down *right now* or she's gonna scream, Harlan," I was an adult.

I think that many times, No Name would come out and not even announce herself. Sometimes in my teenage years, during fights with my mother, I would bring up times when No Name had actually caused great suffering for me, and at that point, No Name herself would come out and refute everything I said. But for the most part, when my mom acted too defensive or had fleeting moments of overprotectiveness, I had a sense it was No Name.

But whether or not my mom was on board, adulthood was coming my way. At the start of ninth grade, I started my actual growth spurt. Boobs, butt, blood, everything. And I wasn't ever left alone. The boys stared at my breasts as if there were three of them sitting on my chest. They all drew penises on the bathroom stalls, which I saw when I wandered in there with friends several times after school.

Snapchat—everybody had it, everybody used it, but only a small number of girls in the school got what I got out of it: an uninvited intro to sex ed. These girls had to be relatively skinny, with mostly clear skin and nice clothes, and all the boys with mostly clear skin and nice clothes would send pictures of their penises to the girls, whether they wanted them or not (it was usually the latter, unless one of the girls wanted a picture to keep and use against the boy later).

I remember my first picture. A boy who had started a conversation off with, "Hey, what's up?" had ended it with an uninvited image of what looked like a mushroom. I hadn't really seen a boy's thing since I was six in Vietnam. *Obviously penises are solely for function, not decoration*, I thought, and shut my phone off.

I giggled to my mother about it the next day. She was my best friend. It was still hard for me to make friends in California, even though I had been there a couple of years. I had a few good ones, but none of them really understood me. This doesn't mean that my mother did, but she came closer. She didn't giggle back. Instead, I got a lecture on what counts as sexual harassment.

I discovered mascara that year. I wasn't very good at makeup. I watched a video on YouTube and began to line my eyes with black quite aggressively. My skin was pale, because I never went to the beach. I stayed home a lot and watched Woody Allen movies and pounded on the piano keys at the most random moments. I continued to resent the idea that I had to practice piano.

Practice for what, exactly? No one practices things they enjoy. I've never heard someone say, "Gosh, I need to go practice riding my bike." Sure, you learn how to ride a bike, but once you've got it, you do it because you love it.

I went to school every day with my mascara and pale skin and eyeliner. I spent time between each period staring at myself in the mirror next to all the other girls doing the same, and I saw a face of freckles that got darker as I got older, and a huge nose that would be ugly on its own, if it weren't for the other big parts of my face making up for it, like the cheeks and the eyes. While I stood there, with the girls all readjusting their bras vigorously and putting on deodorant, I got another picture. A dick pic. It was overall a very successful day.

Trump was elected two months into my freshman year. At first, he was a joke. Boys would wear huge "Trump 2020" flags as capes around school, ironically. But when it came down to the country being run by Hillary or Trump, it wasn't a joke anymore.

I already knew where the school stood on the issue, because even though California is blue, Orange County is as red as blood. "I'm voting for Trump because he's hilarious and better than that criminal," was the main comment going around, and I kept thinking it would never actually happen. He couldn't really be elected, right? What would that even look like?

And then he was. I will never ever forget the night of the election, because my dad was sitting in his chair that was good for people with bad backs, and he looked at the CNN election tracker very calmly while I sobbed hysterically on the floor. Mai was upset at him for voting for the Independent Party. He had read so many books about Mussolini, and he had said so many times before the 2016 election that Trump's tactics harked back to those of Mussolini's.

"You are *throwing* your vote away, my god, Bill," she went. He just looked at her and sipped on his ginger ale through a straw from McDonald's that was probably saved and had gone through the dishwasher ten times because of my mom's orders to his nurses.

So I went to school the next day and entered a sea of red hats bobbing through the hallways. I felt numb, and I felt sorry for my dad because I knew he had worked for a lot of things, he had taught a lot of things in law, and he had done it morally. He was a moral person. He had worked with Justice Ruth Bader Ginsburg when they were both at the ACLU to get the Equal Rights Amendment ratified. He'd worked on voting rights in the South. And the last president he'd see would probably be this guy.

I began high school when it had started to become clear my father was dying. I sat in my room, directly above his, and cried over boys while listening to ABBA. I walked past his bedroom without giving him a second look and went upstairs and wrote my thoughts on my wall and on the wood on my desk, but I never shared them with him. He asked for them, but I never did.

My dad was perfect. My dad was better than everyone else. He was a Van Gogh painting—like a beautiful thing that sits on the wall that I passed by too many times without acknowledging. Now that the painting is gone, the wall is empty. And I'm depressed.

He grew up kicking a can through the streets, fistfighting his older brother over comic books, and picking peaches off of trees. It was the 1940s. How could I tell him? How could I possibly tell him that as I got older, I only became more confused? More unhappy? That every time I looked at Instagram, I saw the girls at school posing in swimsuits with boys who called me ugly but for some reason still sent those pictures to me? That I was a pineapple in a bowl full of freaking watermelons, and no matter how hard I tried, I'd always be spiky and sour? That still, at fourteen, I didn't know how to make friends?

Coincidentally, around the same time he passed, my self-esteem improved. The universe had taken one of my biggest loves from me and replaced it with a love for myself. I began looking in the mirror and seeing the facial features he had given me and thinking that I was actually beautiful. I became more social. The day before his death, January 28, I had gone to the beach with a large group of friends and there was a girl there whom I had heard of and seen around sometimes but had never talked to, Jules Phang. That day, I became much closer to her, and after he died, I think I thought of her as a guardian angel. Because she was so bubbly and social herself, I tried to become that way too.

Michael took me out more and showed me parts of town I had never been to. I even threw a Halloween party, and invited many people from my old school. It was very satisfying when I let everyone come except Justin. And that was the news of the century during the weeks leading up to it. When people saw Justin was barred, they all became afraid they had done something I considered unforgivable and began apologizing profusely for things from the past in order to avoid being excluded as well. That's how fake people can be. Then, when the day came, in the middle of the party, a girl from my old school clumsily stumbled over to me and whispered something into my ear I will never forget.

"Harlan . . . you are, like, so pretty. You're so fucking perfect-looking and just like—look at your house. So big. And your brain is huge. Why do you think we were all weird around you and were assholes?"

After that, I felt as if this olive branch had been extended, but I still didn't go to their parties for a while. Michael encouraged me to try new things, to try to make amends so that I could finish my little journey of finding closure. But he was still very protective of himself in ways I didn't understand at the time but do now. Even as he helped me be more open, he kept his distance. He didn't bring me to any parties where the people from my old school would be; he never even offered. I knew that a part of him didn't want to be seen with me because it could hurt his social life (apart from that one party I had at my house, which was different because

I was the host and he played the part of cohost). He told me the reason was he didn't want me to become like the other "drugged-out, desperate" girls who got drunk three times a week—even though those girls were the ones he always seemed to be around. He reminded me of how I had my heart set on a top university, how I had a career in writing coming, and how I had a family that I could not disappoint. But I knew that wasn't the real reason.

Even when things ended with him, they never really did. My mother and Mai seemed to adore him. It was impossible to leave him completely because I knew too much about him. I knew "Maxwell's Silver Hammer" was the Beatles song of his childhood; I knew his favorite toy when he was a kid was Hot Wheels; I knew he was never really into Legos but did make one Lego building in the form of a police station and jail; I knew that when he ate a meal he'd either have to mix up all the food on the plate or eat one bite of each type of food equally; I knew he had hopes of taking over his father's real estate business and greatly expanding it; I knew he had dreams of collecting black and white sports cars—Porsches, McLarens, Corvettes; I knew he couldn't stand to spend moments alone because he'd become depressed.

I think he saw me as a blessing and as a curse. I was beautiful to him: fun to take naps with, fun to laugh with, unique, smart, open. But I was also perhaps the most confusing and the biggest carrier of baggage out of all the girls he'd ever been involved with. And he had been involved with quite a few before me, and I'm sure some during his time with me. I loved him so much that at one point, even when I had a sneaking suspicion he was cheating on me, or doing something close to it, I didn't confront him. Even when he was right there next to me on the couch, I couldn't bring myself to say anything to him because I knew he'd probably become defensive and whatever he'd say wouldn't be able to satisfy me. So I would get up and go to the bathroom and turn on the tap and cry. I felt he was becoming tired of me—not bored, but resentful. We could spend the whole day together, in which my family would pay for all his meals and give him tons of Christmas presents, and he could go home that night and text some other girl from school. I don't think he knew that I knew he did things like that. But I did know.

On the other hand, as my first love, Michael was close to perfect. I called him one night, two months after we had officially broken up, and asked him to come over and help because I was positive I was going blind (it turns out I had just spent a little too much time on the phone and my eyes had become light sensitive, harmlessly). He came over and held me and stayed there for four hours. He was also the most intuitive boy I had ever been with when it came to small needs of mine. He always took my side.

But he also told me he found me to be selfish and superficial. He said I had bad taste in men, and that most of the boys I had been with before him were quite horrible. He said I was book smart but not street smart. He said I was reactive when I shouldn't be and not reactive when I should be. He said I was becoming my mother. He was right about all of these things.

He and I met just when I was really finding my passion for writing. Our relationship, whatever that may mean, brought me out to be more social, and with that came a new sense of confidence and bravery, which I'm sure has deeply influenced this story. Everything that comes with me—this intensity, my complex relationship with my mother and her dark shadow ghosts, my baggage from the old school, my regrets from my relationship with my father—spilled onto Michael when he and I became close. I'm sure it was a lot for him to handle—it sometimes may have even been a burden. But somewhere along the line, he must have decided it was at least somewhat worth it to be with me in whatever capacity we were together; and so I will love him forever, even when we probably go our separate ways for university.

I heard once from a wise person that if a love of yours doesn't bring you tears of either joy or sorrow, consider that time wasted. It most definitely wasn't.

BUT DESPITE THIS PROGRESS IN MY SOCIAL LIFE, I was still quite peculiar and paranoid by nature. My hypochondria continued to worsen every day, it seemed. My period had been irregular, oddly so, and I went to see my pediatrician, who recommended iron supplements.

"Do you know where to get stuff like that?" she asked.

"Yes, I can go to Whole Foods and get them . . . and so can Harlan," I replied. She stared at me with a perplexed look. I coughed.

"My tits—uh sorry, my breasts. They're very bumpy when I squeeze them," I said.

"And you're worried about cancer, I'm guessing," she huffed.

"Well, yes."

"Harlan. You're sixteen."

"Ten percent of cancer patients are teenagers and someone's gotta be in that ten percent," I said, but I felt ridiculous as it came out of my mouth.

"Show me where the lump is."

I lifted my shirt to reveal the left one only, and pointed at the large *X* I had made with a Sharpie.

"Jesus," she muttered, and put on gloves and began to feel around.

"Do you—do you feel it?" I asked, after ten seconds of this awkward silence where her fingers pressed into my lumpy breast and my legs dangled off the edge of the examination table and I wondered how well they cleaned these tables and if they actually changed the paper sheet on it every time a new patient came.

"Nothin'," she said, shaking her head.

I scrunched my eyebrows together. "That's because you're not feeling the exact middle of the *X*—see? I've checked on the lump every day since I felt it a week ago."

"You've been babysitting your lump?" she laughed. She didn't do it to make fun of me but because I guess this constituted strange behavior. I laughed with her because it felt like the right thing to do.

When the silence hit again, I realized I was acting stupidly, as if I actually wanted cancer. *If the doctor said there was nothing then it is okay, Harlan,* I said to myself.

"You don't have cancer," she declared, and took off her gloves. I shrugged, and was about to ask her about the ringing in my ear and the hallucinations but decided against it.

"Why are boobs so heavy?" I blurted out, and then cringed at myself right after.

"I don't know. Some aren't, others are. Your body is preparing to feed another little human."

"Is it genetic?"

"Sometimes," she said. "They don't hurt your back, do they?"

"No, but they are quite heavy, you know. I weighed them but I can't remember now—"

"You weighed them?"

"Yeah, one at a time. They're definitely different. I always felt the left one was bigger and more aware of her surroundings, you know?"

"Uh . . ."

"Well, it was nice to see you, Dr. Padner."

"Always so good to see you, Harlan. Give my best to your momma."

"I shall."

I went back to the waiting room to meet my momma, a beautiful little tan woman with black hair and pretty lips.

"Hi, Mommy." I smiled at her. Today was a good day. No breast cancer, although this wasn't the first time a doctor had to reassure me of this.

She just looked at me and chewed on her lip. She was disgruntled because I had insisted she wait outside. It just didn't feel right anymore, to have her and all the other moods of hers in the examination room with me while I asked someone to inspect my breasts, although she had seen them many times, from strolling into the bathroom uninvited despite the door being shut, etc.

"Was it good?" she went, with that tone.

"It was fan-fucking-tastic."

"*Harlan.*"

"I'm sorry! I just found out I don't have cancer, so."

She rolled her eyes into the back of her skull and tapped me on the back of my head. "*Shhhh!* Don't say that! Do not put that energy out into the world."

"M-kay . . ."

"I sent about five or six very helpful articles to you about exactly what Ivy League schools look for in applicants. Did you read them?"

The thing about that question was I already knew that she knew I definitely hadn't.

"No."

"Well, that's okay. It's just your world, Harlan, and we're all living in it, aren't we? Just ignore all of the helpful things I send, which by the way were published by the *New York Times*, if that matters to you," she went on.

"I'll read them when I get home, all right?"

"It's not for me. It's for you."

"Thanks."

"You go around gallivanting with Michael, and I like him, I do; he's a very sweet boy. Good, good boyfriend. But he is not a replacement for your future!"

"I didn't say he was."

"Your behavior *implies* that he is."

"Oh."

"I hate to tell you this," she said as she turned on the ignition, "but other than your book project and your unique writing abilities for essays, there are other children who have a four-point-eight GPA and a top SAT score. You *must* research and prepare and strategize to get ahead."

"Everyone knows that kids who sit there doing soccer and somehow also doing freakin' chess club and walking shelter puppies and being head of the debate team are just doing it for college. It looks way more ridiculous than focusing on your passion. *One* passion, which in my case is creating art," I said. I knew I sounded arrogant in the last bit of my sentence, but I meant to. I wanted to get a reaction out of her at this point. I was in a good mood and she had to crush it.

"Those kids are well-rounded. Nothing ridiculous about that," she replied.

"I'm so confused. You know, like, we're all told it's good to know what we want and to go for it. And here I am . . . you know—going for it. Writing a damn memoir at the ripe age of sixteen. And now I'm being told, 'Oh god, you're not gonna get into a good school unless you act like everyone else and act like you don't know what you wanna do with your life.' I *do* know, and I'm showing it by pursuing a passion. If I show up to university and claim to want to write novels and maybe one day . . . you know, scripts and stuff, but they see I spent most of my days cheerleading, then what's the point? Hitler showed a passion, *one* passion, for being an asshole and hating Jews, and look at the impact he made upon this earth. You've never read a history book that said, 'Young Adolf wanted all Jews demolished but he spent his free time giving speeches about equality.'"

A silence settles over the car before she says, "What are you actually talking about? I can't follow. You're saying you want to be Hitler?"

I let out a long hard breath. "Okay, the Hitler thing might have been a bad example. I'm just saying that there's nothing wrong with showing focus on one thing."

"No one knows what you're trying to say. Ever, really," she hummed.

"Well, there's another thing we've got in common, *Madre*."

That night when my insomnia decided it would be a good idea to ruin my sleep schedule, I was startled by a phone notification from "Birthgiver," my mom, who was supposed to be sleeping in the next room.

First was an image of schoolboys on a staircase, all holding their arms up and out in front of them.

3:34 a.m.

Harlan. This is an image of a class of boys all doing the Heil Hitler salute. Look at the right bottom corner. Only one boy is refusing to raise his arm. Be that boy.

Lan

After my first trip back to Vietnam, I returned to New York City restored and replenished. I was still immersed in the world of Wall Street and its fetishizing of efficiency and productivity measured in segments of billable minutes. But I began to make time to write—not legal briefs, but the start of some other, very different kind of writing. I couldn't find stretches of free time, so I wrote in spurts, carrying a yellow pad and pencil with me everywhere. When the subway was stuck between stations, I used the delays to read and write, insulating myself from the unsettling chatter of the daily commute. My lap was my writing desk. I had a view, a moving view of crowded platforms, turnstiles, revolving doors. Vietnam was like the faraway moon, distant, dimmed, but paradoxically almost within arm's reach.

There was no master plan. I already had years of thinking about what had happened to Vietnam, to our family, and to the Vietnamese, North and South. To the millions of refugees who fled when peace came. The many whys and hows of it all. Our edited version of the American Dream and of our refugee lives. I wasn't writing a historical document, but history permeated everything I wrote. There was nothing to research. All the materials I needed were already faithfully inside me.

I had no goal or destination. I just let my story unspool, like dreaming with my eyes open. It was the opposite of wearing a mask, the opposite of molding the face and body to fit the masquerade. English was now my language, and it was big enough to accommodate my intuition. My years of prowling the public library had shown me that despite stacks of books about "the Vietnam War" from a multiplicity of perspectives that included those of American politicians, generals, soldiers, veterans, and antiwar protesters, there were hardly any that reflected the experience of a Vietnamese, much less *the* Vietnamese.

As Bertolt Brecht said, "War is like love; it always finds a way." In many ways, writing is the same. Writers always find a way to write.

I gave myself the gift of writing without expectation.

That was how I began my first novel, *Monkey Bridge*. In Vietnam, I had seen these slender bridges made of bamboo poles peasants had tied with ropes to cross rivers. Crossing these bridges requires the agility and nimbleness of a monkey. It was an apt title because it captures so many kinds of crossing—going from a place of war to one of peace, old country to new country, refugee to American, division to wholeness. I had no formula in mind. I was only writing, drawing from a whirling darkness that was mine, letting characters emerge, seeing what struggles, internal and external, would follow. Out of this came the narrative and plot. But with no top-down plan, I had nothing to be busy for, no schedule to maintain, no order to impose. I wrote when I felt the muscular flexibility of mind and heart that called for it.

The process was nothing like what I had adhered to in high school, college, and law school, or at the law firm, when my days were disciplined by a gluttonous excess of to-do lists and the drill and drum of deadlines. Instead, I let myself roam, though still in a controlled, leashed sort of way, into my many half memories, waiting for me as if they had been perched nearby all along. It felt like the right time to retrieve the gray abandonment of old memories and to write, to recount the sunny but also the rainy stories, a natural follow-up to my return to Vietnam. I was tapping into the least articulated part of myself, the part I already knew but didn't want to know. Writing brought me back to the eternal oblivion of childhood, back to my love of stories, like those in wushu novels and movies and *One Thousand and One Nights* and even the English novels of my high school years; back to the textured backdrop of imagination and magic. I was entering the world of light and shadow, melodies and countermelodies, where history itself, so porous and fractured, is prone to invasion. To my surprise, I had somehow stumbled into a sort of writing life.

I told no one, not even my father, what I was doing. A part of me felt treacherous writing about our experience, as if I were appropriating and expropriating part of their journey and in the process unmasking all of us. And in our refugee world, where conformity meant survival, writing seemed the opposite. Remembering instead of forgetting. Drawing attention to the self and parading our experience instead of blending in inconspicuously. *Monkey Bridge* would tell our story, in fictional form. Oscar Wilde said, "Be yourself; everyone else is already taken."

Writing, even if only in fictional form, nudged me closer to my many selves in America.

Our love for America, maybe like any love, is complicated. I wanted to show this in my book, which I thought of as a kind of love letter to this country that people dreamed about, even if it can be chaotic and dysfunctional and treacherous. We are not here simply by accident of birth or biology. We are the ones who dismantled our lives and risked it all to come here.

But it wasn't just my family I hid my writing from. I told no one, as if it were my dirty little secret. A part of me felt slightly preposterous, self-indulgent, and even fraudulent. Who was I to aspire to write any-thing? Who in America would care to read our stories? Ours are just ours, tangential and particular. I couldn't imagine that we would even register, much less be a presence in the American imagination. And if we somehow registered, it was more like a little pebble or a protrusion in the sidewalk that made people trip. Only then would they turn back to look at what they hadn't seen. Isn't this what I myself wanted—invisibility and erasure? And perhaps even more damning, the project felt comical, ludicrous, even de-lusional on a purely personal level. I felt like an impersonator masking myself as a writer.

Writing is an act of both masking and unmasking. It's also like falling in love. It makes you want to pay attention and listen.

I eventually shaped the book into a mother-daughter novel that re-volves around a mystery about the disappearance of the grandfather in 1975 when Saigon fell. I wanted a story about Vietnam that would show it off as a country with a more than thousand-year history and not just a twenty-year war that was, worse, relevant to the world only because of America's role. I wanted a book about Vietnam through Vietnamese eyes, not American eyes that diagnostically scanned us for weakness and loss. As Orson Welles put it, if you want a happy ending, that of course depends on where you stop the story.

Even as late as 1989, almost fifteen years after the collapse of South Vietnam, the sad story never stopped for us. An American captain of the USS *Dubuque* was court-martialed for leaving a boat full of refugees adrift. Deeming their vessel seaworthy, he did not pick them up and instead left them food and water, which ran out after two and a half weeks. There were four passengers near death who were killed and eaten by the fifty-two survivors.

By now the world was suffering from boat-people fatigue. The *Dubuque* was a minor story sealed off like a ship in a bottle, visible but inaccessible and separate.

For us, our story didn't stop but continued to a sad, fatal end.

I knew nothing about the exotic world of publishing. And ignorance was a blessing; it helped to have a beginner's eyes because if I had done my research, I might not have even tried. But my foray into this blissful new world began unexpectedly and fatefully. I went to the beach in East Hampton, New York, plopped myself on the sand, and watched the waves. Close by was a brown-haired woman with a friendly demeanor, smiling face, eyes bright and alert, having a good time, reading a magazine. We started talking and she introduced herself. She told me she was a literary agent, which meant she represented authors; it was her job to sell their manuscripts to publishers. "I just finished a novel!" I exclaimed without meaning to. I was embarrassed by my spontaneous response. Everyone with a half-formed book probably told her this. I told her what the book was about: Vietnam, the war—from a different and neglected perspective—and the duality of immigration and Americanization, and to my surprise, she asked to see it. I thought it was lucky for me that she had been an anthropology major in college. She was someone curious about culture. Someone with skill and empathy and desire to enter a different world to learn, not to judge.

When I finally connected with an editor, I felt comfortable and believed this story mattered to her. It mattered because she realized it was a story that had not been included in the American cultural and historical production of Vietnam. And although yes, I was grateful to have found sanctuary in this country, gratitude no longer meant servitude or obedience or silence.

When my book was published, I felt like I had given birth to a child. Not in the same way as giving birth to Harlan because the book is not a live, interacting, obstreperous being. But the process of creating the book was like birthing and raising a child. There are oppositional arguments, self-doubt, wrangling and maneuvering to find the right path. The Chinese have a saying about crossing the river while groping for stones. The book has its own ideas and its own desires that one either gives in to or tries to tame and redirect. When reviewers complimented the book, I felt like a parent whose child was being complimented as well.

I never found out if my father or anyone in my family read it. Consistent with his laconic ways, my father never mentioned either my writing generally or *Monkey Bridge* particularly.

As I talked in bookstores around the country, most of the audience were people for whom the Vietnam War was their rite of passage. It was not uncommon for the war itself to be debated at my readings, as the audience used various passages from the book to spin their perspectives on the war—whether it was winnable, whether the United States should or should not have been involved, whether it should have given up and pulled out as it did, whether it was an imperialist power no different from the French, whether the antiwar movement was wrong or right, whether Hồ Chí Minh was a hard-core Communist or a nationalist whose Communist ideology was but a means to achieve independence from France, etc. My novel deals with politics, but it is not political propaganda. I also wanted to talk about nostalgia and the search for home, however problematic and imperfect; the American Dream, however problematic and imperfect; and the quest to assimilate as a necessary but painful process that is sometimes the equivalent of self-mutilation—letting go of, eliminating, or even murdering a part of yourself to become a transformed someone else.

Even though my book was about Vietnamese refugees and the war and our journey out of the country to America, the wider narrative arc that we could not escape was about America and its own Vietnam trauma. America was framed as the father, the hero who left home to save the world, only to have his dream shattered by the pitiful war that wasn't even won. And when he blamed everything on the pitiful people he tried to save but couldn't, lo and behold, he found them now suddenly nearby. Right in the neighborhood. Maybe that was what my math teacher Mr. Wendell was about.

America can be both sweet and bitter.

ONCE, I SAW A PAINTING of a horse eating an apple with the title *It Just Fell into My Mouth*, and this is how I think of my transition from law firm practice to legal academia. It just happened. I was living in my beloved New York City, working at my law firm, and suddenly I heard that Brooklyn Law School had an opening. I decided to apply for the position. It was like buying a lottery ticket.

Brooklyn Law School's appointment committee, which evaluates applicants and makes recommendations to the full faculty, called me in for an interview. I was fortunate that one of the members had also been a clerk for Judge Motley. The committee invited me back for one full day of interviews. At this point, everything seemed more serious. I needed to come up with a "job talk." In legal parlance, this means a presentation with a coherent idea, a theme, setting forth a problem, maybe providing a solution or at least a theoretical framework in which various approaches could be offered. As a practicing lawyer, I had only clients' problems and interests to deal with. There was little overarching normative or theoretical context in the daily work of a lawyer. But I quickly came up with some ideas that sounded plausible enough, drawn from my practical work negotiating and drafting joint venture agreements for investment in China. Why are some countries able to attract foreign investment, which brings with it hard currency, jobs, technology, and managerial transfer, and others not? Why are some countries rich and some intransigently poor? Is the post-WWII international trading system oppressive to poor countries, or does it provide an opening for the poor global South to leverage itself into a higher level of economic and political development? Why is the U.S. dollar the top-dog currency among the other hard currencies of the world, considered as good as gold, even though it is just printed paper? This was an academic way for me to restore the past and circle back to Vietnam.

I had enough to make a presentation to the faculty. I could tell I would get a job offer, and I was right. Soon thereafter, the dean called me to make an offer to join the faculty. My area of research would be emerging economies, international trade, public international law, corporate law, and international business. It was an ideal teaching package, with just the right combination of practical courses that focus on the nuts and bolts of business and courses that are more open to debate about policy and theory.

I had never thought of entering the legal academic market. I never knew how slim the prospects were and that there are many more applications than positions available. Like a sweet apple, it simply fell into my mouth.

TEACHING IS CONSIDERED A NOBLE PROFESSION IN VIETNAM. I was happy to be a teacher. I had control over my time. And I realized what is most precious in life are exactly the things money cannot buy: time, health, love, and friendship. My parents had told me that if a problem can be solved by money, it's not a real problem.

I now had time—and control over my time—to do what I loved, teaching and writing. I was publishing my articles in law reviews. I was on track to get tenure. I loved the art of teaching. I was not just imparting information to students but teaching them to think—to spot the salient facts, identify the relevant legal rules, apply facts to rules, critically analyze, and then beyond that, assess the law from a broader policy and normative framework.

And then another apple just fell into my mouth. My friend Amy Chua, then a law professor at Duke Law School, was due to take a research leave. She recommended me as a visitor and I ended up at Duke for a semester. It was 1998, the year Bill Clinton was impeached. One of the star professors there, William Van Alstyne, who had written a landmark article on the landmark Supreme Court case *Marbury v. Madison*, was invited by the Senate to testify.

I went into the law school on a Saturday to work on a draft law review manuscript. Bill was in his office preparing for his Senate testimony. He wanted to know what I was working on. I told him it was an economic analysis of rotating credit associations used by many immigrant groups to create community capital for community investment. To my surprise, he asked to read my draft article. I told him I would email it to him later.

"You can do it now," he insisted.

"Shouldn't you be focusing on your testimony? Aren't you scheduled to appear early next week?"

Bill was like water—powerful and fluid, taking his cues from the current and the wind, from nature itself, not fixed or defined by any one point. He was always flowing. He turned his attention to my article and sent me three single-spaced pages of comments the next day. I asked to read his testimony, which was filled with references to *The Federalist Papers* and various articles and clauses in the Constitution. When I watched his actual testimony, which was televised live, I realized that the live version was purely extemporaneous. It did not resemble one iota the written, prepared version. It was eloquent and brilliant. The *New York Times* editorial page quoted from it, urging the Senate to adopt the position Bill had advocated.

That was my first encounter with Bill. He was smart and considerate and generous. He lived his life expansively. Like water, he smoothed over my scars easily, without fuss. Water has no problem with jagged or damaged rocks.

When I returned to New York after the Duke hiatus, we made our relationship work despite the long distance. I decided to make a big sacrifice: leave my beloved New York City, my heart's home since losing Vietnam, and move to Virginia, to become a tenured member of the faculty at William & Mary Law School, which was only a three-hour drive from Duke. Williamsburg is a tiny, colonial city vastly different from New York. It is also the place where Harlan was born and raised until we moved to California. And it is the place where I watched, as if through a portal to the past, the live picture on television, not of South Vietnam, but of the twin towers falling, falling, on September 11, 2001. Because I have a bad sense of direction, I had often used the towers as a geographical marker, the way people use mountains to help anchor them and provide them with a sense of place. When those towers tumbled down, I felt like I had lost my mountain too.

Harlan

I still find myself relying on shutting off all my emotions. I find that it keeps me from being hurt and feeling rejected. My mind is an octopus, which sometimes falls asleep and doesn't think at all in order to protect me but then sometimes wraps itself around people I'm infatuated with and doesn't let them go.

When it's awake, each of the eight legs thinks differently. The first two are the reason I tried to hand my boarding pass to the guy at the airport and ended up somehow throwing it over the counter into a trash can six feet away. They make me clumsy.

The other six consume me, wrapping around my entire being to suffocate me, black ink spurting everywhere. One of them holds me every night and helps me to sleep. The other one holds my best friend, Jules, and helps me relate to her. The next one reaches out to my mother. Sometimes she reaches back. The next one helps me cope with all the little miserable things that life offers me, like SATs, or funerals, or flowers at the grocery store that are dyed weirdly, or mosquitos and buzzed haircuts, or rings that rust on your fingers and make an annoying green line. When it comes to funerals, I can't go to them. I laugh and offend everybody who doesn't understand that it's a coping mechanism.

The next one is a morbid weirdo.

Here's what I mean by that. I remember being in Uganda to trek for gorillas and looking out into a nearby field, seeing twelve planks of wood sticking out of the ground, with another plank crossing each one. They looked like the cross Jesus was crucified on. Underneath each one sat tiny little labels with scratchy writing on them, weeds growing over. *That's a cemetery*, I thought to myself. *Everyone died here and now they are stuck under the ground in little boxes. If I ever woke up in a little box because people thought I was dead and buried me, I'd take my fingers and scratch myself until I broke my skin and bleed out so I wouldn't have to deal with waiting for the air to run out.* Then I realized that one of the labels read "parsley" and that it was a garden, and I walked away. The same tentacle also forces me to sleep on my stomach or my side. I don't trust people who can sleep on their back so easily. Aren't they afraid someone will come in the middle of the night and slit their throats, all exposed like that?

The last tentacle has sociopathic tendencies. It can't relate to people at all. It sympathizes but cannot empathize. It watches very calmly with large eyes, watches all the people go by crying and laughing together at things it can't understand or identify with.

I realize that my mother has tentacles too, only most of hers are like my last one, and this is why I've always felt she's so out of touch with the world and so unable to relate.

We were at the dinner table. My mother was holding a knife, slicing into a mango ruthlessly. The knife was released with a clang as she sucked on the mango aggressively, staring at me and squinting.

"I'd like you to explain to me why your physiology test came back today as fourteen out of twenty-three. Are you aware that that is a *D-minus*?"

I stared back at her and curled my toes up. "As I have explained to you, any online test can be retaken up to five times, Mom, okay?"

"But why does one need a retake at all? The first time should be perfect."

"Well, it wasn't. If I take it once and get a bunch of stuff wrong, I can still see what is on the test and use that memory to know what to study for next time," I said back. Mai was as silent as a bat is blind while this exchange happened, the light glimmering off her forehead, which I'd always found adorable, but now it bothered me, with the entire thing wrinkled and furrowed while she listened.

"That's stupid," was all my mom said, turning to Mai with the knife between her fingers again.

They talked about me in Vietnamese, using all the words I could understand. All the words you could use to describe someone as incompetent, or lazy, or difficult, or dumb. They called me all of them, as I sat right there.

"I don't know if you two are aware of this, but it doesn't matter what language you speak in; it's rude to talk about someone while they are sitting right there, especially when the words you use are verbally abusive." I looked down.

My mother scoffed, "I'd hardly call this abuse, Harlan."

"Yeah, well, you wouldn't, since you've seen people without eyelids dying during the war, but you can still be hurt when you see your mom talk about you like that even though you're doing your best."

"You can't even understand Vietnamese," she laughed. Every chuckle ignited a new tiny spark in me, my chest swelling with anger.

They both laughed together—cackled, actually. Did they think it was really a joke? I could understand everything they said, because they used all the words you could use to make another person look bad. And all these words I'd heard since I was a baby.

"Do you ever stop?" I muttered.

"In Vietnam, we would be smacked if we ever talked back to our parents that way, Harlan."

"And that is why I am very proud to be an American, Mom."

"Good for you."

"Thank you."

"Completely *facetious*," she whispered, but it was the kind of whisper where you just know they want you to hear it.

Facetious, as I remembered from one of our arguments two years before, meant "scorning serious issues with humor and the incapability to take anything seriously," according to her.

"You could use a different word that's less obnoxious," I whispered back, purposely mimicking her weird tone. In these moments, I despised the thought of her getting the last word, especially when the argument began with her pointing out a flaw of mine, which I felt hadn't even existed to begin with.

She just shook her head disappointedly, as if thinking to herself that she had made a mistake in having only one child, because maybe if she'd had two, the other could be better than I was.

"I'm just gonna have Jules pick me up; you don't have to take me to Tyler's."

"Fine, if that's what you want," she said with a shrug, returning the keys to the front dish.

"It is," I mumbled, and plucked the orange lanyard off its place on our doorknob, along with the rape whistle, a large orange offensive plastic thing I'm forced to carry because it's attached to the house key. And I had to take the house key, because the door automatically locks itself due to Mom's idea that we could be robbed during the day and held at gunpoint. I stepped outside and pondered my next step. I had not thought anything through. In my mom's head, I had a ride to Tyler's. But Jules did not know she was supposed to come get me now. I couldn't drive; I just hadn't had time to get my license. I had turned sixteen and was working on this book; I had to study every day after school for four hours for the SAT and took the test four times. So, while everybody else got their licenses, I worked. I figured I would get mine later, while they worked. Not to mention the fact that I was not a good driver, from what I could tell. My control over the wheel was fine, perfectly adequate, but my right foot and its idea of when to hit the gas and when to hit the brakes was definitely not.

"Jules," I hissed into the phone.

"Yes?" I could picture her cute little chubby cheeks turning up into shiny apples as she smiled, the happiness evident in her voice. She always sounded as if she was grinning when I called her.

"I am standing at the park across from my house and I need you to come get me."

"I thought Lan Cao was taking you."

"Well, no. I'm now trying to make a point, so I'd like you to come get me," I whispered lowly, as if I was worried Lan Cao herself was lurking behind me.

"Um—why are you talking so weird?"

"Can you just come?"

"Yes, god," she laughed, and I wrinkled my nose a little. The patch of freckles on the middle of it crinkled to form a small brown cluster of frustration. Rude.

"This is no laughing matter. It is ten p.m. and I can see a crackhead wandering towards me, so let's make haste."

"It's a little funny. You need to address a big issue. I don't know what it is but clearly if you choose to stand in the park at this hour when you could be inside the house and face your mother, then there's something weird," she sang, giggling a bit.

"Stop laughing. I can't stand *facetious* people."

Three times that night, my mother called me while I was out. Cecile got on the phone and attempted to persuade me to return many times. She claimed that my mother was sorry for the way she had acted, but I refused to come home until curfew—if she was so sorry, she could tell me herself. But she didn't.

Cecile knew things were more harmonious now; we all got along. There were no more attacks and she seemed to need me more. When I got older, I'm sure she was confused about what to do—I was too old to play, but I wasn't too old to take care of her. She was small and calm.

IT WAS EIGHT P.M. THE NEXT DAY, and Jules and I were supposed to meet Michael and Kaleb at Kaleb's house over an hour ago. But there we sat, with the sound of crickets chirping, peering through her car window at the sight of the keys . . . which she had locked inside.

She took the bridge of her nose between her pointer finger and her thumb and furrowed her eyebrows.

"Do you want me to get my mom? My house is right there," I asked.

"No, no, no. I'm just . . . gonna call my brother," she whispered fright-fully. I didn't understand at the time why she was so afraid. She'd made a simple mistake, and it happens to everyone, doesn't it? "I—I'm such an idiot."

"Dude, do you know how many times I've left my keys in the house? That door locks automatically. I just call my mom when I need help with it," I told her.

"You aren't afraid?"

"Afraid of what?"

"Getting hit."

"I'm sorry, *what*?" I didn't think I'd heard her correctly.

"Or screamed at?" she murmured. Her voice became incredibly low. If her tone was a person it would be a tiny little child, in the fetal position, holding itself gently . . . or maybe a dainty rocking horse, like the one be-hind that shop window I always used to pass when I was a baby.

"Why would I be screamed at for making a mistake?"

"Because it is a stupid thing to do."

"You're calling me stupid for leaving keys inside my house?"

"I'm calling *me* stupid. You're pretty and perfect."

"Jesus Christ, Jules."

"What?"

"You are pretty and perfect too," I said. I had met her just three weeks before. I had only become close to her because my boyfriend Michael's best friend, Kaleb, was interested in her. Now that we were friends, I started to become seriously concerned about her self-esteem issues.

"No. I'm dumb."

"Okay. Enough of this. Do you have spare keys?"

"They're at home." A tear rolled down her cheek.

"Call your brother, and ask him to bring them to you."

"Stupid, stupid, stupid." She dug her nails into her left arm, as some sort of self-punishment, I guessed. Her hands were long, her fingers thin and slightly crooked, her skin soft like the moon. Sometimes, when she was asleep, I'd put my hand next to hers in envy. I'd compare her fingernails, which were beautifully shaped and long, with mine, which were bitten down and attached to chubby baby fingers and a tiny fat hand that got dimples in it anytime I picked up something as simple as a phone.

"Let's call Kaleb," I offered her, and we sat there on the curb bickering back and forth for five minutes, when Kaleb himself called us.

"Hello?" she said.

"Yeah, where the hell are you guys? Are you comin' or not?" His deep voice resonated through the phone.

"Y-yeah, we just had a slight holdup," she giggled, biting on her ring fingernail.

"What kind of holdup, Jules?"

"Uh—well. I locked my keys in the car."

"Of course you did."

"Can you come pick us up? I'll deal with the keys in the morning."

"Uh—hold on." There was a long pause, and I heard him go, "Mike! The girls are idiots and we have to come save them," and then a whole lot of background chatter.

I finally took the phone from Jules and said, "You know what? It's okay. We're gonna fetch the spare keys."

"Are you sure?" Michael asked, after being handed the phone. "I mean, I'd come get ya."

"No, because if you do that, when Jules needs to go home around midnight, you'd need to drop her off back at her car at my house and we're gonna have to figure it out then, and that's even worse."

"Okay, babe. See you soon," he hummed.

I went through Jules's contacts to find Avery, the brother closest to her in age.

"You have to pull yourself together," I said, putting her phone into her left hand, "and stop abusing yourself."

She raised the phone to her ear. "A-Avery? C-can you bring me the spare keys?"

They continued back and forth for a few minutes as I sat on the curb, holding my head in between my knees. I watched a little beetle's journey over some dead leaves in the gutter intently.

"I—I will pay you," she offered, which confused me, because he is her brother and he shouldn't need to be paid in order to help his little sister.

She hung up the phone and we moved toward the park, about a hundred feet from my house and from where the car was parked. I slouched my leather jacket off and put it on the picnic table closest to the road, and lay down on it, closing my eyes.

"Why are you not more panicked?" she inquired, standing awkwardly by the stop sign.

I didn't answer her. I just waved her over closer to me, and she came over, her stomach level with my head, which rested on the table. I took her pointer finger and wrapped my hand around it.

"Enough with the scratching."

"What scratching?" She cocked her head to the side. Did she not know that she was doing it?

"Forget it." I forced a smile, and held on to her finger a little tighter.

"So you're not like . . . worried to ask your mom for help when you forget your keys?" she inquired.

"I mean—I don't *enjoy* feeling her glare at me when I'm just trying to move on with my day, but . . ."

The truth was I knew that if I came back into the house and asked for help it would just be this rigmarole where Cecile would frolic down the stairs and laugh at our stupidity.

"You're very peculiar," she mumbled softly.

The sound of a car approaching loomed, and she swatted my hand away quickly, stepping off the curb into the street. The tinted window rolled down from the passenger's side and revealed a tiny, severe Vietnamese woman. She looked me up and down for a good minute and glared at Jules.

"Hi, Mom," Jules whispered.

I was already confused. I remembered vividly that on the phone, she had told Avery to make sure her mother didn't find out about this. So why was she here?

"Xe ở đâu?" is all the woman said, her tone short and strict.

She had asked, "Where is your car?"

"Over there." Jules pointed to the red Lexus, which was shaped like a ladybug, by my house, and the window abruptly was sent right up, the car rolling over to hers.

"She's pissed," Jules said, coming over to me.

I looked up from my spot on the table and brushed my fingers through my hair. "Well, she should get over it. As if she's never forgotten something in her life."

Jules didn't answer. I watched her follow her mother's car to my house and I saw the window roll down again, the keys being flung at Jules from inside the car, the side of them hitting her in the face.

"Về nhà," her mother insisted, and words of hostility were thrown back and forth before the car sped off, a puff of rage following it.

She had told Jules to go home, and had clearly been shut down.

"Let's go," Jules said to me.

"Why did she come?"

"She listens to our phone conversations and heard me ask for help, I guess," she said.

"So she came to punish you?"

"Yes." She put the key into the ignition and headed toward Palm Avenue.

"You don't find that extreme?"

"She told me we look like whores, sitting there in the park."

"Uh?"

"And she said I can't hang out with you anymore because you're wearing a shirt that shows your shoulders."

I looked down at my tank top, which totally covered my belly button and my cleavage. All that was showing were the tops of my shoulders and the three little moles that had been on my chest since I was a baby. Jules was wearing the exact same shirt.

"She thinks I'm low-class or something?" I asked.

"Yes, but don't worry. I'll still hang out with you." Her lip quivered only a little, and her eyes were still wide. I let it be.

Five minutes passed by before she said, "She told me that if I wasn't hanging around whores in the park selling drugs, I wouldn't have lost my keys."

"*What?*"

"Yep."

"Where did the drug-selling accusation come from?"

"From the fact that we were waiting for her in a dark park," Jules said, nodding, as we pulled into Kaleb's driveway.

We had been sitting there on the couch with the boys for just half an hour before she received a phone call from her father, pleading with her to come home. Her mom was apparently "distraught" with worry.

"Worried about what?" I scoffed.

"She thinks I'm here hooking or something with you," she muttered. "I have to go home now. Can Michael give you a ride?"

"Yeah, yeah, just go." I gave her a hug.

She called me the next night, telling me that when she arrived home, her mother had been waiting there in the garage for her. She slapped her across the face and slammed her keys onto the ground, then confiscated them.

This was the difference between my life and hers, when it came to our mothers. I would never have been afraid to ask Lan Cao to bring me spare keys and to admit I had screwed up and locked mine in the car, but Jules was. She out of her mind with fear.

After that, I don't think we ever misunderstood each other again. Seeing Jules's life with un-Americanized parents gave me an entirely new perspective.

THREE MONTHS LATER, my family took Jules to Catalina with us, with her mother's permission, and we were there all day together. When she returned home that night, she received a very confusing reprimand from her mother, out of the blue, and was told to never see me again; her father told her he couldn't do anything about it, because it wasn't up to him if her mother had convinced herself that we were in a lesbian relationship.

I don't judge close-minded people. I don't think it's their fault, and I actually feel really sorry for them. It must be the saddest and loneliest thing in the world to have been raised in a way that you end up *choosing* to scrutinize your daughter for what kind of person she loves.

My great-grandmother, in Vietnam, had eight children, and when one of them was born in a zodiac year "incompatible" with hers, she gave him to the gardener to raise, in the servants' house, only a few acres away from the rest of the family. And when he grew up to be a traumatized and confused man, attempting suicide a handful of times, the family had to go down to the morgue to confirm it was indeed he who had intentionally overdosed. He popped up from the tray his supposedly dead body was lying upon, and turned out to be very much alive.

It was not anybody's fault. Nobody wakes up and *decides* to be that way. Just like that suicidal, slightly deranged uncle of my mother's, whom she called Father Eight, didn't decide to be that way. He was once just a tiny Vietnamese boy who happened to be born on the "wrong" day.

Now, I don't know what Jules's mom's excuse is for being the way she is, other than that she stayed in Vietnam twenty years after the Communist takeover, so she's definitely a tad behind on America realizing gay people deserve rights like straight people, or maybe she's just behind on civil rights in general. Not that Jules is gay; I can confirm she is incredibly straight based on all the times we've sat together on shopping mall benches and stared creepily at boys.

I love Jules so much that she is the only person, apart from a few other best friends and Michael, whom I would be willing to be completely selfless for. When I witnessed someone doing something to hurt her, the way Kaleb ended up doing, I had to sit on my hands and fight to keep myself from strangling him. Often, I could lie to anybody at any time over anything and feel nothing inside, but if I tried to lie to her, my lips would curl up into a sickly smile and give me away because I loved her so much; there was no option but to be honest with her. My internal strings felt so connected to her by our culture and had yanked me toward her. She was selfless and told me many times she only wanted to help people and found herself suffocating under a pile of that selflessness, which often drove her to allow herself to be walked all over. I spent days with her undoing that pile, while she often did the same for me. In general, I could go to sleep at night soundly and easily, no matter what tragedy was happening in my life—and then I'd wake up and lie and say, "God, I couldn't sleep at all, couldn't stop thinking of [insert troubling event here]. But with her— *her*—I truly couldn't function or sleep if I sensed she was hurting. Because I felt the hurt too. And it hurt more that I couldn't take her hurt away.

HUNTINGTON BEACH IS A TOWN OF STARFISH towel hooks in house bathrooms and signs on foyer walls that say things like "Family Rules: Love each other, pray every day together, always put God first." The only signs I had in my house were made from the back of old coffee-stained law reviews and black Sharpie, saying things like "Take off shoes," "No shoes upstairs," "Keep trashcan away from wall—it will scrape," "Don't put too much toilet paper in toilet," "Don't move the security camera, Harlan."

I remember when we first moved to California, going to so many book readings. When Mom's second book, *The Lotus and the Storm*, came out, she did interviews and events. There was one particular interview that I knew really bothered her, when they asked only what her opinions were on the political fabric of the Vietnam War. They asked questions about the previous presidents of South Vietnam and the Communists, and then they asked the same question everyone asks, one that always makes her close up like a clam.

"How much of this book is based on your real life?"

Her answer was always vague and short. She'd look at me and then her eyes would dart around the room, but she'd still appear quite calm. But I would know. She was erratic inside.

And then we'd go home and lie down next to each other. Her hand is always so small, even though it's bigger than mine. Her fingers are light and bony, thin and pale, but very nimble from pounding on the piano every day and typing and brushing my hair out. When she falls asleep, her lips part, and she snores very lightly. Even when she's asleep, she speaks to me. Even when we fight and I leave, I lie next to her from far away.

———

I'VE NEVER PUT ANY THOUGHT INTO MY GRADES. What I mean by that is I have never really tried to get As. It may have been because what I was learning in school was nothing compared to what I learned at home, in terms of culture, math, music, and literature. But getting As was something that kind of just happened. A part of me wishes I had to struggle a lot more to achieve what I did, because I've realized now that I don't truly know what it is like to struggle or build myself back up, other than mentally or socially. The way my parents raised me has made me almost naturally book smart and emotionally intelligent, but not smart in the world. I know all the ways I could die in my own home, yes, and I have seen and experienced all these different human relationships, but what do I know about failing? Not much. I grew up in an eight-thousand-square-foot house, with life-size stuffed animals and tailored clothing. I watched my mother's heart bleed from the inside out, and I watched my dad disintegrate into nothing but an urn of ashes. I had a purple cat follow me through the school halls, where I felt the most isolated. I sent in my application to Berkeley and then finished my first book. This life isn't meant to be a race. It is meant to be a long, slow dream of perfect confusion, loneliness, deep friendships, and ambition. I'm ready.

There are thousands of people we see and know, thousands of songs we hear together, thousands of words we write, thousands of voices we listen to, my father's among them. All of them are us.

Lan

Maybe because my husband and I were older parents, I wanted to create a lot of memories for Harlan. I took many pictures of her and with her because I love photos, but also because I wanted her to have photographic memories of us when we are gone. I wanted to simulate permanence for her because impermanence was always looming. There was a vein of melancholy in this undertaking.

There were photos of milestones, such as the first day of school and the first swim in a pool, but I liked snapshots of ordinary moments as well. Will she remember the playhouse she had on the little hill in front of our house in Virginia? Will she remember my father, her grandpapa? I took her to see him as often as we could, and took many photos of her with him. Each time I confided in my father about some rebelliousness of Harlan's, he would brush it off and warn me to not push her too hard, an admonition completely out of his character and antithetical to how he had pushed me.

We also wanted to raise a child who was globally aware and cosmopolitan, and so we started early taking her around the world. These trips tended to jolt us out of the normalcy of everyday life. I grew up in a culture that saw land and country as sacred. But I was not a nationalist. I teach international law and all things international; there is an immeasurable difference between the "purity" of nationalism and the "mongrelization" embedded in internationalism. I know the rhetorical and legal devices international lawyers have had to come up with historically to tame and temper the dangerous passions of nationalism.

So Harlan took her first international trip at age five. At that age, everything was new and she was still absorbing the world without the filter of judgment or criticism.

We picked a Mediterranean cruise, which involved a manageably scaled flight to Italy, staying a few days, then embarking on a ship with port stops all over Greece, Turkey, and Italy. The ship was a self-contained vehicle, big and stable and safe, like a giant rock on land.

There were so many things Harlan absorbed just through our travels, which were easier to impart when we were traveling than when we were staying at home. Forcing some of these lessons on her at home would have likely to led to tantrums. But the excitement of the trip and the unfamiliarity of her surroundings made her more open to experimentation. Each trip had some parts that were just for her or that she picked. In Barcelona, Spain, for example, it was going to the ocean or watching street performers on La Rambla. For us grown-ups, in every city, it was going to museums and art galleries. She learned to adapt and accommodate us, finding things to like or entertain herself with when we got to a part of the vacation that was not centered on her. She had never been a picky eater, and going abroad made her more open-minded. None of us were willing to eat crickets, but our unwillingness was a personal choice. Eating crickets was just something some people in different countries do. Meeting people with names we couldn't pronounce was nothing to laugh at, especially since we were in their country. Same with meeting people who spoke English with a foreign accent, which showed they came equipped with another language we probably couldn't speak.

Harlan has been to all seven continents and almost fifty countries. Whenever Bill and I had conferences to attend or speak at, we took her and created a vacation out of the work trip.

She also carried her violin with her, and I was so proud to see the case slung diagonally across her little body, its soft contours pressing against and superimposed on her cute little compact self. When she was five, the violin case was almost as big as she was. As she grew, so did the size of the violin and the size of the case.

One day, on the eve of one of our vacations, Harlan announced she needed a break from the violin. A part of me wondered why. Her teacher had praised her touch, her intonation, her artistry, even her sight-reading ability, and all this flair and skill with hardly any practice at all. If I made her practice, we would fight, and the rapidity with which the fight escalated confused and shamed me. I could hear the strings played off-key; I have perfect pitch. She would insist no, it was correct. I relented, succumbed, and stopped commenting on any aspect of her playing, hoping my silence would give her a sense of freedom and love of the instrument. I even left the house when she played either the violin or the piano. But I feared the day would come when she decided to stop.

And so it was not a complete surprise when that day did come. For the first time in a long time, she went on the plane as we headed for summer vacation and had only a carry-on suitcase. No violin. Which I had always thought of as a portable piano, exquisite, almost a sanctuary away from the vicissitudes of life. Imagine being able to carry music that you make yourself with you wherever you go. But she had given the violin eight years, and it was not bringing her joy. Joy, of course, was the goal here in America. Piano drills never brought joy for me, but there was so much to tangle with that once completed they always did bring a sense of hard-won satisfaction. And now, of course, the piano itself does finally bring me so much joy, and I am thankful my parents didn't let me quit. But I let her quit, and right away I felt like a failure of an Asian mother.

I was not the kind of mother who raised or could raise, through the enforcement of implacable rules, a stereotypically successful Asian kid. But it was a struggle. I let Harlan quit and held my regret inside my own body even as I could feel the freedom in hers.

When I commiserated with Bill, he tried to soothe me by making his face sad-looking, but I could tell he did not share my consternation. No auxiliary support would come from him.

In fact, he was fine with whatever she chose to do. He was a professor of constitutional law and nationally known as a First Amendment expert. Somehow this led to Harlan believing even as a toddler that she had constitutional rights in the house, particularly freedom of speech. He was a philosophy major in college and reveled in philosophical and psychological complexities and nuances, whereas I was more interested in bright-line rules where a child was concerned. Bill was not Asian, was not a refugee or an immigrant, had no anxieties about failure as far as I could tell, liked risk taking, and saw life as something fluid, to be discovered and savored. I worried about this kind of approach to parenting. How could we ensure she would achieve excellence if she was allowed to make her own choices? When I complained about his hands-off, laissez-faire approach, Bill would point to his children from his prior marriage. All three were academic superachievers, schooled at the top Ivy League colleges or their equivalent, relatively happy and normal.

Still, I couldn't just let nature or his side of the family history take its course. While Bill liked to show his motorcycle off to Harlan or have her help him strap a helmet-wearing teddy bear in the passenger's seat (the teddy bear was his regular motorcycle companion), I spent time fighting with her about things like the multiplication table, spelling, grammar, and values to absorb such as delayed gratification, hard work, and persistence. Mai was a high school math teacher in Canada, so she was in charge of teaching Harlan math, everywhere, whether at home, on a beach vacation, on a cruise, or on a plane flying us to a new international destination.

I showed her YouTube videos of the famous marshmallow experiment that focused on children's experience of deferred rewards. "What would you do," I asked her, "if you were told you could have a marshmallow now but two marshmallows if you waited for ten minutes?"

She quickly replied, "Where are the marshmallows while I have to wait?"

"In front of you," I said. "You would be alone with them."

She was silent for some time, looked at me intently, and then said she would wait, but as she grew older I suspected she gave that answer because she could sense it was the one I wanted to hear.

I ALWAYS WANTED A DOG WHEN I WAS GROWING UP, and my father furtively got me Topaz because my mother did not want a dog in the house. Topaz was my beloved pet until I had to leave him behind, so when Harlan asked for one, I said yes. Of course, Bill said yes too. He too had had many German shepherds. But both Harlan and I had developed an allergy to dogs, so we ended up getting a standard poodle, a hypoallergenic breed.

Harlan was only five years old when we brought Figaro home. She was strapped in her car seat. And he lay in her arms, quivering. On the way home, she made all kinds of promises to feed him, groom him, clean his food and water bowls, and walk him whenever he needed it, however long he needed it. He was black and had curls all over his body. We kept him clipped like a lamb and did not give him the stereotypical poodle pom-pom cut, which we thought would make him look silly. Standard poodles, after all, were originally working or hunting dogs, and their webbed feet made them especially suited for retrieving waterfowl.

Figaro was sensitive, eager to please, and eager to be trained. His first night, he was in a crate, and when he whimpered and emitted soft little barks, I shushed him and immediately he stopped. Harlan left our bed and went into the crate to sleep with him, dragging her pillow with her and sharing it with her new friend. From that day on, the two were bonded and inseparable. He was known by many endearing names. Sir Fig. Figgy. Fig. Figster. One name didn't seem enough for a dog so beloved as Figaro.

Figaro was also very smart, and not especially obedient. He knew "come," "stay," and other commands, but would first look up when he heard the command, and then, I could infer from his facial expression, decide whether it was worth it to obey. But thank God for Figaro, because he always made things fun. When Harlan practiced violin, he made funny sounds when she played a high note. At first we thought his ears hurt because they are sensitive and can hear all kinds of pitches, and I would drag him out of range, but he would insist on coming back and being next to her, happily and softly whimpering. And then it occurred to us: He was enjoying the violin, immersing himself in the singular power of music. This observation delighted Harlan. She grinned so widely, even her eyes smiled. And even when she rebelled and talked back sassily, I could see only the disarmingly sweet curls of light brown hair that framed her plump face.

It was Bill, to my surprise, who started Harlan on the piano. He had bought a piano lesson package offered by a student on behalf of the student public-interest organization. It was for a good cause, as proceeds go to help cover expenses for law-school students who opt to go into lower-paying public-interest law jobs. The piano is more forgiving than the violin. A beginner can play a simple song and make it sound better on the piano than on the violin. But whether she was playing the violin or the piano, Harlan had a tendency to gloss over mistakes instead of returning and doubling down to correct them. So mistakes would be made over and over, at the same place in a song, month after month, because she had not untangled the segment that tripped her up.

"Wrong chord," I would say.

"Stop telling me what to do," she would fire back.

Neither carrots nor sticks, praises nor threats worked. Nor did sermonizing. Well, these strategies worked in a limited way. They might get her to do the deed for that short-term time span, but not for anything beyond that. I could not stop the broody moods or the furtive, dismissive glances. Nor the conclusory declaration, "You have no idea what you sound like, Mom." Or if she felt she had gone too far, she would say, "You have no idea what you sound like, Momma," to soften the derision.

If Bill overheard our bickering and fighting and mutual provocations, he would say nothing, but I could tell he felt I was the one who should have been able to stop the escalation.

I realized that I could make Harlan do something, but I could not make her like it. And what I wanted and could not get was for her to want to do something on her own. She had style and flair but no desire to do the necessary drilling to turn natural affinity into true musicality and virtuosity. And if she did end up doing what I wanted, it was always with a heavy sigh, and that was what stayed with me and made everything feel crooked, not the fact that I "got my way." Harlan never understood this and always asked me why I was so upset by a mere sigh.

Her practice over time, and our relationship whenever it revolved around music, became a vicious circle. This was no longer about the piano or the violin but about something deeper. A test of wills, maybe. It didn't help that I was divided against myself. Do I let the child do what is joyful and nurture her own path, whatever that might be? Or do I override the child's short-term preferences by having a parent's fortitude to insist that she stick with the course, by rote, by practice, by sheer hard work, rather than let her flitter and flutter from one whimsical project to the next?

The stars were not aligned for us, buffalo and horse. The buffalo is plodding and doesn't buck. A willful horse does. In the end, she bucked so much it made me queasy and dizzy and exhausted. I let her do whatever she wanted, practice or not, correct the mistake I pointed out or not, and in the end, decide to continue with her music or not. It was a decision I justified by telling myself our mother-daughter relationship was more important than music or Tae Kwon Do or any underlying, valuable lessons to be learned. But a part of me was worried that I had succumbed and taken the path of least resistance. Another part of me concluded that Harlan was simply asserting what every American kid had the right to assert: autonomy, freedom, and independence.

Those rights were fine when it came to extracurricular activities, but for the core of schoolwork, Harlan did what she was told. School was inviolable. She must have known some things were not negotiable, maybe because in that area Bill and I and Mai were a unified front. We are an academically oriented family and Harlan has known since she was a toddler that education is supremely important to us.

But even the way we talked about education was different. Bill encouraged Harlan to do her best, and he had faith that her best would mean, hopefully, straight As. I told Harlan outright she had to get straight As and nothing else was acceptable, because I knew straight As were totally within her reach. She was two grade levels ahead in math, and her writing was natural and spontaneous, though she was characteristically not strong in any area that required adherence to rules, like grammar. Rules were easy for me, but not for her.

Because Bill had faith that Harlan would excel, he did not feel the need to monitor her homework. Until Harlan entered her sophomore year in high school, sitting with her at the table when she did her homework after school was her and my routine. I did my work next to her, which allowed me to oversee hers without hovering conspicuously. It was easy to monitor her progress, now that we were in the digital age. Both her middle school and high school encouraged parents and students to download programs called School Loop and Canvas, which provide instant access to homework assignments, test dates, and test results. I drilled the following rules into her head, my parents' rules that I have followed and that I also impart to my own students:

First, never wait until the last minute to do something. The day before something is due, proofread the completed work, rather than starting or trying to finish. Second, do more than you are asked to do. If a project requires work on odd-numbered questions, try to tackle the even-numbered questions too. Third, always do extra-credit work. You never know when you will need it, and the teacher will notice who does it. There were more rules to impart, of course, but I thought it better to stick with three. One rule seemed too scant, two was better, and three seemed to be a universal favorite.

When I first started teaching, one of my professors, a fantastic classroom teacher, advised: "Don't jam more than three main things into your lecture. They won't remember." He then added, "I follow the Phyllis Diller rule."

"Who is Phyllis Diller?" I asked.

"She's a goddess stand-up comedian. She sticks with the rule of three."

The rule of three means that a trio of principles, events, and characters is usually more humorous (in the case of stand-up comedy) or more effective (in the case of life rules) than other numbers. My professor said that Phyllis Diller would first establish the joke; second, reaffirm a variant of the joke; and third, reaffirm again before twisting and killing it.

Even Martin Luther King Jr. used groups of threes in his magnificent speeches. "Free at last. Free at last. Thank God Almighty we are free at last."

People count to three before embarking on the main event. One, two, three. Or ready, get set, go. Then in the West, there are Three Little Pigs, Three Blind Mice, Goldilocks and the Three Bears. And so on.

Despite the pithiness of threes, suffice it to say that Harlan did not always remember them. Our fights continued. But when it came to schoolwork and academic performance, I did not waver. Anything that could distract or derail her from concentrated study was to be dealt with immediately. Even in elementary and middle schools, when grades didn't count, we still insisted on straight As. Bill supported me fully in this. Once Harlan was used to getting As, she would see that as the norm and continue to work to maintain it, with a sense of confidence and inevitability, he said. So we shepherded her and monitored her schoolwork as early as first grade.

Her public elementary school in Williamsburg, to our delight, was an International Baccalaureate school, which meant the curriculum had as its foundation a broad, international outlook. In third grade, she took several aptitude tests given by the school and was permitted into the gifted program called Visions, putting in place the first steps in Bill's plan to make excellence an ordinary, expected part of her academic life. When we moved to California, she tested into an equivalent program called GATE— Gifted and Talented Education. And when she entered high school, we made sure to enroll her in honors classes in ninth and tenth grades and AP or IB classes in eleventh and twelfth.

I insisted that Harlan keep herself grounded and her eyes on the prize. Follow those three rules, Harlan, I reminded her. The more I brought up the three rules, the more she scuttled off to be with Figaro, who demanded nothing of her.

I could tell high school changed everything. The same mostly normal, mostly stable, mostly nice kids in eighth grade, mine included, transmogrified into something confusing when they crossed the ninth-grade threshold. Even when Harlan argued and clashed with me, we interacted despite our incompatibility. She would still snuggle in bed with me, often sleeping with me even after she had decided it was time for her to move into her own bed.

What I began to see was that everything was both magnified and miniaturized in high school. Feelings of loneliness, alienation, exclusion, marginalization—anything that suggested being and feeling less than— were magnified. Feelings of self-worth, confidence, achievement, inclusion— anything that suggested being and feeling good—became smaller. I couldn't tell where this was coming from—hormones, stress, school environment, teachers, other students?

I set out to do what I had always done when faced with problems: research. I returned with a vengeance to the data-driven self I had developed years before, looking for authority figures who could guide me to understand the mysterious creature in the house, my own child. Harlan had always been feisty and sassy and spunky. Her choices to do or not do something were always defended forcefully, with impertinence and righteous defiance. But she was always easy to return to normality. She let go of bad feelings quickly.

But in her first two years of high school, she mostly skulked and scowled and made a point of sighing impatiently, almost disrespectfully. Her eyebrows furrowed, eyes narrowed, looking at the world neither lovingly nor disdainfully, although I could pick up a whiff of contempt in her ready retort. "You're so lucky, Mom. You should be grateful. You should see how other kids treat their parents. They hate them." It was the first time I had heard of parents needing to show gratitude to their children, the exact reverse of Confucian piety and rectitude.

I was not ignorant of psychology. I knew that children her age would start the process of separation, slowly severing the bond in incremental steps. At the time, her withdrawal and intermittent defiance seemed to be within the standard parameters of teenage development. I comforted myself with the famous Mark Twain quote: "When I was a boy of fourteen, my father was so ignorant I could hardly stand to have the old man around. But when I got to be twenty-one, I was astonished at how much the old man had learned in seven years." Still, the change in my daughter was shocking when it happened. I thought I would be an exception. That she would be an exception. Or at least that the Asian part of her life, which must have some influence on her, however subliminally, would restrain and dampen the more conspicuous expressions of American individuality.

She interacted minimally with me, her ears plugged with the ubiquitous earphones attached to her iPhone. When she came out of her room, it was to visit her father, who was debilitated by back pain. He'd had a laminectomy for stenosis before our move to California, but the operation did not work as we'd expected. Bill was on a high daily dosage of federally controlled substances such as oxycodone and fentanyl patches. I couldn't discuss any of Harlan's boyfriend issues with him. He was in physical agony every day. And the pain medication had many side effects—nausea, dizziness, lack of appetite, depression.

One day she confided that she had a boyfriend. I encouraged her to bring him home. I'd had no friends in high school, much less a boyfriend. The boy seemed nice. I noticed he took off his shoes before entering the house without being asked. Harlan reverted to what I considered her old self. When his mother drove him to our house, I met her and liked hearing what she said about him, which was that he was an extremely kind and sensitive boy.

And then he broke up with her. And she cried and was understandably sad. To spend alone time with her in her sadness, I took her to do mother-daughter stuff together. I offered to buy her a manicure and pedicure. We went shopping at her favorite store. We walked around hand in hand and felt the bright California sun all around us. Of course the first breakup would be painful, but I consoled myself with the thought that it was better she experienced heartache while still at home, with her family, than while away in college. For several weeks, I let her have sleepovers with her girlfriends. She was still quiet, but there was no hint of pain or sorrow of the kind that was cutting and searing.

And then the test results for Trig came back. A C! Knowing that I considered a C the equivalent of failure, Harlan preemptively snickered, gesticulating wildly in the process before unleashing her tirade. "You always tell me it's important to learn how to deal with failure. Now look at how you're acting. So what if I get a C?"

I could feel a fury rising and could barely believe what I heard. I could have dealt with the situation better if Harlan had shown sadness or panic about her grade. Or if she had said she was struggling but would try harder next time. Instead, she used it to make her point that I was a hypocrite. It was true that I wanted her to know how to survive failure, but I was thinking more of small failures, like losing an inconsequential Tae Kwon Do match. I could even imagine spectacular failures that came from setting aside the fear of failure and taking a big, dazzling risk. But failure in education was not something I had contemplated or could tolerate because as long as you follow the three rules and maintain equilibrium, the Confucian template guarantees success.

She had lost equilibrium, and equilibrium is everything in Asian culture.

I couldn't tell who did what, but someone was spreading nasty rumors about Harlan. Like a virus, the rumors shape-shifted as they were regurgitated by various students on various social media platforms. I was relieved she was sharing what was happening at school, and I wanted to do something to help, unlike my parents, who would not have known what to do even if I had included them in my problems. When I suggested various solutions, she snickered contemptuously.

"All you do is fix things, Mom. And you don't even do it right." And worse: "You're always trying to improve me. You're not maternal. You're not caring in the least."

I coaxed her into letting me make an appointment with the vice principal. I used the language of rights: "We need to stand up when someone violates our rights or our dignity." Silence. I switched to the language of compassion, for her and even for the boys who were bullying her. "You'll feel better when someone else listens to your problems." And "They shouldn't think this behavior is okay. You'll be helping them realize they need to change. There is still time for them to change." When she finally agreed, she and I went to see the administration. Based on what Harlan recounted, there was no doubt bullying had occurred, the vice principal agreed. But the boys denied any wrongdoing when they were later called into the office. Because Snapchat posts disappeared and other social media posts were deleted, there was no documentation or hard evidence, and what we were left with was an uncorroborated story that could be doubted and dismissed. More troubling was the fact that the act of telling the school authorities was itself viewed as snitching by other students, which subjected her to additional ostracism. I asked if she wanted to see a therapist and she said yes.

In the end, Harlan confided in me that she was eager to move to a different school. I did not know the depth of her internal suffering, but I agreed immediately because I too thought a change was necessary, although I hadn't pushed for it because I was worried transferring to another school and starting anew could destabilize her further. We had bought our house in the neighborhood precisely so she could walk to our local school. The friends she had made since our move to California were from this neighborhood and went to this school. But now the emotional toll and turmoil had crescendoed. It was almost the end of April of her sophomore year, a most inopportune time for an unmooring as drastic as a transfer to another school.

I plunged into research. Our options were limited. Even schools in the same district would not allow a transfer until the start of the next academic year. I tried various exorbitantly expensive private schools but an end-of-year start was also not feasible. I looked into homeschooling and discovered it was legal in California and that even respectable universities have admitted homeschooled kids. I filed the necessary paperwork and created a private school in my own house for one student. And then I found out that homeschool credits would not be recognized by the requisite accrediting agency.

We urgently needed something for her from April to June. Finally, I located a public high school in our district that offered classes online. All tests and finals must be proctored at the school. And her classes would be accredited, treated just like those from any conventional high school.

Harlan excelled academically. But she suffered emotionally. She was an extrovert, preferring the company of others to time spent alone, opting to do rather than to quietly be, and the isolation of home study was debilitating. "I have no friends," she said. Depending on her mood, she might add, "How can I when you took away my phone? For two years! Without my phone, I am isolated."

I had given her a flip phone so she could make calls. It could also text, but not with the ease of a smartphone. She hated it and barely bothered to charge it, which meant I was not always able to reach her. She shrugged. "You ruined my life, Mom. You have no idea. You're so extreme." She still mentions it as an example of how not to parent.

In the meantime, I explored alternatives for the next academic year—a private, Waldorf high school in the adjacent city and a smaller public high school in another district, which, in the latter case, would have required us to establish residency there. There was only one option left—another midsize high school about a fifteen-minute drive from our house. We asked for a school tour. As the guide took us through a labyrinth of halls, I saw something that brought a lilt to my heart. There, hanging on a huge wall, were flags of various countries representing, I assumed, the countries of origin of the student body. For Vietnam, I saw the familiar flag I had grown up with, the flag of the now defunct South Vietnam: bright yellow with three red stripes. I looked at Harlan and knew that she noticed the symbolism and its significance as well. It seemed like a good omen.

HARLAN AND I HAVE GONE TOGETHER TO VIETNAM TWICE, once when she was six and the second time when she was fifteen. On the surface, I wish Vietnam could be a country like any other I have visited with my American child. But Vietnam was my birthplace. And it was the place where I discovered one of my primal truths: Everything can fall. What remains can still be beautiful, but only if you understand real beauty.

Our first trip, in July 2009, I took her to Vietnam with Mai for almost two months for a specific reason. I found that, for me, a directed purpose made a trip there less emotionally treacherous. In this case the goal was to immerse Harlan in Vietnamese. Mai and I both spoke it, obviously, although not very often in America because we didn't want Bill to feel excluded; on this trip, we thought it would have a bigger impact on Harlan if she could hear our conversations in a natural setting, where everyone else was speaking it too. Also, she would attend a Vietnamese school run by Catholic nuns. Private schools were allowed only up to a certain grade level. So our only choice if we didn't want her in a state-run school was this school.

Harlan took to Saigon immediately. She loved its constant busyness, traffic jams, street vendors, noises, food, energy. Nothing bothered her— not the oppressive summer heat or the torrential downpours that turned parts of the city into little brown lakes. Even the lopsided, buckled sidewalks intrigued her. Harlan treated everything as if it was just how things were and how they were supposed to be.

She seemed perfectly fine when we left her at the school. At six years old, she was the oldest kid there, but it was fine because she was there only to learn Vietnamese, even if it was rudimentary.

Soon our day had an easy routine. Breakfast at home, a two-bedroom serviced apartment, usually consisting of chocolate croissant and Vietnamese yogurt, which was rich and a little sweet as well as tart. Taxi to the Catholic school. Mai spent time with friends she had met after the Communist takeover in 1975. Many had tried to escape by boat and were caught, imprisoned, and ultimately released with black marks on their records, probably forever. I returned to the apartment to do my summer research and writing. I would pick Harlan up after lunch, around two p.m. We would then wander from one neighborhood to the next, going into a café for air-conditioning or a cold drink. Everywhere she went, the Vietnamese indulged and fussed over her. And if she spoke any Vietnamese to them at all, shopkeepers would insist on giving her ice cream, candy, or chocolate for free. I realized that they saw her as an essentially white child; only if people looked carefully would they notice the slight Asian features.

Even in 2009, years after Bill Clinton had taken the momentous step of normalizing relationships with Vietnam, the Vietnamese in the country still saw us overseas Vietnamese, dubbed the Việt Kiều, "foreign Vietnamese," as an exotic breed they didn't quite know what to do with. We came back to Vietnam carrying our foreign culture.

I took Harlan to Givral, the ice cream shop that had been famous since before 1975. Except now all around it were luxury designer stores, such as Armani and Versace, and air-conditioned malls. Since the institution of market reforms in the early 1980s, Vietnam and Saigon in particular have welcomed foreign investment inflows in the billions, fifteen billion of which came from international remittances sent by people like me, the Việt Kiều. So integral have we become as a vehicle for hard currency that in 2004 the government passed a law deeming the once outcast Việt Kiều "an integral part of the nation." And in 2008, the government amended the Law of Vietnamese Nationality, allowing overseas Vietnamese to hold dual citizenship. It was a law meant to lure the Việt Kiều back to Vietnam through various tax breaks and relaxed limits on property ownership. But it caused immense anxiety for us. We return to Vietnam knowing we have the safety of American passports. If we could be considered Vietnamese nationals, would we be ensnared in Vietnam's murky labyrinth of whimsy laws and decrees and regulations?

We were in Saigon and I spoke Vietnamese with a southern accent, just like other Saigonese there. I should not have stood out. But after I ordered and the waiter brought our food, someone from the next table asked me where we came from. Seeing the surprised look on my face, the stranger added, "Aren't you a Việt Kiều?"

I nodded. "Why do you ask?" I said, surprised by the question. What I meant was "how did you know."

"You said thank you to the waiter. No local Vietnamese would do that." She paused and grinned broadly, showing teeth.

Conversations and salutations between strangers are tricky in Vietnamese. When meeting someone for the first time, one must assess the other person's age and rank, derived from socioeconomic status, and decide whether to slot them in one's family or friendship circle. There is a different word for each permutation within the familial circle: male, female, age, status, down to whether the person is presumably from the mother's or father's side of the family. There is an "I" that is gender-free and formal, which originated as an "I" used by a servant speaking to the Emperor, but this word has evolved so that it is now used when one wants to be formal and restrained. With this "I" form, boundaries are up.

When in doubt, put yourself in the lower-ranking position and accord the other person higher status.

"So where are you from?" She used the word cô, which meant she considered me higher ranking than herself but not as high as her parents. It was a diplomatic choice.

I have always hated this un-American question, but I wasn't in America, so I couldn't even be mad. "Are you from America?"

"Yes."

"My family tried to escape in nineteen seventy-six and nineteen seventy-seven, but we got caught three times. How long are you staying?" she whispered.

"About two months. I'm here so my kid can get to know Vietnam and learn the language," I said, pointing at Harlan.

"Oh, she's your kid? So pretty. She looks American."

I smiled.

"There are language classes here. Nearby."

"She's in a Vietnamese school for little kids," I replied.

"No, I mean language classes for the Việt Kiều."

"Oh . . ." Was she suggesting I take Vietnamese language classes or was this just general information sharing? We were communicating without difficulty in Vietnamese.

"Many Việt Kiều come back with very bad Vietnamese. And they can't write or read. Where are you from in America? Cali?"

Cali is the endearing nickname for California, which is the American Dream to the Vietnamese here. I noticed that in Saigon, there were pho shops called Phở Cali, evoking a sweet dreamscape, whereas in America, the pho shops were meant to evoke nostalgia, named after famous places in the pre-1975 days.

"No. Not Cali." In 2009, we were still in Virginia, though Cali would beckon in three years. "Virginia," I said.

"Oooh, Virginia. Very pretty?" she asked. "Four seasons. I want to go there too. And Cali. That's my dream."

EIGHT YEARS LATER, Harlan and I flew back to Vietnam yet again, but by this time, we had made our home in California. We met up with a group of friends, including my editor, Carole. We had brought my two novels to life together, and it was poignant to show, to introduce—dare I even say show off—Vietnam to her.

A part of me saw it as a forlorn little country, nothing to show off. I wondered if anyone would even come here to visit if there had been no "Vietnam War." I always resented Vietnam being viewed as a war and not a country, but it is, frankly, the war and America's defeat that catapulted Vietnam into international consciousness, prompting tourists, especially American ones, to come and witness its despairing beauty, its sorry sights, to understand who these scrawny sunbaked people are who defeated the most powerful country on earth, inflicting trauma on its national psyche, stealing the spirit of its youth at places like Kent State and its soldiers in battlefields like Khe Sanh and Hamburger Hill years and years after.

I had started teaching international trade again, and some of the most important trade rules are the rules of origin. Products nowadays are not always manufactured in one country, but in many. If an orange was grown in Florida but was pressed and processed in Colombia to make orange juice and the orange juice was then sent to Argentina, should Argentina consider it a product of Colombia or of the United States? The answer: Colombia, if processing from orange to orange juice met the "substantial transformation" test.

I too am hybrid. Born in Vietnam, different parts, geometrically imperfect, assembled in the United States, substantially transformed by America. With me was my American-born kid, all-American prototype, flawless English (pure American accent, though grammar could be improved).

When I was in America, I used to think I was hybrid because I wasn't in Vietnam. Asian American, hyphenated American came with an implicit qualifier, diminishing, miniaturizing. Uncredentialed. An appendage that stuck like an albatross, connoting geography, demographics, good for census takers but useless for imparting anything complex like identity. Vietnamese American was even more drastic. Like a casualty of war. And as it turned out, being in Vietnam didn't lessen hybridity. A lot of us "return" in search of wholeness, only to find bewilderment. In turn, locals in search of the almighty dollar greeted and welcomed us. We were no longer the hollow men who fled with our failed hopes and righteous fury. We'd become the prodigal children who plotted our resurrection and came back not repentant, but victorious. Hauling cartons and suitcases stuffed with material goods of all kinds from America to bestow on remaining family still in Saigon. Wallets lined with credit and debit cards.

American vets also "return," still booming even in their frailer, aged bodies, seeking something in a place they were suckered into called "Nam." What a strange word. Truncated, not quite a moniker. Obviously short for Vietnam, but always seeming to shortchange the country and everything associated with it. "I was in Nam." The sentence carried different undertones that I tried to decipher. Grasping the tails of reconciliation, acceptance, pride, remorse, anger? All of those?

On this trip, we ventured outside Saigon. We would start in Hanoi and make our way south. Hanoi, Sapa, Hội An, Saigon. Famous cities. But they felt like destinations unknown. Unified in name, with the North having gobbled up the now defunct South. In name, because North and South are very different—divided in the 1500s for more than two hundred years. War and politics aside, the two regions are culturally separate.

What the Việt Kiều call Day of Mourning or Black April, April 30, is referred to as Day of Reunification here.

Hanoi was new to me. Everywhere, streets seemed warped and crooked or spiraled or weirdly wedged, maybe because it was the movement of the traffic that lanced the asphalt and distorted the roads. Roads in Hanoi were more narrow than those in Saigon, the traffic more manageable and sedate. Old French colonial villas, beautiful remnants of subjugation, faded but elegant, lined the tree-canopied boulevards. The streets were divided by guilds and known by the specialized wares sold on each one. At night, the sidewalks turned into nighttime cafés, as peddlers and res-taurants edging outward brought hibachi-style portable stoves to grill their offerings on red hot, sizzling coals.

Walking with my friends, white foreigners to the locals, I was buffered by Westernness and whiteness. Peddlers, hawkers, diners, motorcyclists, all jostling, elbowing, scavenging, grubbing—even beggars, an endless crush of them, modified and tempered their whooping and dodging be-havior around white foreigners as they panned for opportunities.

Guidebooks described Hanoi as charming. Vietnam is no longer lean or, more precisely, poverty-stricken like it was right after government con-fiscation of private property post-1975. It's been fattened by capitalist money and investment. Even austere Hanoi, where foreign and Việt Kiều investors must trek like supplicants at the temple's gate to apply for invest-ment licenses. I observed it through my alien viewfinder eyes. It's as foreign a city to me as to my friends. Harlan seemed to love Vietnam, although she made a point of praising Saigon, perhaps feeling an obligatory loyalty to the South. Mai, whose family was originally from the North but fled south in 1954, spoke to the locals in her northern accent, which could be eliminated at a moment's notice in favor of the southern variant when needed. Southerners were charged more for everything, so she put on her northern accent. Our hotel was in the Old City. Streets were lined with diminutive cafés, somewhat dilapidated but quaint. Việt Kiều—all of us having fled our homes upon the South's downfall—are like tourists in our home country, even more so in Hanoi. This city had no emotional meaning to me whatsoever. My heart didn't dip at the sight of it, and I was glad. It was just another place to visit. Time had passed, of course, but I was indifferent to its passage here.

We treated all our culinary experiences with gusto and caution. I would have loved to eat the way I used to as a kid, sitting on tiny low plastic chairs the height of footstools, hovering over flimsy aluminum tables while slurping noodle soups that came with plates of fresh, uncooked purple-stemmed twigs and leaves with fancy names like garlic chives, perillas, rice paddy, sawtooth, spicy mint, and fish mint. But our bellies had become more delicate, no longer accustomed to the kinds of bacteria that thrived in Vietnam. We avoided ice. We made sure bottled water contained safety seals. Of course, with Carole and gang, this extra precaution made sense. When we entered a restaurant, if there were white tourists, I felt immediately more secure.

Sapa and Hội An, north and south of Hanoi respectively, were lighthearted places outside the old war zones, with no hidden alcoves of the past. Nothing to suggest where old buildings had been felled and new ones had gone up. In Sapa, terraced rice fields in succulent green, mountain peaks veiled in swirling gray fog, and indigo-dyed cloths drying on clotheslines were just that. Same with the ancient port city of Hội An. Graceful, atmospheric, historic. Walls painted yellow ochre. Roofs with clay tiles. Colorful lanterns. Gridlike idyllic streets. Everywhere there were vendors carrying food baskets of all varieties, glutinous rice cakes stuffed in banana leaves, flat rice cakes steamed and topped with toasted shrimp and scallion oil, even elaborate concoctions like variations of noodle soups. I experienced these places mostly as an ordinary tourist would. None of it required the repression of personal memory.

Instead, we made new, wondrous memories together. Harlan insisted that she be allowed to learn how to ride a motorbike in Hội An. I started thinking like a lawyer. What's the state of tort law in Vietnam? Are there safety standards? Is there mandatory insurance? What's the medical system like? All I could see were Harlan's light brown eyes winking at me with hope. *Let me, let me, let me.*

Mai took her down a dirt road and showed her how to ride it. I was anxious. I didn't know whether it required shifting gears or using a clutch. I only knew it had a motor and it was on two wheels. Which was all I needed to know to be nervous. We would be riding in traffic. Not crazy traffic like Hanoi or Saigon, but traffic nonetheless, including fuming buses, other motorcycles, cars, bicycles, mopeds, three-wheeled tuk tuks, even ox-drawn wagons and pushcarts.

But the thought of riding on her own motorbike was exhilarating to her, this kid who was the last one in her preschool class to know how to walk, who could never even crawl, who was reluctant to go down a slide even as everyone in her preschool was whizzing down fearlessly, who was scared of learning how to ride a bike, insisting she would be more than content to be the only kid in the entire world who didn't know how. Now I was riding on the back of Mai's motorbike, looking back as if into a time portal every few seconds to check on my little girl riding on two spindly wheels powered by a motor. There she was on the motorbike, working the horn and gas and brakes even as honking buses and taxis zoomed by her in a free-for-all flow. Whether on highways or in meandering alleys, other motorbikes were so close you could reach out and touch them; your knees jutting from the passenger's seat could graze theirs. And it seemed every-one honked in Vietnam—not to scold fellow drivers but apparently to alert others of their proximity. The constant blaring and blasting was annoying and scary. The helmet was tight on Harlan's head. I had read that head injuries were commonplace in Vietnam.

Her face was intense but beaming, and she was happy. Even while we were idling on our motorbikes, waiting for traffic to move, vendors, some scrawny and as young as seven or eight years old, descended upon us, thrusting fruit, bottled water, and trinkets at us. Little men, little women, little children. Waifs everywhere in dusty loose garbs flowing like Western pajamas. All it took to bestow beneficence on them was a few dollars—which, faced with incredibly adorable and hauntingly hopeless street chil-dren who followed us, we sometimes did and sometimes did not, for no reason other than the inner random beast of mood or whim.

When the air started to throb, wet and salty with the sudden onset of high winds, thunder, and rain that, due to bad drainage, gave us almost ankle-high water in a flash, I wrapped my arms tightly around Mai's torso. Curses, screams, laughter, animals bleating. I was frightened being just a passenger, but Harlan remained calm and joyful, thumping the accelera-tor, following us closely, spooling into one intersection, then another, all of us cavorting to our destination to evade the rain and thunder.

IN SAIGON, I had arranged to teach a one-week course on international sales at the University of Economics and Law. The students had been cho-sen for their English-speaking ability and their legal acumen. They bowed when I entered the room, and stood up when they answered questions. Commercial law, business law, corporate law, trade law—these were the subjects I regularly taught. The government had no problem with the rule of law, as long as it was of the sort needed to attract business. Nonethe-less, politics and commerce are not always so easily dichotomized and segregated. I worked the principle of shareholder lawsuits in corporate law into my lecture, emphasizing the right of the owner—that is, a shareholder (and not just an administrative agency)—to sue even those who were "higher ranking," the managers and the directors. This was how individual rights could be folded into an innocuous lecture on business law.

Many of the students, quiet in class, were full of conversation afterward. This was the South, so they all had relatives who had made it to America in 1975 or after. These were students who had received help in the form of overseas remittances, and they had now accepted the responsibility to do what was necessary, through education, to take care of their parents, siblings, and the entire sprawling clan. It says a lot that the most famous and most beloved literary hero in Vietnam is Kiều, the protagonist in an epic poem written more than two hundred years ago. Kiều was a prostitute who suppressed personal happiness for the benefit of her family. Despite her profession, the country revered her nobility and dignity.

Outside the formality of the classroom, my students wanted to know more about America. How much money do people make? Do they own houses and land? How many people live in a house? Can the government take your house? Is it true that there are places in America with hundreds of thousands of Vietnamese? That you can just stay there and speak Vietnamese all day and not even learn English?

I could feel it building up in my chest, something I wanted to say now, or it would never be said, even to myself. The yanking, tugging feelings. A crushing weight, sorrows and sins, pangs of shame, even, for having fled, for leaving everything behind. For coming back with more money and more than that—more savoir faire, more status, more opportunities, more privileges than the average Vietnamese, all because of an American passport. To be fair, however, there are many millionaires if not billionaires in Vietnam now that it has embraced unadulterated capitalism, laissez-faire capitalism, rogue capitalism, drawer capitalism—capitalism governed by unpublished, nontransparent regulations mysteriously hidden in a bureaucrat's drawer, to be whipped out to spook Việt Kiều and even foreign investors who have plunked down enough cash to feel they have no choice but to plunk down more to grease the wild-scheme projects through. We Việt Kiều nonetheless snickered at and felt superior to these millionaires and billionaires. So much money, so little class. But in the end, the truth was that purely by some incomprehensible, serendipitous turn of fate, destiny, or randomness, our roles could easily have been reversed. I and mine here in a place where if the lampposts had legs, they would leave—at least, in the immediate postwar years of reeducation camps, starvation and poverty, and confiscation and elimination of private property in the name of equality. They and theirs in America, chasing the improbable possibilities rattling inside the American Dream.

What was I now seeking and clearly not finding? Home? Forgiveness? Redemption? Moving from one in-between place to another, each absent of center, each enough in its own way?

The students became more familiar, more eager as the week progressed. Do they like the Vietnamese in America? they asked.

I didn't know the answer to this question. But it didn't matter. I was teaching them law, so I blurted a legal answer. I smiled and told them that America is a country of laws; the rule of law reigns. That is enough. The Constitution promises equality and due process of law. The Declaration of Independence gives all of us the right to pursue happiness. That too is enough.

LATER ON THIS PILGRIMAGE, I started dreaming in a sputtering of Vietnamese. My birth language was slipping back into my heart in Saigon. Even the new version of the city, where supposedly high-end concrete, glass, and steel structures have supplanted old, graceful villas, I noticed that I sometimes formulated my thoughts in Vietnamese. The Vietnamese side I thought had withered was capable of being reactivated. The six tones, the southern cadence, all around me, made me feel like I was back in old times. Nothing looked the same, but Saigon is not about visuals. It's about the senses. Bikes, taxis, sedans, three-wheeled vehicles, mishmashed, chaotic, pinwheeling, zipping, roaring in hyperdrive, almost psychedelically, oblivious to pedestrians. We must somehow find our footing and bull-headedness through all that adrenaline wail. And we did. It was purely a matter of timing as to when you angle and smooth and oscillate your way across the street. Awfully sweet.

I did not go looking for my house or the spot where it once stood. Home was not a place you could return to. Home was a place you could lose.

But as my friends told me they were loving the trip, seemingly overlooking the country's multiple and conspicuous foibles, heat, dirt, fumes, and congestion that not even history and exoticism could erase, I absorbed their enthusiasm.

MY LAST BIRTHDAY IN SAIGON WAS AUGUST 1974. Forty-three years later, after many seasons of strangeness and unraveling, I had my next one there, surrounded by friends who had made the trip with me from America. Sometimes being there felt like getting to the finish line, but, of course, in reality, that is not so.

All of us decided to take cyclos all over Saigon and Cholon. In America, none of us would get into a car without buckling ourselves into the obligatory seatbelts. But here, we were willing to sit in a three-wheeled cyclo that would compete in the city's lunatic traffic over chewed-up roads. The cyclo drivers wearing half grins had all been youngsters once, buddies from the withered shells of the defeated army of South Vietnam, with perpetual chains around their necks that could be yanked tighter anytime by the government. Cyclo driver was all they could be here.

Mai and I were in charge of getting all our individual cyclo rides. We did not bargain. Harlan could have sat with either Mai or me, but we let her have her own as she wished, plus that meant one more cyclo driver would get a job. The old man who pedaled mine had been imprisoned for many years after 1975. I wanted to know how many years was "many," but I didn't ask.

In a cyclo, passengers are basically on a platform scaffolded by a flimsy frame covered by a sheet of canvas and propelled by human effort—totally vulnerable and exposed. Sitting in a cyclo, you could almost be part of Saigon itself, its weeping asphalt, its consoling shadows, its raw, choking heat, traveling slowly enough to see and savor everything, but with the floating-flying giddiness of the surrounding traffic, everything could feel fast and fleeting at the same time. Skinny dogs dodging traffic. Grabbing, needy vendors in a perpetual pioneering search for customers. Beautiful little children, the "dust of life," as they were called, begging tourists with reverent eyes. Our cyclos traveled in a snarling herd, like wildebeests or zebras in Africa in a contest of life and death, veering this way, then that, in synchronized movement. Waiting when necessary at the intersection or traffic circle for an accumulation of other bicycles, cyclos, and pedestrians before our contingent blasted our way forward together through the drift of humanity. This was life in Saigon. Treacherous. Fast. Exuberant. Exciting. Touch and go.

We crisscrossed our way through ramshackle outdoor food stalls and itinerant peddlers. Slabs of pigs' ears, beef and pork, live chickens and ducks hanging barbarously upside down in close proximity to vegetable kiosks and silk and taffeta bins. Pungent, aromatic, odorous, fermented, and stinky, I would say, if I didn't have to judge myself for thinking it. Shirtless men sucking on cigarettes, naked toddlers being scrubbed in washbasins no bigger than their little bodies, women squatting, scrubbing black-lacquered teeth with betel nut husks, staring at our cluster of cyclos, two Việt Kiều and a half-breed child with white foreigners. There was no sense of outdoor versus indoor, as public sidewalks were taken over for tasks normally associated with the private sphere. All overwhelming to my Westernized sensibility. Then on to a temple, the most famous in Cho-lon, which venerates the Empress of Heaven, goddess of the sea and pro-tector of seafarers and fisherfolk from treacherous waters. The temple is practically ostentatious on the outside, with ceramic figurines depicting ancient fables. Walls are covered in intricate friezes, gold-leaf inscriptions on carved tableaux. The curved roof is adorned with dragons and serpents. Inside is a different story. A contrast of solitude within ancient walls. Coils of incense hanging from rafters wafting aromatic fog. Incense sticks burn-ing in rows of giant steel pots.

Carole was writing a novel about women pirates and oceans and tem-pests, and we all took as an auspicious sign the fact that the temple was devoted to the Goddess of Heaven, who was also a protector of the ocean. Prayer flags, which were basically red strips of paper that could be used to write prayers on, hung like banners from the ceiling. A carved wooden boat representing the goddess's connection to the sea looked as if it were suspended from the air itself.

After about an hour, we finally made it to the place that still gnawed at me. Not my house, because I knew it had been torn down, but the once-gray church that was one street away from my house. It was now pink, this church that I used to visit for its beautiful piano, for the amputee beggar outside singing Creedence Clearwater Revival, for the six busy cross streets that tumbled in front of the church.

Of course, the beggar was not there, visually. But I and all the dark selves within me, sturdy and more or less unified, felt him viscerally. His echo was there, a vanishing but strong presence reverberating through me. Like Saigon itself. Hurt and flawed and fragmented. But forever here.

ACKNOWLEDGMENTS

Lan Cao

I have always loved boxes. When I was a child, I put both my treasures and my fears in boxes to respectively safeguard or segregate them. This book is like a box. Nearly everything I've felt or seen is in here. I thank my therapists, Dr. Christine S. and Dr. Sarah K., who have given me the gift of being seen and helped me in ways that words cannot adequately express, even for a writer. My gratitude to Sarah, for guiding me toward a path of "inner wisdom"; and to Christine, for her cosmic soup perspective on life. This book is in many ways a declaration of love and gratitude for them, for going hand in hand with me on a journey toward air and light that would have been impossible to accomplish alone.

For nurturing my love of literature and for giving me kindness, which in turn gave me hope and faith, I thank my high school English teacher, Ms. Helen McBride. I give thanks to my friends of many lifetimes, Stephen Bohlen, Nancy Combs, Carole DeSanti, Jessy Fraser, Naja Pham Lockwood, Arthur Pinto, Alicia Retsof, Lisa Rothmel, Jane Stromseth, and

Cynthia Ward, for giving me the gift of their presence in my life. Carole DeSanti was also the editor of my two novels, and I am thankful for her advice and her faith, for she did not just search for diversity, which is nice, and she did not just take it seriously, which is also nice. She always understood, in ways that matter deeply for me as a writer. For family, history, love, and other tangled branches of connection, Lê Phương Mai.

For my huge family: the remaining reigning matriarch of our sprawling brood, Mother Six, and my many cousins, especially Numbers Eight, Five, and Two.

Without the following people, I would have no book and no opportunity to write this acknowledgment. Ellen Geiger, my longtime literary agent and friend, how lucky I am to have encountered you on a beach the very first year you ventured to East Hampton, an encounter that resulted in wonderful collaboration and conversations. Rosemary Ahern, for her editorial insight and guidance. I am fortunate to have as my editor Wendy Wolf. Thank you for believing in this book from the beginning, even before the first draft. "Delete, add, what does this mean, just say it, no need to be coy," etc. Thank you, I guess. Absolutely, thank you, and to Terezia Cicel as well. Both of you made the book sing in six tones.

Harlan Margaret Van Cao

I'm not really sure how these things are supposed to go, but when I'm told to write acknowledgments, I really think of my father first. I find myself comparing everyone to him all the time because I miss him so much, and I feel like the luckiest girl in the world to have had him as my father, even if it was for a shorter time than I wanted.

I want to thank my mother. I think this book pretty much speaks for itself in terms of how I feel about her. Despite whatever we have disagreed on, I think it is incredible that our story of being together will stay in this world forever in the form of a book. Books are permanent. I love you, Mom. There is also Mai, my other mom. I know that she never intended to have children and actually had gone out of her way to not do so, but she ended up raising me better than I'm sure others' biological parents have done for them. She taught me how to ride a bike, how to fight back, how to have an opinion and be sure about it. She and I share secrets and loves that will always be precious to me because they're just for us.

I want to thank Wendy Wolf for taking a chance on and investing in that fifteen-year-old girl who came to her office in yoga pants and a leather jacket and sat in a spinny chair and promised to write as well as she could. Wendy has been amazing, and I feel very lucky to have my first writing experience be under her mentorship. Likewise, I'd like to thank Terezia Cicel for her meticulous and insightful reading of my drafts. She notices everything, large and small, that needs to be fixed and took a lot of time to get to know my writing. Although working with such a prominent company like Penguin was intimidating, it will always be what I think of as one of the highlights of my life. I'd like to thank my literary agent, Ellen Geiger, for managing my mother and me and for committing to my mother's work for so long, and eventually taking me under her wing.

I want to thank "Jules," my best friend. The year 2019 was definitely our year. Simply living and coexisting with her as her best friend is an adventure. She is the shoulder I cry on, the brain behind all my big decisions, the heart I confide in, the mouth that smiles when I succeed, and the eyes that leak when I don't. I'd like to thank Bella, one of my other closest friends since middle school. Her love is unconditional and her sweetness is unending. She is the kindest person I know. Every time I think I want to quit or can't do something anymore, she reminds me of how strong I am. She sees the world artistically and as an opportunity to give. There is also Taylor, the first person to reach out and show me true kindness when I moved to California. She taught me to be adventurous and to trust. When we were little, one day in PE I told her she could be a track star someday, and she told me right away that I could be a writer. And we agreed to never let the other give up. Today, she has a scholarship to a university and is one of the top ten heptathlon All-American athletes. We kept our promise to each other. I would like to thank Robbie and Elizabeth, two close childhood friends. I'd like to thank Lauren, my close friend since birth. She and I met before I even became confident in walking, and I hope to be there for her until we die. I would also like to thank Mikey for being my rock. Lastly, I'd like to thank everyone, friend or not, who inspired me to pursue writing and who formed all the experiences that have made me into the person I am now, even if I don't always like that person.